MADAM SPEAKER

MADAM SPEAKER

The Life of Betty Boothroyd

PAUL ROUTLEDGE

LONDON   NEW YORK   SYDNEY   TORONTO

This edition published 1995
by BCA by arrangement with
HarperCollins*Publishers*

Copyright © Paul Routledge 1995

The Author asserts the moral right to
be identified as the author of this work

A catalogue record for this book is
available from the British Library

CN 4089

Set in Linotron Janson by
Rowland Phototypesetting Ltd,
Bury St Edmunds, Suffolk

Printed in Great Britain by
HarperCollinsManufacturing Glasgow

Contents

List of Illustrations

The third bid for Parliament: she stood in the by-election for Nelson and Colne and 1968 but failed to hold the seat for Labour (*Courtesy of* The Times/*Camera Press, London*).

Winner at last: Betty finally got to Parliament at a by-election in the Black Country seat of West Bromwich in 1973 (*Courtesy of* Birmingham Post & Mail).

SECTION III

Betty speaking on the NEC in 1981, the year she joined the Committee (*Courtesy of News Team International*).

'Speaking for the people' was Betty's address in the 1992 General Election. She was already hot favourite to become Speaker.

Madam Speaker, accompanied by Black Rod, leads the Members of the House of Commons to the House of Lords to hear the Queen's speech at the State Opening of Parliament (*Courtesy of PA News/Jim James*).

Madam Speaker meets her deputies.

Order, order! (*Courtesy of PA News*).

A packed House of Commons at the start of the day's business (*Courtesy of the House of Commons Public Information Office*).

Betty in full ceremonial robes at the entrance to the Speaker's House in the Palace of Westminster (*Courtesy of PA News/Adam Butler*).

The Great Bed of State. (*Courtesy of and* © World of Interiors. *Photo by Fritz von der Schulenburg*).

The first woman Speaker's coat of arms (*Courtesy of PA News*).

Introduction

An immediate conundrum faces the writer wishing to attempt a full-length portrait of the first woman in British history to become Speaker of the House of Commons: what to call her? Madam Speaker is her correct title, but that is too formal, except for official usage. Besides, as in real life, she does not achieve that goal until three-quarters of the way through her story.

Madam Speaker is not of the generation that is happy with 'Ms', and though she has often used 'Miss' herself and has no objection to others using it, that too seems inappropriate. Too stuffy, too redolent of the schoolroom. Betty, as her first name appears on her birth certificate, may sound a little too familiar. But that is what everybody calls her at Westminster, except in formal surroundings, and that is how she signs her letters to MPs. Accordingly, Betty is the form I have most often used. No presumption or undue mateyness is intended.

This has been an enjoyable book to write, not least because I admire its subject. I regret that Madam Speaker did not feel able to co-operate, but one must assume that her own book will eventually appear and she is saving her reminiscences for that occasion. It will make a fascinating read.

In the interim, I hope that this first essay at writing the story of her life will interest the general reader who wishes to learn how an unprivileged girl from the back streets of a mill town can, by hard work, perseverance and commitment reach one of the highest offices in the land. This is not designed to be a 'political' book in the customary sense, even though it is about a politician. Betty's life is about more than politics.

Under pressure as usual from my publisher to meet an early deadline, I have not been able to talk to every single person whose life has touched on Betty's. However, what follows is the result of hundreds of hours of research and more than a hundred interviews. To those who have given so freely of their time (including those, particularly at Westminster, who wished to remain anonymous), I am deeply grateful.

I wish to record my thanks to Doremy Vernon, former Tiller girl and author of *Tiller's Girls*, the excellent history of a unique British showbiz institution. Doremy was unstintingly generous with her time and assistance. Thanks also to my agent Jane Bradish-Ellames for her support, and to Richard Wheaton and Mike Fishwick at HarperCollins.

I have drawn on all the published sources going back more than fifty years, including the many interviews with Betty. Easily the best is by Rebecca Abrams in *Woman in a Man's World*, to which I am substantially indebted.

I am also particularly grateful to Brigid Walsh, a fellow journalist in Dewsbury, who has conducted interviews on my behalf in and around Betty's home town. Without her painstaking and highly professional assistance, this book would have been much the poorer. Thanks, also, to my political editor on the *Independent on Sunday*, Stephen Castle, for his forbearance over the last year; a patience much tried, I fear.

Finally, I must express my gratitude to my wife Lynne, for driving me around the Pennines and elsewhere when gout reduced me to a hobble for so many weeks, for putting up with the selfish indulgence that book-writing brings, and for being a quiet inspiration always.

Often, when writing, memories would come flooding back of my own upbringing in a mining town not far from Betty's birthplace. The privations that she faced were common to generations of Yorkshire people. My mother's life has been even harder than Betty's, and accordingly I dedicate this book to my mother Anne.

COWLING, NORTH YORKSHIRE
NOVEMBER 1994

CHAPTER I

MAKING HISTORY

I T WAS A quintessentially British moment of history. The time: mid-afternoon on 27 April 1992. The place: a crowded House of Commons, with Members of Parliament standing excitedly around, packed tightly on the green leather benches, even squatting in the aisles. There was a hum of expectation in the air, and then applause broke out, initially polite but becoming more like the first night of a new show. Betty Boothroyd, daughter of an impoverished mill hand raised in the grim stone terraces of the industrial north, was ceremoniously 'dragged' from her place on the back benches to take the chair as the 155th Speaker of Parliament. She was to become first woman to hold the post since it was instituted in AD 1258.

Betty pretended to be fearful, anxious not to take the job. A voluptuous figure in a dark red and black dress adorned with a diamond brooch in the shape of the crowned portcullis of parliament, her thick wavy hair almost as white as the Speaker's wig, she stood, leaned back and stretched out her arms, spread her hands and cried: 'No, no!' She was acting out a drama that is today merely theatrical, but once was only too real: eight of her predecessors had been executed by the sovereign of the day. And as a former professional dancer, Betty knew how to play to the gallery. This was a performance to relish. She had waited a long time, and endured many vicissitudes, to give it.

Quite contrary to parliamentary lore, the cheers and handclapping grew louder. Hilary Armstrong, a young woman Labour member sitting next to her, made pushing gestures with the flat of her hands. John Biffen, her mild-mannered but tough-minded Conservative sponsor, strode across the Chamber and took hold of both her hands, pulling her towards the floor of the House. He cracked a joke that broke the

ice – it sounded as if he was asking if she would like a dance, and
everyone knows the stories of her being a Tiller Girl – and MPs around
her laughed. Gwyneth Dunwoody, her Labour seconder and close
political friend, then took her right hand and together she and Biffen
led her down the steps of the Labour back benches towards the
Speaker's Chair.

Amid the press of emotional legislators, by the Table of the House
with its ceremonial mace in brackets beneath the leathern top to denote
that parliament was not formally in session, her sponsors let her go.
Now, she was on her own. Betty strode along the government Front
Bench, passing a smiling John Major, the Prime Minister, and his Tory
Cabinet – the epitome of all she had fought against in a political life
spread across forty years – to the carpeted steps below the chair.

Pausing on an upper step, she exclaimed, 'Order! Order!' to quell
the hubbub. Speaking from a small note-card, she said: 'Before I take
the Chair, I wish to thank the House for the very great honour it has
bestowed on me. I pray that I shall justify its confidence, and pledge
that I shall do all in my power to preserve and cherish its traditions.'
The unparliamentary (but understandable) applause reached a fresh
crescendo, upstaging the Prime Minister who was due to speak.

Madam Speaker-elect – she was not confirmed in the job until the
next day in the Upper House by the Lord Chancellor, acting on behalf
of the Queen – intervened again, this time betraying her working-class
Yorkshire origins: 'Now then! Now then!' she cried. Then, with spectacles off, her hands folded in her lap, her face often wreathed with
smiles, Betty sat back in the wide, ornate, green-leather Speaker's
Chair with its finely carved high oak back, and savoured John Major's
tribute.

Though he was later to prove he had a less gentlemanly side, on
this day the Prime Minister was chivalry itself. He must have known
before the vital election began little more than an hour earlier that his
own party's choice for the Speakership, the outgoing Secretary of
State for Northern Ireland, Peter Brooke, had been outmanoeuvred
by Betty's supporters in all parts of the House. His speech was prepared
and ready for her swift victory. It was no less generous for that.

'Many people will remark that you are the first Honourable Lady
to assume the responsibilities as Speaker,' he said.[1] 'I shall not dwell

on that point, except to note that you have made history today.' She had made history, he argued, not simply because she was a woman – and it was Betty herself who appealed to MPs 'elect me for what I am, not for what I was born' – but because 'the House trusts you. It believes that you enjoy in abundance the qualities necessary to protect and sustain the House, and to safeguard its rights.'

That day was historic for another reason, he added. It had been only the third contested election for the Speakership this century, and the sixth since 1800. Beating the other candidates added to her success, and would enhance her authority. It had been a 'House of Commons occasion', and those privileged to be present would not readily forget it.

As a former Conservative Whip, wise in the ways of parliament, John Major was under no illusion about the job of Speaker. She would need a vast array of talents and virtues. 'She must know when to turn a blind eye and when not to do so. She will sometimes need the wisdom of Solomon and, if I am strictly honest, she will sometimes need the patience of Job.' All her predecessors had found their patience sorely tried from time to time, not least Speaker Sir Fletcher Norton, who was in the chair in the 1770s. When the ennui got too great, he would cry out: 'I am tired! I am weary! I am heartily sick of all this!' She would not face the physical dangers experienced by some of her forebears, but there were new perils and burdens. Day after day she would be heard and now seen by millions of listeners and viewers, and deal with the steady growth and complexity of parliamentary business. Long gone were the halcyon days recalled by Elizabethan essayist Francis Bacon, who wrote: 'When Mr Popham was Speaker in 1581, and the Lower House had sat long, and done, in effect nothing, coming one day to Queen Elizabeth, she said to him: "Now, Mr Speaker, what hath passed in the Lower House?" He answered: "If it please your Majesty, seven weeks." '

There was much more in this vein. It was a vintage parliamentary occasion that had MPs searching for historical precedent and entertainment. In her manifesto speech not many minutes before, Betty joined in the fun. She quoted a Speaker of 400 years before, Sir Christopher Yelverton, who thought the office demanded 'a voice great, a carriage majestical, a nature haughty and a purse plentiful'.

How did she measure up to that? 'Not very well, I fear. I certainly do not possess a purse plentiful. I do not believe that I have been endowed with a haughty nature. It is true that in the past I may have been granted some physical agility; but my carriage is not all that majestical now,' she told MPs. What was left? Perhaps only what Speaker Yelverton described as 'a voice great', which she could use strongly in fairness and justice when the occasion demanded.

This joyous afternoon was the climax of a long career in parliament, beginning as a secretary to a Labour MP almost exactly forty years before. 'Becoming Speaker wasn't something I had thought of doing, but then I never analyse myself,' she said later.[2] 'I just take everything in my stride. I am not a fixer in any way. Of course, once I became Deputy Speaker, I thought the Speakership might come my way so I had to be prepared. But it wasn't until after this last election that I thought it could become a reality and then I thought: "By God, go for gold, Betty."'

There was a little more to it than that, but gold she got. And to secure it, she was willing to abandon all her previous commitments to the Labour Party, the 'family' that had nurtured her from her teens. A gregarious woman by nature, she was also nonetheless ready to give up the camaraderie of parliament, the easy-going cross-party friendship of the bars and tea rooms of the Commons, where as Speaker she would no longer be welcome. Labour's first Speaker, Horace King, tried to keep his favourite corner in the Strangers' Bar, but was discreetly chased out. 'It will be a lonelier life than I have known before,' Betty confessed.

Then why take it up? What is so attractive about the Speakership of the House of Commons that can make politicians quit their party and the affability of what is sometimes called 'the best gentleman's club in London'? It cannot simply be the lure of chairing debates in the House and appearing live on afternoon television, nor is it. The compensations are substantial, in terms of social status and indeed materially. The Speaker is the second-highest commoner in the land after the Prime Minister, and all MPs entering the Chamber must bow to her, even if for some it is only the most perfunctory nod. Her salary is the same as a Cabinet minister: £65,038 a year when she was first elected, £69,928 today. She lives in a luxurious state apartment at the

Palace of Westminster, has her own carriage, personal staff and an entertainment and travel allowance in excess of £120,000 a year. Betty has also appointed the Speaker's first personal public relations manager, Terence Lancaster, a former top Fleet Street journalist.

There is a formidable array of responsibilities to match. Madam Speaker is normally in the chair for three sessions a day, the first two lasting two hours each and the last sometimes as long as it takes to end the day's proceedings. All speeches by MPs are conducted through the chair – direct argument with the other side being forbidden. She must control the ofttimes unruly members, and if she gets to her feet they must sit down. She is responsible for keeping an orderly House. If an MP breaks the rules, for example by calling another member a liar, the Speaker asks him or her to withdraw or leave the Chamber. Refusal to go results in being 'named', and could end in suspension for the offending MP. In extremis, the Sergeant at Arms can be asked to eject an MP by force.

In debates, Madam Speaker decides who shall be called. For this, she has a Speaker's Conference each day at noon in Speaker's Office to go through the business of the day. After that, she repairs to her private office with her three deputies to assess which of the clamouring multitude of MPs seeking to speak should be permitted to do so. Her task is to balance the rights of ministers – the executive – to announce and explain government policy of the day, and of Her Majesty's Opposition to oppose it, with the claims of the smaller parties and those of individual back-bench members who may not share the views of their parliamentary party. As she once said: 'There is only one thing I am intolerant about, and that is intolerance. People sometimes forget that all points of view must be allowed in this House. Some may well be unpopular, but everyone must have the right to speak.'[3]

There are many other tasks, both political and administrative. Madam Speaker must decide which amendments to Bills ought to be debated by the House. This is a critical function, as was shown by the furore over the Bill ratifying the Maastricht Treaty in 1993, when Betty overruled her deputy, Michael Morris MP. She allowed a debate on a Labour motion to accept the controversial Social Chapter on workers' rights, a bruising parliamentary passage that John Major only just survived. She also determines which are Money Bills, and therefore not open to change by the House of Lords, and what issues are sub judice and cannot be discussed by MPs. She is responsible for issuing the writ to allow a by-election to take place.

Madam Speaker is the also guardian of the privileges of the House of Commons. Historically, the Speaker served both the Commons and the Crown, but by degrees from the sixteenth century onward, the office veered towards representing the Commons. Perhaps the most famous example of this loyalty, quoted by Tony Benn MP in the debate on Betty's candidature, took place on 4 January 1642, when King Charles I entered the Chamber to arrest five members for treason. Speaker Lenthall refused to comply, saying: 'May it please your Majesty, I have neither eyes to see, nor tongue to speak in this place, but as the House is pleased to direct me, whose servant I am here, and I humbly beg your Majesty's pardon that I cannot give any other answer than this to what your Majesty is pleased to demand of me.' Betty is deeply conscious of the great historical tradition she has inherited, though she could scarcely forget it. Her apartments are hung with their portraits in oils. Nowadays, Madam Speaker is more likely to have to deal with attempts to offer payments to MPs (as in the celebrated *Sunday Times* case in July 1994), or 'leaking' evidence given in confidence to a Committee of the House. She may summon offenders to the Bar of the House and reprimand them.

Above all, the Speaker speaks for the Commons. She represents the elected parliament in external relationships with the Queen, the House of Lords and other outside authorities and bodies. She represents the Commons at royal weddings and state funerals, and services for those whom politicians respect like the late broadcaster Brian Redhead. Betty loved 'the sunshine in his voice'.

Madam Speaker receives visiting foreign dignitaries, and entertains sumptuously in Speaker's House, her home in Westminster. Hers is a palace within a palace. The newly refurbished state apartments, entered by a fan-vaulted 'cloister' in the northernmost courtyard, are situated between the two towers at the eastern end of the palace, overlooking Westminster Bridge and the River Thames, and just beneath that most famous of London landmarks, Big Ben. Betty is apparently deaf to its well-known chimes, saying: 'I live under Big Ben, and I never hear it.'[4]

MPs and other guests to Speaker's House never fail to marvel at its treasures. The elaborately decorated apartments were completed in 1859, to the design of Sir Charles Barry who rebuilt the Palace of Westminster after the destructive fire of 1834. The hand of his collaborator, A. W. N. Pugin, the master Gothic revivalist, can be seen everywhere. Tim Willis, one of the very few journalists allowed access to Speaker's House, wrote: 'For Betty Boothroyd, every day is like living in a Pugin exhibition. She finds the date on a Pugin calendar, fills her pen from a Pugin inkstand, warms her hands at a Pugin fireplace. She keeps Pugin's own china in her cabinets, lights her way with Pugin candelabra, and when she looks up from her Pugin settee, rests her eye on Pugin friezes. Still, she says: "I don't get carried away by all this splendour. I'm north country. Down to earth." ' [5]

Betty unburdened herself to her interviewer with characteristic frankness. Of the imperial Speaker's Bed with scarlet silk hangings, made by Holland and Sons in 1858 and officially never slept in, she chuckled: 'Of course I've bounced on it, and it's far too hard to sleep in. I prefer my comfy one upstairs.' And the drapes? 'I helped to choose all the curtains. The old ones were so tatty and torn that the waitresses were horrified. They used to stand in front of them so that visitors wouldn't see how threadbare they were.'

The entrance to Speaker's House, topped by a tower decorated with gargoyles and heraldic lions, leads through heavy double doors into a small porch, the colours of its glass as deep as the day they were stained. Minton tiles, heraldic lintel-carvings and Gothic standard lamps lead on to the *pièce de résistance*: a red-carpeted staircase of blindingly burnished brass. 'The effect on newly elected MPs arriving for their first audience with the Speaker must be humbling,' wrote Willis. 'Before them, a massive fireplace soars skyward. Flanking them, heraldic beasts bear the royal standards. Turning at the half-landing, they grasp a hand-rail supported by riots of scrolled foliage to confront insanely tall candelabra. To sufferers of Stendhal's Syndrome, it must be a relief to duck into the cool of the lacily carved cloister.'

Ahead, he found reception and dining rooms, to the right, the Speaker's Study, with its massed portraits of previous Speakers. With their fireguards like little cathedrals, gleaming brass and mirrors, the apartments succeeded in their purpose – to impress, judged Willis.

But he asked: do they lack personality? 'Not to Betty Boothroyd. She knows her Speakers like old friends: her "hero", Sir Arthur Peel, "the mere rustle of his robe could quell a noisy chamber"; John Trevor, "he was cross-eyed, which must have made it difficult to catch his eye"; and William Lenthall, who faced up to Charles I and now watches her at work.'

For Betty, this is both home and office. She wears formal parliamentary dress, a black coat and skirt, white blouse with decorated cuffs and neck, for meetings with her staff and deputies. Westminster officially insists that the Speaker's normal day, while different from that of an MP, is no less busy. Indeed, it begins not so very differently from that of the rest of us. First thing in the morning she reads the papers and listens to the news.

But she is looking for something different: events that might prompt requests for an emergency debate, or a Private Notice Question calling a minister to account on an issue too urgent to admit of delay. She consults with her clerks, who during business sit before her on the Table of the Commons (even the table takes initial capitals in the serious world of Westminster). The party managers – the Whips – may also wish to speak to her about getting business through the House, and backbenchers usually put in their bids to speak at this time.

After lunch, Betty is dressed in her official robes ten minutes before the session begins at 2.30 p.m. There then takes place a Speaker's procession from her state apartments to the Chamber. In front goes the Commons Bar doorkeeper, clad in knee-breeches, silk stockings and white gloves, wearing a 250-year-old messenger's badge. After him comes the Sergeant at Arms, bearing the Mace which symbolizes the authority delegated by the sovereign to the Commons and without which parliamentary proceedings cannot begin. Then comes the Speaker, her train bearer, her chaplain and her secretary. The procession takes her through the Central Lobby, the busy circular atrium with hard benches and a post office, where MPs meet their guests and constituents. Betty's radiant progress is a show-stopper. Friends say she still gets a kick out of this traditional pageantry, which many imagine dates hundreds of years ago.

Her sponsor in the Speakership contest, John Biffen, himself a former leader of the House, confesses he 'still gets pleasure in watching' this daily event. 'The noise of conversation has been stilled. A path has been cleared for the procession. The advancing footsteps echo, almost like a slow march. The policeman's cry goes up, "Speaker," and respect is enjoined by his stentorian cry, "Hats off, strangers." I have never seen a man remain "covered", to use the parliamentary idiom.'[6] Prayers are said in the Chamber by the chaplain, and then the press and visitors (always known as 'strangers') are allowed into the galleries. Madam Speaker then opens the day's business.

This is the rewarding, if wearing, part of the job. There is also a heavy administrative burden. Madam Speaker chairs the House of Commons Commission, a body of senior MPs, which formally employs the thousand or so full-time staff who work to provide services for MPs: the library, the refreshment rooms and bars, security, the reporting of debates in *Hansard*, the verbatim record of the work of parliament. Managing the palace is a massive task. Inside its Gothic splendour are two miles of corridors and 1100 rooms. Even with the gradual introduction of hi-tech security devices, simply keeping the building safe is a non-stop anxiety that still troubles Betty, many years after Irish republican terrorists murdered Airey Neave, the Tory MP, with a car bomb in the underground car park exit in New Palace Yard on 30 March 1979.

At least her own person is secure from the quarter where danger historically came: the throne. Though the office dates back to 1258, when Simon de Montfort presided over Henry III's 'Mad Parliament' in Oxford, the first Speaker to be so designated was Sir Thomas Hungerford, chosen in 1377. It was not long before Mr Speaker was in trouble with the monarch. Sir John Bussy, Speaker for three parliaments was beheaded by Richard II in 1399; his nervous successor, Sir John Cheyne resigned after two days. Thomas Thorpe, holder of the office for less than a year in the mid-fifteenth century, was beheaded during Henry VII's reign in 1461, as was Sir Thomas Tresham ten years later. Richard III carried on the tradition, chopping off William Catesby's head in 1485, after he had been in the Chair for less than a month.

Henry VIII beheaded two Speakers, Sir Richard Empson and Edmund Dudley on the same day in 1510 – not because they would not do his bidding, but because they did his father's bidding rather too well. Empson and Dudley were 'extortioners without parallel' on the Tudor monarch's behalf, enriching themselves hugely in the process.

Parliamentary historian Philip Laundy relates: 'Circumventing the compliant Commons, they exacted illegal taxes and ransoms by means which they were devoid of every scruple. Verdicts were dictated to judges and savage fines were imposed for trivial infringements of the law. In addition, they assured the packing of the House of Commons by intimidating the sheriffs into returning their own nominees.'[7] Such was the hatred they roused among the people, that even the despotic Henry VII felt obliged to incarcerate them in the Tower of London. His son spent the money, and beheaded them on trumped-up charges of constructive treason.

For many years thereafter, perhaps because subservience to the crown became more the rule than the exception, the Speaker's neck was safe. Even so, it was not always the most attractive post. Queen Mary's second parliament in 1554, called to ratify her marriage to Philip of Spain, was presided over by Sir Robert Brooke, the Recorder of London, and the first Speaker to represent the City of London. He lasted precisely five weeks. He went on to pursue a brilliant legal career, becoming Chief Justice of the Common Pleas.

Almost exactly 438 years later, his descendant Peter Brooke, another lawyer, was Betty's chief opponent in the Speakership stakes. Aged fifty-eight, and MP for the City of London like his famous forebear, Brooke was undoubtedly a 'man of Westminster'. His father, Henry Brooke, had been a Tory MP and Home Secretary in Harold Mac-millan's government in the 1960s. A famous cricket buff, he is the archetypal Englishman, a courteous charmer with a ready wit. At the dissolution of John Major's first administration in March 1992, he was Secretary of State for Northern Ireland, though with no great expectations of retaining a Cabinet post.

That Peter Brooke was candidate at all is proof of the remarkable pother that the Conservatives got themselves into when faced with the prospect of a battle with Betty. Formally, of course, the office of Speaker is supposed to be a consensual expression of the will of the House. In modern political history, it has in practice been a fix between the two Front Benches. The ruling party usually knows that it can enforce its will when a vacancy arises, simply by demanding loyalty.

But the Prime Minister does not always gets his or her way. In 1983, when Mrs Thatcher was finally obliged to replace the accommodating former Labour MP, George Thomas, rewarding him with the title Viscount Tonypandy, her choice was Sir Humphrey Atkin (now Lord Colnbrook), a former Chief Whip, who she imagined would be just as compliant as George Thomas had been. The House evidently shared her view, and plumped instead for Jack Weatherill, a former Deputy Chief Whip. It was the right choice. Weatherill was judged on all sides to have been a good Speaker, of the mould of 'Shakes' Morrison of the early 1950s and Selwyn Lloyd, the former Foreign Secretary who was wished on to the Commons by Harold Macmillan after his 'night of the long knives' in July 1962, but who made a fine Speaker nonetheless. Weatherill's choice as his successor (private, but discreetly circulated) was Betty Boothroyd, his deputy since 1987.

Peter Brooke clearly fancied doing the job rather longer than his illustrious antecedent, but his party could not bring itself to make him the sole Conservative candidate. Four or five others were jostling at the margins, hoping to catch the Chief Whip's eye. Technically, it was none of the Whips' business, the election for Speaker being a free vote of the Commons. But they were very active, nonetheless, pushing the unfortunate Brooke as hard as they could in telephone canvassing during the weekend before the critical vote. The Labour Whips were also active drumming up the Boothroyd vote, but their task was easier. Betty was her party's sole candidate.

Brooke brought some dignity to a contest that, with the benefit of hindsight, was a foregone conclusion. Too many Tory MPs – 72 in all – voted for Betty for him to succeed. They were partly motivated by the consideration that Brooke was an outgoing Cabinet minister, and back-bench MPs do not like rewarding ex-ministers so swiftly with such a plum job.

David Wilshire, Conservative MP for Spelthorne, articulates that view. If anything needs to be kept out of the hands of the executive it is the Speakership, he argues. Yet here were the Tories offering a former Cabinet minister 'clearly identified with the establishment', he said. 'I have no confidence in the Speakership if it is in the Cabinet's gift. Betty owes her position to the votes of MPs, not to some discussion in the Cabinet – and that must be good. It must concentrate their minds occasionally, I suspect.'[8]

Brooke was candid and characteristically generous in defeat. 'I knew from my canvassing that Betty would win, but I also realized that my Party wished there to be a candidate from our side. Betty won. She has made an excellent Speaker,' he confided later.[9] The patrician with half a millennium of history behind him failed where the parliamentary charms of the daughter of a humble mill worker succeeded. It was a political fairytale of sorts. But the apparently easy outcome disguised one of the longest and toughest campaigns of recent parliamentary history.

It was a long haul from the back streets of Dewsbury to Speaker's House. Born into Labour Party activism as she was, it was still an enormous ambition to realize simply to get into the Commons in those bleak post-war years, when Labour parliamentarians seemed to be either trade union worthies or careerist intellectuals – and certainly male. Unlike Harold Wilson, from nearby Huddersfield but light years away in cultural preparation for politics, Betty has no battered photograph of herself as a child standing at the doorway of 10 Downing Street, awaiting her inheritance.

Indeed, some years before she became Speaker, Betty confessed she had never expected to enter the Commons. Asked by Jean Denham, then working as a Labour Party press officer in Transport House, if she had ever imagined as a teenager that she might become an MP, she replied: 'Oh, my dear, the first time I ever saw the Houses of Parliament, I had come to London on a coach, on a works outing, and there was Big Ben. No, I would never have dreamt that I would be an MP.'[10]

Yet becoming an MP did quickly become her dream, and one she was convinced she could achieve by sheer hard work, dedication and self-belief. As she has so often and so eloquently put it, Betty came out of the womb into the Labour movement. Her mother, Mary, and father, Archie, were both members of the party and of the Textile Workers' Union in the heavy-woollen town of Dewsbury where she was born in the Depression year of 1929. She was used from childhood to seeing her home given over to political activity: party meetings, election campaign sessions, the nuts and bolts of local political work that made the district a byword for municipal socialism.

Betty was a quite boisterous, fun-loving teenager who enjoyed life to the full, as much as any girl could in drab, post-war Britain. She was a keen dancer, and dated the local boys. But she was serious about politics. She joined the Labour League of Youth just as soon as the rules allowed, at the age of sixteen, and apart from a brief, unhappy spell as a professional dancer on the London stage, immersed herself in local politicking and the national activity of the party's youth arm.

As a schoolgirl, Betty sang the wartime favourites to servicemen, travelling round her native Yorkshire in a converted bus with a band called The Swing Stars to give concerts at airfields and army camps. As an older teenager, she trained her voice for a different purpose: public speaking. Even her lunch-break was not sacrosanct. Just before she landed a job at Transport House, Labour's London headquarters, she worked as a secretary to the manager of a British Road Services depot in Batley, the 'shoddy' capital of the woollen district. Sheila Goodair, her workmate there, recalls: 'On a lunch-time, we used to grab a sandwich, and she used to practise her speeches in front of me.'[11] That was in 1952, when Betty won a national speaking competition organized by the old *Daily Herald*, newspaper of the labour movement.

Moving to London at the age of twenty-two opened up a whole new vista for Betty. Working as a secretary in the research department at Labour's HQ, under the brilliant but roguish Wilfred Fienburgh, she came into contact with the great political figures of the day and saw the bitter Left–Right battle within the party at close quarters. She soon moved to Westminster to work as a secretary to a stridently Left-wing MP, Barbara Castle, and then also for Geoffrey de Freitas, a brilliant, debonair old Haileyburyian (like Attlee, for whom he was Parliamentary Private Secretary) and lawyer. Barbara Castle, born just a few miles from Betty in the Yorkshire coalfield, and Betty's other pals in the ardently socialist Hornsey Labour Party brought her into contact with the Keep Left group, which looked to the fiery hard-liner Nye Bevan as its political guru. De Freitas, an internationalist with strong European and American sympathies who nurtured unfulfilled ambitions of his own to become Speaker, drew her into a centre-Right, Atlanticist-European circle.

Betty could not have wished for a more comprehensive grounding in politics. She also began to look the part of a would-be MP. She was always perfectly groomed and as well-dressed as her meagre salary would allow. Her father had taught her to spend that little bit more than she could really afford for clothes that would make the most of her natural sense of presence, a stylishness that had been honed by the discipline of professional dancing. As one old friend from her Dewsbury days observed: 'Betty had a great feel for fashion, and always seemed to be in fashion before others – and long before the fashions were up north. She was always very smart.'

Smart in other ways, too. Betty slaved away in the basement room off Westminster Hall, the oldest part of the House of Parliament dating back a thousand years, working with the inadequate facilities given to MPs. But her conviction grew that she could do as well as any of them. There were two big obstacles: her inexperience, and her sex. She could do something about the one, nothing about the other.

When she was still in her mid-twenties, Betty approached Labour's National Agent and asked if she could be considered for a parliamentary nomination. He told her she was too young and needed 'to get some age on my shoulders'. So she ran her own little investigation into the average age of Labour and Conservative MPs. On her own side, it was 'near pensionable' – that is, in the early sixties – while on the government side she found a deliberate policy of bringing on younger candidates. Determined to succeed, whatever the odds, by sheer force of personality she won the nomination to stand at a by-election in rural Leicestershire South-East in 1957, and at Peterborough in the General Election in 1959 – before she took off for the States, temporarily disillusioned with the 'old men of Europe'.

Even today, there are only thirty-eight women Labour MPs out of 272, though it is now party policy that half the winnable seats becoming vacant before the next election will be given to women. By comparison, the party was in those days neanderthal. This was true not only of the men, but often the women too. David Wood, the canny political editor of *The Times*, once wrote: 'Women selectors, it seems, are not merely unsparing judges of their own sex. They also want to keep other women in their place.' Betty agreed. In her experience, women selectors in

Labour constituencies seemed to judge women harder than they did men.

'Many times I have been told I need the experience of bringing up kids and standing at a kitchen sink,' she said.[12] 'Perhaps it springs from the limited horizon some women have set for themselves. Or do they hope a male candidate will marry their daughter and they will get to see the inside of Number 10? I sometimes wonder.' She disclosed that 'certainly there is a hostility to glamour', while conceding that top-drawer aspirants from the right background would always do well. 'Women like Shirley Williams who scale unscalable heights will be few. Others, like myself, remembering school reports which read 'she is a trier' will proceed with the determination of a resilient tortoise.'

It should not be forgotten that in the fable, the tortoise did get there. And so did Betty. In all, she stood five times over a period of sixteen years before being elected – if not an entry for the *Guinness Book of Records*, certainly a testament to determination. Yet it was characteristic of the woman that she could not only carry on regardless after every setback, but find room to joke about her predicament. 'There was little doubt I was destined as the girl most *unlikely* to succeed,' she used to grin.

She made it to Westminster as the choice of the people of West Bromwich, a Black Country constituency steeped in the industrial revolution, doubling Labour's majority in a by-election. Almost immediately, she was taken into the lower rungs of government, as an assistant Whip, responsible for keeping fellow MPs in the West Midlands in line, ensuring that they were there and that they voted for Harold Wilson's government. It was the beginning of a career in parliamentary supervision that two decades later would ensconce her in the Speaker's Chair.

En route, there were some diversions: to Strasbourg, for an eighteen-month stint as a nominated EuroMP (when she was also Whip to Labour's ill-assorted delegation), to diverse parliamentary committees on such key issues as abortion, and to Liverpool, where as a hard-line moderate on the party's national executive committee she took part in the long investigation that finally destroyed the Militant Tendency's 'entryist' tactics.

But it was to the Chairmen's Panel that her interest was directed:

that body (almost entirely composed of men MPs) whose interest lies in directing and administering the work of parliament. Its members chair the committees that examine parliamentary Bills line by line, where Opposition MPs fight to water down government measures, and ministers and their backbenchers strive to get their way. It is an unsung role, because the MP in the chair is there to expedite business rather than to make a name for himself or herself.

It is also lethal to orthodox political ambition. Sir Marcus Fox, Chairman of the Conservative MP's 1922 backbenchers committee, who went to school with Betty but travelled a different political path, says: 'Membership of the Chairmen's Panel is usually given to people who have shown an inclination towards it. It is not normal for somebody who is going to achieve ministerial office to go on the panel. It usually happens a bit later in your parliamentary career, when you have experience of committee work, and you look to that rather than making speeches in the House and trying to get noted. It does, in a sense, map you out.'

Once on the Chairmen's Panel, her progress to Deputy Speaker in 1987 and then to the Speaker's Chair itself in 1992 appears in retrospect to have been natural, inevitable even. It was not. Her astute and hard-working chairing of legislative committees – which prompted one gallant Tory MP to present her with a bottle of perfume – was not enough to guarantee her the job; not enough, in fact to guarantee the nomination of her own party. Her supporters (most notably Gwyneth Dunwoody MP, fellow hammer of the Left on the NEC) campaigned quietly but sedulously to secure Neil Kinnock's backing for her bid for the Speakership. Outright self-promotion for the post is strictly out of order, but Betty herself worked behind the scenes to secure her candidature: a soiree for 'Betty's friends' at the Westminster flat of Lady Helen de Freitas here, and word in the right ear there.

From the outset, she realized the importance of winning the votes of as many Conservative MPs as possible, just in case Labour did not win the election and have the Speakership in its gift. She had the remarkable good fortune early on in the campaign to win the backing of one of the most respected MPs on the Tory benches: John Biffen, former Conservative Leader of the House, ex-Cabinet minister in Margaret Thatcher's time, and a true 'House of Commons man' who had written an insider's account of how Westminster works. The very fact that he was on side did much to dispel fears of a partisan candidature, allowing Tories to vote as their conscience dictated rather than as the Whips told them. The total support of all the minority parties completed her broadly based coalition, which delivered a much bigger majority than even her most committed supporters had dared hope.

There are those, like political commentator Tony Howard, who believe that 'it is quite possible that she decided very early on that she wanted to be Speaker'. Certainly, it became a fixed ambition as the years went by, probably as far back as 1983, after Labour's disastrous showing at the polls and possibly even before that. Long-range aspirations of that nature require just the fixity of purpose that took Betty Boothroyd from the back-to-backs of Dewsbury to the pre-eminence of second-highest commoner in the land.

The friends of her formative years were not surprised. Jean Megahy, her close 'comrade' in the Labour League of Youth, pays tribute to her achievement, while noting wryly that she expected nothing less. 'I certainly thought Betty would make her mark, because politics became her life. And once she became Deputy Speaker, I almost saw an inevitability about her becoming Speaker. People who know I know her say what a good job she is doing, and how much they enjoy watching Parliament – because she made it more interesting.

'I think, because she's a woman, it's very different. And her appointment was an issue because she was the first woman Speaker in seven hundred years. But I think, certainly in this area, people see somebody who has come from the same background as themselves and has achieved something like this. People say – isn't it wonderful that somebody from an ordinary house in an ordinary street in Dewsbury has achieved this in competition with the highest in the land. There is a feeling that she is one of us. And I think it is a mark of her greatness that she hasn't tried to hide her past. People who are themselves are always impressive. She never tries to be anything else. She is never ashamed of her roots. She talks about them, and they are important to her, and I think this is a mark of her greatness.'

Has the goal of becoming the first woman Speaker been worth the struggle to achieve it? Unquestionably, Betty has sacrificed much to win her 'gold'. Looking back on her life, a few months before she was elected to the chair, she said: 'I don't believe that I have any regrets. If I have any, I think it's family. The fact that I have no family is a regret. Not just parents, because parents have to pass on, but that I haven't created a new generation. I don't regret anything I've done in my professional life, that's all right. But I would have to have liked to have, to have had, a husband, a partner, and to have created, to have seen a family round me.'

But she is a person on 'a very even keel'. Though she would be 'down' after losing elections – and there were too many of those in the early years – Betty has had no depression or real sadness other than family deaths. 'I don't think I've had periods of great gloom. I don't think I have suffered in that way. Maybe it's because of my make-up, my resilience. I always think that there's nobody really to look after me but me. I have got to earn a living, I have got to do my job, because nobody is going to do it for me. Nobody looks after West Bromwich if I'm ill or depressed. So I just do it. I'm not introspective at all like that. It's a stoic thing – I think this is a lot to do with being north country, I really do. I don't analyse my feelings, I just get on with it.'[13]

In this view of the world, Betty may be counted characteristic of her home town. A 'Descriptive Account of Dewsbury' published around the turn of the century observed that the heavy-woollen town had not reached its position of 'commercial and industrial eminence' at a single stroke, or even by a number of brilliant and successful efforts. 'Rather is it the result of patient plodding effort, of difficulties surmounted one by one with a courage and pertinacity that all must admire, and which is ever characteristic of the reliant, independent denizens of the Yorkshire hills and dales.'[14] Those qualities were evident from her childhood, and stood her in good stead when she took on the male-dominated citadel of Westminster.

CHAPTER II

A YORKSHIRE UPBRINGING

B ETTY BOOTHROYD was born on 8 October 1929, at 24
Marriott Street, Dewsbury, in what was then proud to be
known as the West Riding of Yorkshire. The rented house,
long since demolished, was a stone 'back-to-back' cottage typical of
the Pennine mill towns. The front gave out directly on to the street,
and the back formed the back of the next street. The terrace, like
much of the Eastborough area where Betty spent her early life, was
demolished in the slum clearances of the post-war years. Eastborough
was a tightly packed community at the foot of a steep hill, surrounded
by woollen mills and warehouses. Life was not easy, even when 'trade'
was good. When it was bad, and the millworkers were laid off, it was
perilous. When they could, husbands and wives both worked full time.
Betty's family was no exception.

Dewsbury, situated in a flat hollow just north of the River Calder,
is a very old place that has spread out among the surrounding hillsides.
Tradition has it that Paulinus preached here in the year 627, and local
historians contend that the town owes its name 'God's Town' to this
visit. Certainly, it was known as Deusberia in the Domesday Book,
though more recent experts suggest that the name derived from Dui,
a god of the Brigantes, commemorated on a Roman altar nearby.

The town remained something of a rural backwater until the coming,
first of the canals that connected Dewsbury with the great ports of
Liverpool and Hull, and then the railways in 1840 which linked Dewsbury to the great manufacturing centres of Leeds and Manchester.
Dewsbury was constituted a municipal borough in 1862, but as late as
1891 – when Betty's father was five years old – the parliamentary
electorate was only 12,093. However, industry was by then booming.

Dewsbury specialized in the manufacture of heavy goods: blankets, kerseys, flannels, baizes, serges, druggets, rugs and carpets as well as cloth of the finer sort.

In the years before the First World War, the Descriptive Account of Dewsbury said that 'constant work is found for the teeming population in the huge mills and factories that abound on every hand, and contentment and prosperity is indicated on every side.' If such a commercial idyll was true then, it did not last. But in the no-nonsense climate of the 1920s' Depression years, families got by as best they could. 'Life was very hard,' recalls Alf Ramsden, a family friend of the Boothroyds who later went on to become Labour Mayor of Dewsbury. 'The women did all kinds of extra things to earn extra money. It was a very close-knit community, with it being back-to-back housing. Every neighbour helped each other. It really was a pleasure to see.'[1] The houses usually had two bedrooms, a single living room and a cellar which doubled up as a 'keeping room'. There were no gardens. Bath time was Friday night, in a zinc bath in front of the fire.

Betty's own first recollections are of those back-to-back dwellings. 'My earliest memory is of coal fires flickering in our house in Eastborough in Dewsbury,' she told Yorkshire Life more than sixty years later. 'In the background, I was aware of my father's presence. He was always there, even more often, perhaps, than my mother, in my childhood memories. He was in his mid-forties when I was born so it was obvious to me, long before I could think rationally, that I was something special to him. He was my first playmate, doing all he could to capture my attention to make me happy.'[2]

Her mother, Mary, née Butterfield, had married Betty's father Ben Archibald Boothroyd a little more than seven months before Betty's birth, at St Ignatius Roman Catholic Church, Storrs Hill Road, in nearby Ossett. She was a Catholic, but he was not, and the church's instruction 'that all the children of both sexes who may be born of this marriage shall be baptized in the Catholic Church and shall be carefully brought up in the knowledge and practice of the Catholic religion' was not carried out.

The wedding certificate for the marriage on 1 April 1929, shows that Archie, as he was almost invariably known, was a forty-three-year-old widower, and gives his occupation as 'weft man in a woollen mill'.

Mary Butterfield, at twenty-seven some sixteen years his junior, was a spinster, a woollen weaver living at 1 Zion Street, Gawthorpe, Ossett, a village on the road out to the county town of Wakefield. Her father, Harry, was a blanket finisher. Archie's father, Walter, by now dead, had been a chemical worker.

The timing of Betty's birth so soon after the wedding, is of some interest. Either she was born very prematurely – and there has never been any suggestion of this – or Mary Butterfield was carrying the future Speaker of Parliament when she went to the altar. If the couple did marry when it became clear that Betty's mother was pregnant, this would not have been particularly unusual, even for those more censorious times. But the gap in the couple's ages was not so common, and must have been powerfully influential in the sense of reverence that young Betty – as she is named on her birth certificate, she was never Elizabeth – felt for her father.

The couple evidently met at work, at George Harry Hirst's woollen mill, up the hill from Eastborough in the adjoining town of Batley. Mrs Marjorie Edwards (née Teale), now aged eighty-three and living in Boothroyd Lane, Dewsbury (an indication of how common the name is locally), recalls: 'Betty's mum worked at Hirst's mill, and her dad worked there some of the time. All us lasses worked in the mills. People used to work two looms after the war. Mary taught me how to weave cloth on a loom. She started working in the mill at thirteen. She had it hard, but she was always full of life, and full of talk.'[3] Marjorie's sister, Sally, now Mrs Rhodes, aged eighty-seven, said: 'Betty's dad was out of work a lot. Everybody was out of work. Her mum was a weaver and her dad was a weft man. There was more work for weavers. I think that's where they met, at Hirst's Mill.'

When they met, Archie had not long been bereaved of his first wife. He had married Mary Hannah Bould in October 1912, when they were both aged twenty-six. Their certificate of marriage at St Philip's Parish Church, Dewsbury, gives his occupation as 'mill-hand', and his address as 20 Marriott Street, four doors down from the house where Betty was born. He appeared to move quite often in the warren of narrow streets that made up Eastborough, but again that was by no means uncommon. The houses were all rented. Mary Bould came from Back Lawson Street, Dewsbury, and was listed as having no occupation.

The marriage lasted fifteen years, until her death. Mrs Rhodes connects this childless marriage with Archie's fierce devotion to Betty. 'He had been married before, but they did not have any kiddies. He thought there was nobody like Betty.' On BBC Radio 4's 'Desert Island Discs' decades later, Betty disclosed to interviewer Sue Lawley that her father had originally wanted to call her Hannah, after his first wife. Presumably this was too much for the new Mrs Boothroyd.

However Archie and Mary Butterfield met, it seems to have been a good match. Betty told an interviewer nearly half a century later: 'I think they had quite a happy marriage, they were very devoted. My father married late in life and he was very much older than my mother and I think that they hardly expected any children at all. When I came along, it was quite a surprise. I was an only child and a little indulged by my father; he must have been late forties when I was born. The fact that I came along perhaps even brought them closer together.'[4]

She worshipped her father, as is clear from her many references to him, and was very deeply affected by his death when she was only eighteen years old, struggling to find an adult identity. 'My father was a very splendid man. We had very little money, but he was always extremely smart,' she recalled. Like him, she still brushes her clothes and hangs them up before going to bed. 'And his shoes would be stuffed with newspapers to keep them in good shape – as mine are today.'[5] To make the family shoes last longer, Archibald bought bits of leather from Dewsbury market, and hammered them into place on a last on the kitchen table of a Sunday morning. 'And he would polish them. You could see yourself in the shoes that I wore. He was a very proud man.'[6]

Both her parents worked in the woollen mills. It was a long day, from 6.30 a.m. to 5.30 in the evening, and until lunchtime – or, as it was universally known in West Yorkshire, 'dinner time' – on Saturday. Like most working-class households, the Boothroyds lived by a set weekly ritual. Once Archie had got the coal-fired boiler going on Monday night, Betty's mother would do the washing. On Tuesday night, she did the ironing. On Wednesday night, she 'did' the bedrooms. On Thursday, it was the turn of the downstairs rooms. And on Friday night, she did the baking for the weekend. All this on top of working at the mill. 'It really was a full-time job for women. They had a very hard time indeed. Many of them were the only breadwinners of the family. My mother used to say to me, "You know, I am not employed for my sex appeal. I'm employed because my rate of pay is lower than that of your father's. That's the only reason." '[7]

There were long periods when her father was out of work, and he would stay at home doing the housework. Many, many others were on the dole in the 'Hungry Thirties', but even so Archie's house-husbanding was unusual. He closed the door and the curtains so the neighbours would not see him about his chores. 'A lot of men, particularly during that period, didn't want to be seen doing what were considered to be women's tasks,' said Betty later. 'But my father always did his share of the work.'[8] It was not until the advent of war in 1939 that trade picked up again and there was full employment in Dewsbury. Then, the skills of the Boothroyds and thousands of others were needed to make blankets and uniform cloth for the troops.

Betty has often talked readily of Archie as the inspiration of her life – 'my father imbued me with his sense of optimism that you *could* do things, that everything was possible. Even when he was unemployed, which was for most of my childhood, he never got depressed.'[9] Archie's life was typical of the working class at the time: a struggle against material odds, in his case made doubly difficult by his socialist convictions and his trade union activities with the Textile Workers' Union. He was often out of work, and Betty remembers periods before the war when 'we used to pray for snow so that on Monday morning he could go down to the council offices and get a job shovelling snow'.[10]

Betty's dance teacher Mrs Vivien Meakin describes him as 'a small fellow who always wore a cap'. Alf Ramsden, a former Labour Mayor of Dewsbury, recalls that he worked for 'a very low wage' at one of the mills in Dewsbury. There is anecdotal evidence that he was victimized by the millowners for his outspoken trade unionism, and had to find alternative work in Sowerby Bridge, another mill town further up the Calder river valley, almost into Lancashire. He travelled there by early morning workmen's train, often in the company of a local preacher who was also a socialist. However, Archie seems to have been less interested in the Labour Party than his wife. Ramsden recalls, 'Betty's mother, rather than her father, was involved with the Labour Party, but both were members.'[11] Another local Labour councillor,

Jack Brooke, said, 'Mary Boothroyd was a strong Labour supporter and supported the rights of women. Mary was forthright for those days, and very strong willed. She had grown up the hard way.'[12]

Betty was more inclined to see them as a husband and wife team. 'My parents were politically minded because they were mill workers in Dewsbury during the Depression years. That sort of experience made you politically minded. As a matter of course they became members of the Labour Party. Our home was used for ward meetings and as committee rooms at election times.'[13]

Another interest in Archie's life, as for so many of the men folk living in the tightly packed back-to-back streets was 't'club'. Eastborough Working Men's Club and Institute was – and to a substantial degree remains – the centre of social life in the neighbourhood. It began life in a rented corner property in Battye Street, where Betty was later to live, in 1910. The club was an immediate success, and the committee bought the premises in 1912 with cash loaned by the members.

A contemporary list of names and occupations of those who loaned money provides an insight into the social mix of working men in Dewsbury in those days just before the First World War. The largest group comes from the textile trade: warehousemen, card cleaners, a teamer, a rag merchant and mill labourers. There were four coal miners, not surprisingly as the pits of the west Yorkshire coalfield penetrated almost to the centre of Dewsbury, and for many years the constituency had an NUM-sponsored MP. There is a blacksmith, a tailor, a french polisher and a clerk. In 1913, the now-flourishing club bought a vacant piece of land virtually alongside the old premises to expand, but the war and the slump of the 1920s put back those ambitious plans for more than twenty years.

Archie Boothroyd, then in his late thirties, was a member of the club's eighteen-man committee in 1925. He is pictured on the official photograph, a serious-looking man with just the hint of a wry smile playing about his mouth. In contrast with the other committee members – most of them much older, and looking more like figures from the Victorian age – he eschews white shirts and wing collars for a rather dandified, high-neck patterned shirt with a broad cravat. Parted fashionably in the middle, his full head of hair is combed to each side. The eyebrows are strong, eyes a little hooded, his nose is strong and his jaw quite firm. Much the most artistic-looking of the group.

Within months of that picture being taken, the club was pressed into a new role as calamity hit the community. In the General Strike of 1926, 'conditions were so acute in Dewsbury, along with the whole of England, that the neighbourhood was almost in a state of famine.'[14] Eastborough club officials, almost certainly including Betty's father, visited local tradesmen in small parties 'with a view to begging or buying as cheaply as possible meat and potatoes and any other vegetables'. For the duration of the strike, the club was turned into a soup kitchen, and no child who turned up with an empty bowl was turned away.

Given his trade union and Labour background, and the close-knit nature of Eastborough, the General Strike – in which Archie must have taken part – would have been devastating for Betty's father. He lost his first wife, Hannah, a year later. She died, in Archie's presence, aged forty, in 24 Marriott Street (where Betty was born) on 18 August 1927. After that, he seems to have dropped out of the working-men's club hierarchy. When Eastborough WMC celebrated its silver jubilee in November 1935, he was no longer a member of the committee. But by then he had a new wife, and a six-year-old daughter.

Betty may have virtually hero-worshipped her father, but she also concedes that both parents were a great influence. Archie taught her discipline, taking care of her clothes, working in a team and being responsible to other people. Her mother, who worked tirelessly for her during the sixteen-year struggle to get into Parliament, was the rock of the family. Betty sees that more clearly now. 'She was enormously supportive and, as I've got on in years and looked back, I realize that I probably didn't value the support she gave. She quietly enabled me to do the things I wanted to.'[15] Betty remembers her mother as 'very quiet and very modest', a woman who hadn't much confidence in herself outside her own home, but 'a very loving, warm person, extremely kind'.

She paid a much more generous tribute later in Rebecca Abrams's anthology, *Woman in a Man's World*, recalling that her father's death in 1948 made it extremely difficult for Betty to pursue her political ambitions in London. 'That really was heart-breaking. I always look back on that period and think what a very brave woman she was. She never put any obstacle in the way. I went home at the weekend, and whenever I could, but she must have been very lonely, being on her own, going out to work, looking after herself, nobody to come home to, nobody to look to or to do anything for. I was probably rather callous, looking back. She always came to help, fighting elections, enormously supportive, on the doorstep, knocking on doors, very proud of me. She never let me know that she was proud of me, but she did say so to others.' Betty remembered one by-election count in particular, when she was over-tired and over-emotional, weeping, 'I've just lost, I know I've lost.' Only her mother was in the room. She reassured her, 'Oh, never mind, never mind. Win, lose or draw, you're still my daughter.'[16]

Despite the privations forced on them by the Depression, which must have seemed almost natural at the time, being shared by most of their neighbours, Betty believes she had 'an exceptionally happy childhood'.[17] 'It helped, of course, that I was a much-wanted child.' Like any family, it had its strains, 'But, my goodness, we managed to be happy.' If it was a very poor household, it was a very happy one. 'I don't recall really going short of anything. If anybody went short, it was my parents. I always went to dancing class, and my father made a sleigh for me in the winter. I didn't perhaps have the best of every-thing, but I never really went short.'[18]

Working-class life in those pre-war days was still characterized by a strong sense of community. People helped each other without asking, and they virtually lived in each other's houses, as much out of necessity as anything else. Mrs Sally Rhodes, Mary Boothroyd's next-door neighbour in Battye Street, recalls, 'Betty's mum used to carry her into our house on a morning. She was only a baby, and she would put her in our bed while she went to work. We were all aunties to her, but we are not related. I used to wash her hair in Fairy soap, and I used to say, "Come on, Betty, I will make you a fairy before your mum comes home." '[19]

In later years, Betty used to say, 'Some fairy I've turned into!' But even then there were some signs of performing precocity that would later take her on to the stage, not to mention hints of a bit of the devil in her. Sally remembers, 'She used to stand with her hands behind her back and her back to the fire and say nursery rhymes when she was about three or four. I used to wash her. There was another girl called Sheila. I used to put them both in the bath and wash them together. I used to wait while my mum was done with the tub, and wash them outside if the weather was nice.'[20]

She loved eating next door, too. 'Betty used to run to our house and knock on the door and say, "I've bought my tick-tock plate for my dinner." It had a clock printed on it. She used to like Brussels sprouts and my mum used to buy them. She went in one day and said to her mum, "Why don't you have those little cabbages like grandma?" But Archie didn't like Brussels sprouts, so Mary didn't buy them.'

Sally's sister, 'Aunt Madge', has similar recollections. 'My mother [Mrs Charlotte Teale] said she would look after Betty when she was born. Betty's mum used to bring her to our house at six o'clock in the morning, before she went to work at seven. Betty used to call us – there were nine altogether, six girls, two boys and a step-brother – all aunties and uncles, and my mother grandma. Because we were a big family, she used to get all the attention because we were all a bit older than her. If my mother went on a bus trip, she would take Betty with her. She'd go to Leeds shopping, or Scarborough, but she wouldn't go much. We couldn't afford to in those days.'[21]

Sally adds, 'Betty was a bonny bairn. She was always a bit sunburnt. You couldn't help but love her. She hadn't a bit of edge on her. Her dad thought the world of her. He used to teach her all sorts of bits of poetry and nursery rhymes, and she used to stand in front of the fire, with her hands behind her back and recite them. She used to say "damn big spider" – only it should have been "great big spider". She would only be three years old then. She lived in our house more than her own. It was lovely living in Eastborough.' Betty also had scarlet fever at the age of ten, at the same time as Mavis Teale, and went into hospital for a week, Mrs Edwards recollects.

Eastborough, a densely populated area of Dewsbury just off the busy Leeds Road, has its own school, a Victorian Board School opened in 1879. Originally divided into three sections – infants, boys and girls – it was built to accommodate 900 pupils, large by the standards of the day. Here Betty came at the age of four in 1934. Another well-known contemporary of the school, Baroness Lockwood, who lived in the next

street to Betty and who later went on to become the first Chairman of
the Equal Opportunities Commission, remembers its disciplinarian
head mistress, its board of honour of pupils who won scholarships to
the Wheelright Grammar – and its tiny, concrete playground. 'Most
of the children came from the streets around, and went home for
lunch,' she told the author. 'There was one feature of the school: every
Tuesday morning we were encouraged to take our newspaper to school
and discuss current issues.'

Enlightened as the Board school was, its pupils were no strangers
to poverty. In 1902, Miss H. B. Walker, one of the school managers,
bought boots and socks for twelve boys and sent them on holiday to
Scarborough. In the year of Betty's birth, one of the women teachers
gave doses of Virol 'costing a halfpenny' to the infants. Electricity was
installed the year before she began attending, and the milk sold to
children was reduced in price to ½d (around 0.2 new pence). Even so,
parents in the 30s had to make sacrifices so that their children could
attend school regularly.

Their sacrifices were not in vain. Eastborough was a model school
of its kind. A copy of the report by Her Majesty's Inspectorate for
February 1939 still exists. In it, Mr L. J. Gibbon says of the girls'
section: 'The important thing about this school is the training in general behaviour which the girls receive there. The actual teaching is all
sound and competently given; but it is the manner rather than the
matter of instruction which is of deep and lasting value.' Praising the
inspiration of the headmistress, he observes, 'Just as each member of
the staff is encouraged to make her own contribution in her own way,
so each child is taught to be a responsible individual. The result, for
the school as a whole, is discipline in the true sense of the word as it
applies to a vigorous, interested community.'

The inspector found the school ill-equipped in some respects,
pointing out the shortage of up-to-date books in the school library
'both reference books and "light" tales for private reading'. He also
commented on the lack of indoor accommodation for physical training,
and recommended hiring a local hall. But he discovered no academic
faults, and admired 'the excellence of the children's handwriting'.
Indeed, Betty's firm, rounded script has not altered in half a century.
Mr Gibbon paid tribute to the headmistress and all her assistant

teachers, saying they 'deserve great credit for the maintenance of a school which is, at all points, alive'. Betty can still bring back those very early days, particularly the learning discipline practised in the school that has remained strong in her mind. In the infants' school, she recalled for a centenary edition of the school magazine in 1979, 'There was lots of sand to play with and beds to sleep on in the afternoon, and one classroom where what looked like enormous playing cards were pinned to the wall, which we used to point at when learning to add up. I still think of those large playing cards now when adding figures together.'[22]

Boys and girls were segregated when they reached the age of seven, and Betty was upset – though not because she was leaving the boys behind. 'I didn't want to move up to the girls' school, because the headmistress was called Miss Mackay, and everybody said she was awful.' There may well have been something awe-inspiring about Miss A. Mackay. She became head of the girls' school in 1900, and stayed in post until 1942. 'As it turned out, I liked her, but she left soon after my move.'

Miss Fox, who taught English, was her favourite teacher 'though I cannot remember why other than that I enjoyed her lessons the most'. Then there was Miss Smith, who taught the senior class. She travelled a good deal, especially to Australia 'and we all liked her to tell us of her adventures'. Miss L. Ganter was headmistress, and Betty was not too keen on her 'because she was terribly strict. One of the things I learnt was never to be late for school, because I had to walk through her class.' Pupils stepped right into the headmistress's class as soon as they entered the school. From her desk perched on a small platform, she could see right across the school. 'She would stop latecomers in front of the whole class and want an explanation. I'm sure as a result of Miss Ganter's discipline I learnt it is better to be five minutes early for an appointment rather than a minute late.'

At Eastborough, by Betty's time a Council School, great emphasis was placed on traditional learning. 'I remember Miss Fox, when we were having English lessons, used to get very annoyed when we put the apostrophe 's' in the wrong place in the word 'Girls' School'. She used to take us outside to the front door and point to the sign above the door and say, 'Girls has an apostrophe after the "s" because the school belongs to all the girls and not just one – you must remember the plural by that example.'

With the advent of the war, the arches under Eastborough School were bricked up and converted to an air-raid shelter. Betty recalls, 'Because I lived close to the school my family and neighbours used to come to the shelter at night and sleep there on bunks and would go home in the early morning. Because of that area being used as a shelter there was not much of a playground, but some of us used to play in the shelter at break-time in pitch darkness. It was the best fun I can remember, playing hide and seek and catching each other in the dark. But our little group got too large, and the teachers found out and we got into a lot of trouble and it had to stop.'

Perhaps this was the offence that she later related as a brush with authority that brought out both her sense of filial duty to her working parents and her youthful self-assertiveness. 'I remember vividly when a teacher at school was seeking to keep me in for something I had done wrong. I don't quite remember what it was, and I refused to stay because it was winter and both my parents were working and I had to get home and lay the table for tea and light the fire. And no teacher was going to keep me in after school, and deny my parents that little bit of comfort. I stood up against that and I won the battle. I explained that I'd come in Saturday morning, I'd come in Saturday afternoon, but my parents were not going to be deprived. There are times when one has to assert oneself like that for other people. I was extremely determined that nobody was going to deter me from the thing that I believed was right for me to do.'[23] She told the same story to *The Times* in 1992, adding that she was adamant her parents who had worked damned hard in the mills all week would not come home to a cold house. 'I guess I was always assertive.'

Betty brings back another fond memory of her school days: the Christmas parties, when the wood and glass partitions separating the classes were rolled back for the 'very good' parties organized by the teachers. 'I used to rave about the sandwiches, which were wonderfully tasty,' she remembered in the Eastborough centenary booklet. She told her mother they never had such lovely food at home. Puzzled, Mary Boothroyd went to the school to see what the sandwiches were made of. It was perfectly ordinary potted meat (a sometimes glutinous form of paté, still much favoured in traditional working-class homes) from Alfie Wilson, the butcher in Battye Street – 'the sort of stuff we had frequently at home. It tasted much better at school parties.'

In the days when potted meat at school was an event, there was not very much social life. Young Betty grew to value small diversions, and not expect to be indulged. 'My parents never promised me anything. I sometimes envied other kids when they said things like, "We're going to Blackpool on Sunday." But when I asked my parents if we could go somewhere, it was always "Wait and see." You had to wait and see whether it was possible.' There were no promises, so there were no real disappointments.

Once in a while, but not very often, the family would go to Leeds, 'the really big city for us', less than ten miles away. Unusually for a child, it was once again the simple gastronomic delights that became embedded in Betty's memory. 'I remember at about half past four, we would go to a cafe in Leeds market where the market stall-holders used to go, and I remember having glasses of milk and lovely ham sandwiches with lashings of thick, beautiful ham in, all hanging over the sides and lovely soft bread.'[24]

At home, there was genuine austerity. There was no television or radio. In the evenings, they would sit by the fire and tell stories. 'We had an electric meter, but if we weren't doing anything, there was no point in sitting there with all the electric lights on, so we would turn them off and sit in the firelight and just talk.' The thrift born of necessity has proved abiding. She still recalls, 'Once we got a good coal fire going we would turn out the lights. I still switch off lights today whenever I leave a room.'[25]

Archie, described by fellow Labour Party activists as 'a very quiet man, happy to do his bit', would go to the local Working Men's Club on Sunday dinner (lunch, that is) time, but only for an hour. 'My mother would slip him a bit of money. She paid all the bills; she had boxes where she put the rent and rates and money for the electric meter, and then she'd give him a little bit of money to go off and have a pint or two.'

While Archie and Mary may have had few pleasures, they were determined not to stint their daughter of her childhood passion: dance. Her next-door neighbour Sally Rhodes remembers, 'She used to like dancing. When she was little, she used to dance round the room. She would be about five years old.'[26] When she was only eight years old, Betty was enrolled in the Vivienne School of Dancing in Dewsbury, run by Vivien Meakin at the Temperance Hall, Willans Road. She charged a shilling (five new pence) for four hours, and the lessons usually took place once a week on Saturday mornings. Vivien had four troupes, and the girls would be moved up a class as they got older.

Apart from teaching the elements of dance, the Vivienne School put on charity shows in the area's numerous non-conformist chapels, and in nearby Ossett Town Hall. Vivien also did four matinees at the Dewsbury Empire, then a thriving music hall just off the Market Place in the centre of the town. They were very popular. 'We used to get full houses at the Empire and at Ossett Town Hall,' she recalls.[27] 'It was lovely because they had nice scenery. We used to love to go there. We put on some good shows, and everybody used to be waiting and asking, "What's your panto this year?"'

Betty swiftly made her mark at the Vivienne School, and was already being cast as principal boy by the age of twelve. Why? 'Because she was the type. She had the nice legs, the figure, the voice, well, everything about her. She wasn't frightened like some kiddies when you have to say to them "keep smiling". Betty had it off to a tee.'[28] She was attracted to tap-dancing, but Vivien put them through the whole routine – troupe dancing, chorus work – the lot. 'I think Betty started like a lot of the girls did. She wanted to go to dancing classes and she loved it. A lot liked to do it and say, "Oh, I go to dancing classes," but they didn't keep it up. It was a hobby unless they were really outstanding.'

Of course, at that age, it was merely a pastime for Betty, too, even if it was a consuming one. 'Even as a very small girl I loved dancing,' she confessed to *Yorkshire Life*.[29] 'The interest grew as I became older. I was devoted to tap-dancing and ballet. I soon found, though, that I wasn't all that good at ballet.' That was Vivien's judgment, too. But Betty had other qualities that her contemporaries did not. 'She wasn't acrobatic or a ballet dancer,' said Vivien, now Mrs Vivien Meakin, aged seventy-three, living in retirement in Ossett. 'But she had a voice that could carry. When I hear Betty now, I think, "Well, you always had a good voice." You couldn't always hear some of them. They had little voices.'

The stage presence and voice that would make her the second-highest commoner in the land fifty years later won her the role of principal boy three times before she left the Vivienne School at around thirteen years of age. 'She was Prince Charming, Robin Hood and Aladdin,' remembers Vivien. As Aladdin, she sang 'Far Away, Long Ago'. 'She had quite a good voice. She was a good all-rounder. She was a good attender too. You know, some of them would hit and miss, and they never got anywhere.' But Betty stuck the course. 'When it got nearer to the pantomime, around September/October, we would put on an extra rehearsal. But she was always there, and she soon learned her part.'

A fading photograph from 1941 shows Betty as the Baron in *Robin Hood* and in *Babes in the Wood*, which (said the *Ossett Observer*) 'filled Ossett Town Hall with a delighted audience on Saturday afternoon, the proceeds being in aid of the central hospital supplies and comforts for local servicemen'. A profit of around £20 was realized. The panto had been written and was produced by Vivien, and was played entirely by children aged three to thirteen. The local paper said, 'Their dancing and acrobatic skill, coupled with remarkable versatility, and sense of showmanship, were obviously the result of careful and thorough training.' Praise was showered on the costumes, mostly made by the girls' mothers.

In the group photograph, Betty, then aged twelve, is on the extreme right of those seated. Her appearance in *Robin Hood* and *Babes in the Wood* is an extraordinary anticipation of her role as Speaker. She wears a judge's wig, a white ruff, and a frock coat – almost precisely the costume worn by speakers down the century until she took the chair. Her face and mouth are full, the dark, arched eyebrows already well-formed. Her strong – almost podgy – hands rest calmly on her knees. She looks for all the world as if she is about to call a particularly persistent backbencher. It is a remarkable piece of innocent premonition.

Dance was a great liberating experience for Betty, even if she finally expressed herself through the very different medium of politics. The stage lifted her horizons from the grimy terraces of Dewsbury to a wider world. Mary Boothroyd pushed her daughter's natural passion, and even persuaded her reluctant Archie to allow Betty to become a full-time chorus-line dancer in the sinful capital.

Even in Dewsbury, scarcely a risky neighbourhood despite it being wartime, Archie Boothroyd was anxious for his daughter's welfare. 'I always wanted more freedom as a child, because my father was always so much more protective of me than my friends' parents were of them,' she acknowledged much later.'[30] 'It was always an embarrassment to me that I wasn't allowed to stop off at someone's house for a coffee after the dances at Dewsbury Town Hall. But the cloakroom attendants at the town hall, Mr and Mrs Whiteley, lived at the end of our street and there was no question that I could be home later than they were. My father would walk down the street looking for me if it was getting close to the time.'

By contrast, her mother pushed her for all she was worth. There wasn't very much spare cash, but what there was went on Betty's dancing lessons. Like most people in Eastborough, the Boothroyds belonged to the local Cooperative Society. To this day, Betty can remember their membership number 12249. All the family groceries were bought at 't'Co-op', and the 'divvi' (a quarterly dividend bonus based on spending, and paid in cash) was saved 'for me, for my dancing and for any equipment I wanted'.[31] 'I loved to dance. I loved the music and the movement, and for a time that was what I wanted to be then.'

Betty was not the only subsequently famous political name attending the Vivienne School of Dancing at this period. By a quirk of fate, so was Sir Marcus Fox, now Tory MP for Shipley, west Yorkshire, and Chairman of the Conservative 1922 Committee, which comprises all the party's backbenchers. 'I used to attend the dancing school with my twin sister,' admits the boy hoofer, who does not make much of the episode these days. 'Our mother insisted that we learned ballroom dancing.' He also went to Eastborough School with Betty, which he remembers as 'extremely disciplined, as most schools were in those days. It was in an area of some deprivation. The staff were absolutely superb, no other word for it.'[32]

A mutual understanding grew up between Vivien Meakin and Mary Boothroyd. 'Her mother, she was a nice lady, I knew her very well,' remembers the dancing teacher. 'It was always "our Betty". She worked hard for Betty, she did. And she was so interested. She had Betty's costumes made for her. She always had lovely costumes. A lot of the mothers made the costumes themselves, but there was a lady called Mrs Whitworth who used to do it for a living and she started to sew for me. She was the one who made Betty's costumes. She always had the best. They always had lovely costumes. People often used to say so. You'd go to these professional shows and watch the opening chorus coming on, and they could look quite tarnished because they were used a lot. But ours were new every year. Of course, a lot of them were used as sundresses afterwards, or as shorts. But of course the principals' didn't because theirs had all the satin and a lot of feathers and all that. We had some very happy times.'[33]

'Her mum was a very ordinary lady. Well, she would be very proud of her now. She was proud of her just being in the dancing class, never mind on the stage. She was the only one, and her father was a lot older than her mother and he was out of work a lot. It was the times. But Betty didn't want for anything because her mother worked two looms, I know that, and she worked damned hard for Betty. They only lived in a small house. But with her mother working hard, Betty got what she wanted. I mean, to come to a dancing class – a shilling was worth a lot more than it is today. And when it came to the shows, there was the expense of the clothes. But Betty had everything.' Through the period flavour of this testimony comes the real voice of working-class pride in a talented child, for whom no sacrifice is too great, particularly by the mother.

It was soon to be rewarded. Eastborough School was designed to educate the children of its catchment area from five to the school leaving age of fourteen. But about this time, the education authority decided to turn the school into a junior and infants', and pupils aged eleven and over who had not passed their eleven-plus examination for the Grammar School were transferred to a secondary school, Park Mansion, an imposing building with tennis courts in the middle of Earlsheaton Park.

Betty went there in 1942 in the year of the big change-over, at the age of twelve. It was a big intake that year. She 'hated the thought of leaving Eastborough', where she had been so happy. But her talents were quickly spotted by one of the teachers, Mr Hardisty. More than fifty years later, her classmate Jean Holroyd (now Mrs Jean Walshaw) recalled, 'He was right proud of Betty. She was very bright. Mr Hardisty always knew that she would get on.'[34] At Earlsheaton, there were A and B streams. Betty was in form 6A, a small class composed of potential high-fliers. 'She was only twelve months at Earlsheaton before she passed for the technical school,' remembers Mrs Walshaw.

This was Betty's passport to the great outside world. At the age of thirteen, she won a scholarship to Dewsbury Technical College. It was 'the happiest day of my parents' life. It meant I would be doing subjects like English, English Literature, French, book-keeping, shorthand, typing and grammar – all the things which would help me earn a better living than they had ever had.'[35] She later told Vince Hall, principal at what is now Dewsbury College, that her father wanted her to go to the technical school so that she would not end up at the mill. She recollected that the teaching had been 'very formal', and her teacher was 'a very remote and severe man'. And in those days, teachers were addressed as Mr and Mrs – 'not on first name terms like they are nowadays'. Betty would have qualified either with the Royal Society of Arts or with the Yorkshire Regional Examining Body.[36]

Archie was delighted. 'He felt it was the sort of an education that would earn me a living. It was enormously important to him that I had a job where I could earn a living.'[37] Her parents did not want the sheer drudgery and insecurity of the mill to be Betty's life, as it had been theirs. For her father, the pinnacle of ambition, painful in its modesty, was a job working in the town hall. 'That was security to him,' reflected Betty. And secure it would have been, but she was looking for adventure rather than a safe haven.

CHAPTER III

ADVENTUROUS YEARS

IT HAD TO BE bright lights. If not the footlights, then the dazzle of a department store. Dewsbury was a considerable provincial town and from miles around drew shoppers to its famous covered market and its substantial stores. These attracted Betty from childhood. She later confessed, 'My first ambition was to be a window dresser. I used to love walking round Dewsbury and looking in shop windows. There was one particular shop which was full of wonderful things like whalebone corsets, pins and needles and haberdashery.'[1] By the time she had made it to the Technical College, the height of her ambition was to work in an office – and then become a professional dancer.

After leaving Dewsbury College, Betty was taken on in the finance department of the town's largest department store, Bickers, on Northgate in the heart of the town. Betty thought of it as 'a very posh shop, which we could never afford to shop in ourselves, so it was wonderful to be able to go work there'. She described it later, 'It was a grand shop. Lots of lovely smells of perfume and cosmetics and lovely clothes that I could never afford to buy. It was one of those shops where, when a customer pays, they put the money into a cylinder and they pull a lever and it goes "Whoop!" through the shop and into the office, and one of my jobs was to check it out, stamp the receipt, put the change back in the flask, "Whoop!" and send it back again.'[2]

Her starting wage was £1 a week, a reasonable sum for a school leaver in those days. But she must have made a strong first impression on the store managers. 'I started work for one pound a week and I got a fifty per cent increase the first week, so I was on one pound ten shillings (£1.50) from the first week,' she said later. 'That was the first job I had.'[3]

Alf Ramsden, then an apprentice upholsterer at the shop and later

Mayor of the town, said, 'Bickers was a real high-class departmental store. It sold furniture, lingerie, clothes; it had a ladies' outfitting section, electrical goods – everything a department store sold.'[4] The store maintained a small fleet of delivery vans, which were a common sight on the cobbled streets of Dewsbury. Years later, it fell victim to the changes in retailing fashion, and closed down.

But not even the whoosh of a 'posh' department store like Bickers, the acme of commercial success and propriety in her home town, was good enough for Betty. She still hankered after the stage, and despite her youth she was determined to dance professionally. While still attending college, she had become acquainted with Laurie Ward, a local boy attending Dewsbury's Wheelwright Grammar School. They met while walking up Halifax Road to school classes. This was during 1944, in the closing months of the Second World War. Their chance encounter brought her first break into showbiz.

Though still a schoolboy, Laurie Ward was the trumpeter in a teen-age jazz band that called itself the Swing Stars. The average age of the seven-strong band was 15. They were all Dewsbury lads, their names a roll call of Yorkshire surnames: Jack Booth (leader), Stuart Leach, Jack Spink, Jack Coulson, Vernon Preston, Derek Bramley and young Laurie. Fifty years later, he remembered, 'During the week we did normal dances. Good money it was, too.'[5]

The Swing Stars also did a gig – for nothing – on Sunday nights, as their contribution to the war effort. They performed for the Voluntary Entertainment Service, an arm of the forces' national organization ENSA. Betty and her dancing friend Sheila Jackson, another product of the Meakin Dance School, performed a tap routine with the band. Jackie Coulson, the drummer, says, 'We regularly played Sunday night shows at aerodromes and Army camps, and you can imagine the impression Betty made on the boys in the audience. She was a stunner, with lovely legs and a real mane of hair.'[6]

Indeed so. Contemporary photographs show her as a striking young woman, with curling hair cascading down over her shoulders. She wore a very short pleated skirt, well above the knee, with a bodice and blouse – a far cry from the home-stitched panto finery of just a few years earlier. 'We weren't a bad outfit and looked the part in our bow ties and white shirts,' recalled Coulson. 'But Betty's tap routines and songs gave an extra zing to our shows. We built up quite a following.'[7]

The Swing Stars played their VES concerts with other turns. 'We were part of the act,' said Ward. 'There was also a conjurer, a ventriloquist, and classical singers. Most people were grown up. We were the only children, the band and the two dancers. All the others were mature people, you know, in their forties and fifties.'[8]

Even by wartime showbiz standards, it was an extraordinary life. The VES concerts toured in a converted coach, a single-decker owned by a local firm in Wakefield. 'That coach took us also over the place entertaining the forces,' recalled Ward. 'If there was nowhere to do the show when we got there, we used to do the show in the coach. It had a piano inside, and some little curtains and two or three rows of seats taken out.' And, just like the servicemen they entertained, they had no idea where they were going until the last minute. The hinterland of Yorkshire was full of army camps, and the county's flat plains to the east were dotted with airfields.

'We used to be picked up at two or three o'clock on Sunday afternoon,' said Laurie Ward. 'No one knew where we were going, except the leader, Jack Booth. We had to travel about seventy miles, with no motorways, no lights or street lamps as there was a total blackout. As you can imagine, it took a long time. We used to go all over the place. Yorkshire, Lincolnshire, to army and RAF camps. We even went to an American hospital once. We also played one Sunday night at the Leeds City Palace of Varieties. It was just one of those things. There were soldiers stationed in Leeds, so we played there.'

For the teenage Swing Stars, it was exhilarating. Jackie Coulson brings back the memories. 'If we were playing at an airfield, we used to watch the bombers returning home from their missions. They were exciting days for young musicians. We rushed all over, playing one venue, packing up our instruments and heading for the next.'[9] Laurie Ward, who went on to become a professional musician and joined the Oscar Rabin band in London, playing the Strand Lyceum and the Hammersmith Palais, agrees: 'We had a damn good time. But it was quite demanding as we were still at school, and we sometimes didn't get back until two in the morning. Our parents used to tear their hair out, as you can imagine, leaving home on a Sunday afternoon and not coming back until late.

'Nobody got paid. It was your bit for the war, if you like. Our only payment really was food. We got army or air force food. There was nothing special, but I remember once we went to an American camp and we got food that we'd never seen before: steak and corn. I'd never seen corn on the cob before.'

Betty and Sheila did a dance routine, but the future Speaker also sang. The rest of the band thought she 'wasn't a bad singer'. The Swing Stars played the popular hits of the day and traditional jazz. Betty sang the wartime favourites, and Laurie Ward thought her 'very talented'. He added, 'She would be only fourteen or fifteen when she was with the band. She was still at school.' During the week, their venues were rather less exotic: the town halls of the heavy-woollen district – Batley, Dewsbury, Ossett and Morley, and once the Ravens-thorpe ambulance rooms. They also played the Batley Gaiety, which was above Burton's the tailor's shop. 'All of Burton's shops seemed to have a room above which got turned into some sort of dance hall. We would get full houses, but the forces were press-ganged into going to see us. There were a lot of people at the local ones, too. There were no such things as discos in those days. This was the wartime equivalent, I suppose,' said the Swing Stars trumpeter.

Even at such a young age, Betty could turn men's heads. 'She was a smashing person, she was quite adult really,' said Laurie Ward. 'Betty was a very pretty girl, there was no doubt about that and she went out with various lads. She was a normal girl. She was a fun-loving girl, more boisterous than Sheila.' With her dancing partner, Betty was also expected to make the gauche Dewsbury lads presentable to an audience. 'When we were on stage, we had to have make-up, so Betty and Sheila used to help make us up,' Ward adds. 'I mean, we had no idea how to do it. We used to wear dinner suits or sometimes grey trousers, a white shirt and a red tie, depending on where you were going. Betty and Sheila had various costumes which I suppose they made. They dressed alike so I presume their parents got together and made them.'[10]

Both Jackie Coulson, the drummer, and trumpeter Laurie Ward thought that Betty would go far. Jackie says, 'I used to wonder if Betty saw herself in a showbusiness career. She had the personality and the figure for it . . . I am thrilled by what she has achieved, and proud to have known her. It was always a pleasure working with her.'[11] Laurie concurs, 'I'm quite proud to have known her as a person, not just as the Speaker. Looking back, she did have a strong personality. There was no doubt about that. When she spoke, people listened. I mean, it was just normal conversation – but there's always one, isn't there?'[12]

Betty herself remembers her Swing Star days with affection. After becoming Speaker, she wrote to Mrs Audrey Grant, the widow of Jack Spink, a piano-accordionist who also played with the band, asking for a photograph of the good old days. Betty said in her letter, 'I well remember Jack and many of our other friends who were with the Swing Stars. I can picture Jack now on the piano-accordion and me saying to him "Play it faster, Jack, play it faster." We had a lot of fun in those days.'[13]

Mrs Grant was full of praise. 'It's obvious Betty knew how to turn heads. Her outfit was quite daring for those days, but she made an attractive front for the Swing Stars. They were unforgettable days, and her letter expresses the affection she still has for them. She was a vibrant young lass with a love of life and being at the centre of things. It took a lot of nerve for someone so young to sing and dance before a crowd of soldiers and airmen, but it seems the experience stood her in good stead. If she could handle them, I can't see how a bunch of MPs are going to cause her problems.'

What shines through these recollections and tributes is the sense of a pretty and strong-willed young woman, a 'bobby dazzler' in the vernacular, but assertive beyond her years. It is easy to relate the Speaker we now know to the glamorous young dancer who could command the attention of hundreds of men. But it was not all short skirts and gallivanting round USAF bases. While she was learning the rudiments of a professional stage career, Betty did not – could not – forget her origins, and the political struggle being waged by her parents to improve the lot of textile workers and the working class in general.

The other Swing Stars noted her humble background. Laurie Ward saw the little house in Marriott Street, but only from the outside. 'It was a one-up, one-down kind of house in Eastborough. In those days, Eastborough was very dingy, very turn-of-the-century, dark and dismal. The people were all right. It was just the area. We were quite ordinary and equal: nobody had any more worldly goods than any other.'[14] He remembered Archie, her father, as 'a small fella, and very sociable. I think he had political inclinations, but you're asking me something. From a young lad's point of view, it didn't enter my head, didn't politics, then.'

It had certainly entered Betty's, almost umbilically. As she later confessed, 'I came out of the womb into the Labour movement.' Her parents were active members of the Labour Party, 'so it was always there'. Politics fascinated her, and what she really wanted to do was change society. 'I hated the dark satanic mills and the narrow lives and houses that people that I was brought up with had to live in. All of that made me even more concerned about changing society.[15]

'But it was always there. I came from a family that was interested in politics, it wasn't something that I had to get accustomed to. It was part and parcel, like miners' coal dust that you can't scrub out of your nails. There was talk always of politics, local more than national.' Her uncle was a councillor on the local authority, so the family always supported him. Neither Archie nor Mary Boothroyd stood for the council (though Betty did, unsuccessfully, of which more later) but they were both members of the Textile Workers' Union and of the Labour Party. They knocked on doors, canvassed for the party, and attended political meetings. It was a classic Labour childhood.

'My mother belonged to the Women's Section of the Labour Party,' she recalled, 'so we used to go to Women's Section meetings. We would go to Huddersfield Town Hall, or Leeds Town Hall, and see the great speakers like Nye Bevan and Clem Attlee. It was a great occasion. We'd take a flask, because we couldn't afford to go to restaurants, and we'd go along with the Dewsbury women's section, maybe on a coach and take sandwiches. My mother used to say, "We'll take jam and hope for spam that we can swap around a little." It was a very happy period.'[16]

Betty joined the Labour League of Youth as soon as the rules allowed, at sixteen, finding fresh energy to pour into politics as she did into her stage work. These were heady times. It looked as though her career could go either way – politics, or the stage, though in some respects both professions require similar qualities. Many MPs behave as if they have an Equity card in their wallet or handbag, and not a few stage professionals are strongly attracted to politics – Glenda Jackson, the Oscar-winning screen star who became Labour MP for Hampstead being the most obvious case.

In the immediate post-war period, with Clem Attlee in Downing Street at the head of a reforming Labour government with a handsome parliamentary majority, the League of Youth was a happy, optimistic band of comrades. Anything must have seemed possible. They paid a penny a week, and were entitled to send two representatives to the executive committee of the constituency party. There were speaking competitions, socials, and tramps across the moors.

Those days were recalled by Molly Walton, a Labour councillor, of Crossland Moor, Huddersfield. 'We used to do fund-raising to keep the party going. It was a very active social life. We used to hold socials every Sunday night throughout this area. They cost three shillings (15p), and we would provide food – but no drink. People would come from Sheffield, Bradford, Dewsbury, Brighouse. That's how you made your money. And the summer schools were really superb. We would have a weekend at Wortley Hall (near Wakefield), odd day schools, then week-long schools at Matlock, Derbyshire. Then, in the winter, we used to go and hike every Sunday in the snow. My dad used to say, "If I told you to go, you wouldn't," but I used to go with the group. We would go over Scammonden moor. I suppose Betty would have gone with her group.'[17]

Another young Leaguer, Mary Hansom, from Marsden, deep in the Pennines on the Yorkshire–Lancashire border, found her unforgettable. 'Betty was always very smart. She used to wear a tailored suit, and had great long fingernails. I can see her now: upright and hands down by her sides. Of course, she wasn't as plump as she is now. She was very slim.'[18] Mary Hansom went on to marry Harold Sims, who was Yorkshire organizer of the party for many years. Harold remembers Mary Boothroyd making an impact in the women's section, which in those days could fill Leeds Town Hall for its annual rally. Recollections of Betty in her first years in the League of Youth are less clear, but he was to meet her again as her political ambitions matured.

The Labour League of Youth met in the Ben Riley Hall, a three-storey building in Union Street, Dewsbury. An amusement arcade occupies the site now, though there was probably more fun in the old days. Ken Sharpe, secretary of Eastborough Working Men's Club, reflects, 'In about 1945/46, they used to have a youth group downstairs, upstairs there were four snooker tables which were open every night. You could have a game for twopence (less than 1p). Betty was secretary of the youth group. She hasn't altered much. She always had the upper hand then. She was in charge, and she was only sixteen years old.

'It was more of an organizing job. She was the kind of girl who got on with everybody. They used to go on little outings, hiking and the like. The youth group was about all there was in that day. We were glad to have something like that.'[19] But the League had its serious side. 'I can remember on voting night we used to go out canvassing, making sure people would vote. Betty used to get involved, and go to the town hall counting at elections. It was something that just grew on you. It was always a Labour stronghold, and she was always into politics.'

These two worlds, showbiz and politics, intertwined in other ways. The ubiquitous Alf Ramsden ran the Central Youth Club in Eastborough School, and Mrs Winnie Kettle used to go there with Betty. 'We would be about fifteen years old. We used to enjoy dancing and jiving to big-band music. The big thing was dancing in those days. We all went to the youth club together, and then to Dewsbury Town all dancing. We were all so proud carrying the tap shoes around with us. We also went to Huddersfield baths dancing. They used to put a floor over the pool. It was all big-band sounds like Glen Miller doing 'String of Pearls'. And there used to be a bandstand in the Crow Nest Park (on the heights above Eastborough), which we used to dance around on lovely summer nights. Me and Betty had a pair of shoes alike, with gorgeous wedges. She got hers in America, and my brother bought me some from Bombay. Betty was very fashionable.'[20]

The suggestion that Betty got her 'gorgeous wedges' *in* America is puzzling, because it was another fifteen years before she would go there. But Mrs Kettle does supply one missing link: the transition from enthusiastic amateur to would-be professional. 'There used to be a pub at the bottom of Daisy Hill [in Dewsbury town centre] called Fryer's Vaults, and there used to be a dancing class upstairs.

'My friend and I went there, and Betty came too. The second time we went, we were told a dancing teacher was coming over from the

Fedora Dancing Class in Bradford – and she wanted some girls for panto. It was only the second time at the class, but I got a contract off the Bradford teacher, along with my friend and Betty. Betty was a good dancer. Betty went in *Cinderella*, but I don't remember where. We would be about sixteen years old then.'

Three pounds, a sizeable sum in austere, post-war Britain, and on the boards 'professionally' at last! For a time, the West Riding, its intense Labourism and its accessible showbiz, appeared to be enough for the zestful young Betty. But suddenly, everything changed. Shortly after her seventeenth birthday, in late 1946, she announced that she was going to London to go on the stage as a professional dancer. Her teacher, Mrs Meakin, says 'Betty got the idea. She said to me "I'd love to go and do a pantomime like you."'

Now it was Betty's turn. 'She did it off her own bat. I don't know if she wrote up, or what. I just remember her coming to tell me she'd got in. I never remembered where it was, but it was somewhere in London, because she's mentioned it in her interviews. She loved it, but she came back because, like me, she didn't warm to it. She had been in panto like I was, the only thing was, it wasn't a number one company. I mean, the number one companies for pantomime were Francis Laidler, he was king of the pantomime, and Emile Littler. Betty wasn't with either of those, but there were other pantomimes. I remember Betty coming and telling me, 'I've got in, I'm going in pantomime!"' [21]

This short paragraph may hold the key to the Great Tiller Mystery. For almost a decade, Betty has been billed as the Tiller Girl who made it to the top. When she was elected Speaker, the London *Evening Standard* strap headline ran: THE COMMONS GIVES EX-TILLER GIRL A STANDING OVATION. Next day, the *Daily Express* shrieked BETTY TAKES THE TILLER, with a strapline EX-CHORUS GIRL IS FIRST WOMAN SPEAKER IN 734 YEARS. Even the 'heavy' broadsheet papers dwelled on the fact that a former high-kicker from the chorus line had become the second-highest commoner in the land. But was she ever a Tiller girl?

It may be instructive to ask first what a Tiller girl was, and why being one was such a showbiz cachet, when chorus girls were normally rather looked down upon. Doremy Vernon, whose invaluable history

Tiller's Girls tells the story of nearly a century of a remarkable stage act, traces their origins to a pantomime at the Prince of Wales Theatre, Liverpool, in 1885. John Tiller, a successful businessman who could not dance a step, presented four 'ordinary little girls from Manchester' as Les Jolies Petites. They were an instant success. Their encore was greeted with a standing ovation, and the lavish praise that followed persuaded Tiller to give up the cotton trade for the stage. He was thirty-six, with heavy family commitments and a mysterious past, having been born the illegitimate son of Maria Frances Tiller, in Blackburn in 1854.

Tiller, a choirboy whose deep love of music enabled him to win prizes at the Royal Northern College of Music, was taken under the wing of his uncle, John George, wealthy owner of a prosperous cotton agency in Manchester. There, he prospered sufficiently to allow him time for theatricals. He became stage manager of the Minnehaha Minstrels, an enthusiastic group of businessmen amateurs who gave charity shows in Manchester theatres. The troupe was certainly unique. It had a deaf flute player, who had an understandable but disconcerting habit of carrying on playing when his fellow musicians had stopped.

Tiller graduated to become director of the city's Comedy Theatre, and began to teach young girls to dance. Asked to provide a quartet of children for the pantomime *Robinson Crusoe* – inexplicably sub-titled 'The Good Friday That Came on a Saturday' – he chose four of his ten-year-old pupils – Dolly Grey, Tessy Lomax and Cissy and Lily Smith for his first troupe. They all had to be the same height and shape, and to be malleable. 'They had to be. Relentlessly, he made them repeat every movement and worked them for hours on end until they were perfectly in unison. Most evenings they were so exhausted they had to be carried home on their parents' shoulders.'[22] The Tiller Girls were born.

Parents were reassured by Tiller's description of his stage tuition as 'training', which had the ring of an apprenticeship about it. Women were often eager to sign the necessary permission for their daughters, arguing, 'Let her go, give her a chance to see the world.' Fathers, often unemployed and perhaps even envious, were more likely to object. More than fifty years later, when the Tiller Girls were a household name for glamorous precision chorus-dancing, there was the same divide in the Boothroyd household, though Archie was more anxious for, than jealous of, his gorgeous daughter.

Every interviewer and profile writer has tried, with varying degrees of failure, to pin down the facts of Betty's showbiz career. But Madam Speaker has been reticent on this score. She told Glenys Kinnock and Fiona Millar this version: 'I loved to dance. I loved the music and the movement and, for a long time, that was what I wanted to be. My father didn't want me to go away from home and it broke his heart when I did go, at seventeen.

'My mother, who was rather more indulgent, obviously realized it was better for me to get it out of my system, so in that terrible winter of 1947 I left home and went to dance at the Palladium and at Luton. It came to an end because I had a nail in my shoe of which I wasn't aware, which gave me a very bad foot. I also hated being away from home and they missed me so much that I just packed it in after a year. It is an episode which, since then, has been blown out of all proportion.'[23]

This interview, published in late 1993, indicates some irritation with the media obsession with her short professional career. Indeed, in 1988, when Ewen MacAskill, political correspondent of the *Scotsman*, profiled 'Miss Betty Boothroyd, tipped to be the next Speaker', he got short shrift when he raised the subject. 'She is not interested in talking about her days as a kicker,' he wrote.

'When I told her I had asked her assistant for a picture of her as a Tiller girl, and had effectively been told to get lost, she laughed and said she would give her a rise. She added she had long since destroyed pictures of those days. "If I thought that is all you wanted to talk about, I would not have given you an interview," she said in a Yorkshire manner that is half laughter, half a threat.'[24]

Betty's vexation may be understandable, given her new-found eminence and her quiet ambitions for the future. But Betty has only herself to blame for setting the newshounds off on her showbiz past. She has insisted that the papers only got on to the story when she became Deputy Speaker in 1987. In July of that year, she told Sandra Parsons of the *Wolverhampton Express and Star*, that she had been discreet about her dancing career when standing for the West Bromwich by-election (which she won) in 1973. 'I kept the Tiller Girls connection quiet, because I knew that if the press got hold of it, I'd never get away from it. When I was made Deputy Speaker it came out, I don't know how, but I don't mind now anyway.'[25]

There was some economy with the truth here. In fact, Betty herself had given the game away as early as 1982, in *The Times*. In a feature-length article on the page facing the leaders and letters – headlined: WESTMINSTER WOMAN TELLS ALL – SHOCK – Betty was sharply critical of the way the political system sometimes discriminates against women, and pretty women in particular. 'Certainly, there is hostility to glamour,' she wrote. 'I was once a professional dancer (dammit, I was once a Tiller girl).'[26]

You can't get much clearer than that, although she was never so clear again. Rebecca Abrams got closest in her October 1991 interview,[27] done while Betty was in the thick of the campaign to secure the Speakership, but before she ascended to the chair. 'I became a chorus girl,' she told Ms Abrams. Not, it may be noted, a Tiller Girl. And Tiller Girls would die rather than call themselves chorus girls or show girls. 'I'd always been very much interested in dancing and I was quite good at it. I knew a girl, she was called Betty too, who lived in Dewsbury and we both wanted to become professionals. My father thought it was a dreadful idea, my mother thought it was okay if I wanted to do it. So we went for an audition, and we became professionals.'

She danced in Luton and London, but the Palladium was not specified on this occasion. 'I was part of a dancing team and I liked the teamwork: you all turn your head to the right at exactly the same angle, and you all kick your left leg up at the same height and the same time. I've always been an individualist, but I'm also a teamworker – that is why I like politics; politics is teamwork, to some extent.'

The Girls lived in Soho, in the Theatre Girls' Club in Greek Street. 'Everyone thinks if you're a dancer, men drink champagne out of your shoes every night, but we were never allowed out; we always had a matron. It was the winter of 1947, and it was a terribly harsh winter when the nation had no coal, no heating. I found it a very hard life. I enjoyed the make-up and the sparkle, but there's quite a lot more to it than just the glamour that one sees when the curtain goes up.'

Betty recalled licking her finger to pick up sequins that had fallen

off the dresses, and giving them to the wardrobe mistress to be sewn
back on again for the next performance. 'I thought it was going to be
terribly exciting and frightfully glamorous, but it was really just like
politics: damned hard work. My father thought it was a terrible job
for a working-class girl to do and he didn't approve at all. After about
six months I gave it up and came back home to Yorkshire and had a
very dreary job as secretary for the Road Haulage Association.'

In neither of these long interviews did Betty repeat her insistence of
some years previous that she had been a Tiller Girl, and corroborative
evidence that she was is hard to find. Even though John Tiller had
died many years previously, the routine was pretty much the same.
Girls from the north and the Midlands were brought down to London
for 'training'. The founder's dictum still stood. He wanted 'a troupe
of girls trained like soldiers, to dance with the precision of a Guards
regiment on parade. Not a leg to rise above the waist, every head shall
turn together and feet are to stamp a single whiplash on stage.' The
discipline and training was so tough and methodical it was akin to
brainwashing. The Girls talked of being 'Tillerized'.

Aspiring Tiller Girls would receive on note paper headed 'The John
Tiller Schools of Dancing Ltd (telegrams: "Tiptoes")' an invitation
to come down to practise their kicks 'with all the other girls'. For
rehearsals, they would receive half salary. Salary was £5 a week. The
letter added, 'We like our girls to have Black Pants or Shorts, White
Blouse, and Black Tap Shoes as Practice Kit. If you should have some
slacks available you will also find those useful – when you are not
actually dancing – to keep you warm . . . If you will write to Miss Bell,
Theatre Girls Club, 59 Greek Street, Soho WC2, and say you are
coming to rehearse with us – I am sure she will find room for you,
and you will find some of our other Girls are staying there – so you
will get to know them.'[28]

So she was in the right hostel for the Tillers. But then, so were
many other showgirls, including ballet dancers and Windmill girls.
The Theatre Girls Club, now used as a hostel for homeless women
with high support needs, was home from home for many young women
on the stage, though it wasn't particularly homely. The girls were
allocated cramped cubicles, boasting a dressing table but with only a
curtain for privacy. Meals were spartan, and taken communally in the

dining room. Breakfast was cornflakes, toast and porridge. The girls got a ration of one spoonful of sugar, which was locked away after breakfast. 'Dinner' in the evening was usually corned beef or sausages. But at thirty shillings (£1.50) a week, it was a bargain in central London.

Lunch was taken at the Moo Cow or Express Dairy coffee bars in Soho – standing up. The girls who still had some cash left after buying cigarettes – smoking was rife and Betty still smokes – would often have Welsh rarebit and chips, jacket potato, or cream cakes. They bolted down milk shakes in tall glasses with long spoons, just like in the films, and unquestionably a cut above Dewsbury. At night, the Theatre Club front door was locked and bolted, in apparent defiance of the fire regulations. Men were not allowed into the building – not even fathers dropping off their daughters. The fearsome Miss Bell, who had run the place since the 1920s, walked round with a bunch of keys at her waist as though she was in charge of a prison. With bars across the windows, at times it felt like one. There was even supposed to be a ghost in the club chapel, of a Tiller Girl who had 'died after an operation'.

Rehearsals for the Tillers took place round the corner in West Street, in a former Wesleyan Chapel that had been bombed in the war. The rules were strict: no visitors, no smoking, naked lights nor intoxicating liquors allowed in the dressing room or in places of rehearsal. Tiller Girls had to dress their hair 'in such style as required by the managers, and shall not change the colour thereof'. The girls used 'spit black' made by spitting into a block of mascara for eye make-up, and wet white for their legs in place of stocking. At the end of a show, sometimes sixteen girls would jostle for four sinks to wash it off.

'They would train every day,' says Doremy Vernon. 'And by the end of two days they could probably hardly walk. They would certainly have difficulty getting up and down the stairs. They used to bath with Epsom salts – and walk backwards down the stairs, or slide down on their bottoms.'[29] And in the Theatre Club they were subject to a curfew. 'We all had to be in by 9.30 or 10 p.m.,' recollects ex-Tiller Girl Vera Norwood, now a pillar of the local establishment in Stow-on-the-Wold, Gloucestershire.[30] 'It was very respectable.'

Outside, however, rather less so. Prostitutes plied their trade in the street while the innocent provincials gaped from upstairs windows. This was 'the best pastime of all at the Club', according to Doremy Vernon. 'The girls could hardly wait to finish their meal and race upstairs to watch business being transacted there.'[31] Some timed the women as they disappeared down a side-alley. The record was three minutes, inclusive of departure and return.

Despite being crammed together, the theatre girls were often lonely, Doremy Vernon notes. This is scarcely surprising. They had left home at an early age. They were engaged in physically punishing work and living under a repressive regime. And it was the coldest winter in living memory. Small wonder, then, that Betty's professional ardour began to cool. Her father was unwell, ill with the heart disease that was to kill him at the age of sixty-two only a year later. She was homesick, and she knew he was missing his only child, in whom he had vested all his hopes for a better future. The nail in her shoe pricked more than her foot. It got to her conscience, too. By her own account, her career in the chorus line lasted only six months. It may have been less, much less.

But was she a Tiller Girl? Apart from her own assertion, the evidence is slight. According to her dance teacher, Betty went to London to be a chorus-line girl in a pantomime. In the panto season of 1947, says theatrical historian Doremy Vernon, there was no pantomime with a Tiller Girl line-up at the Palladium. There *was* a pantomime at the Coliseum, *Snow White*, which played from February to mid-April 1947. It featured the Sherman Fisher and Izna Roselli Girls as 'Ladies of the Court'. But among the fourteen kickers, there was only one Betty, and she was not a Boothroyd. There *was* a Tiller Girl line-up in *Mother Goose*, which played at the Casino from just before Christmas 1946 to 10 February 1947, but Doremy Vernon has re-interviewed the survivors of that troupe and none remembers Betty.

And despite telling Glenys Kinnock and Fiona Millar that she had played the Palladium that season, she had earlier disavowed any such suggestion. On 11 May 1992, Betty wrote to another theatrical historian, Chris Woodward, who is writing the history of the London Palladium, saying, 'I regret I have no specific recollections of the London Palladium and I am, therefore, unable to help you.'[32]

Within days of her becoming Speaker, the *Evening Standard* launched an investigation into Betty's claims. Under the headline: THE FIRST QUESTION MADAM SPEAKER MUST DEAL WITH: WAS SHE REALLY EVER A TILLER GIRL? Investigative reporters John Passmore and Allan Ramsay delved into the available evidence and came up with no very powerful conclusions. They found a theatrical historian in Bradford, Peter Holdsworth (former drama critic of the city's *Telegraph and Argus*) who insisted, 'I don't think she was a Tiller Girl. I know she was a tap-dancer and we have clippings which mention her in pantomime locally. She started saying she had been a Tiller Girl during a local election in the 1950s but I think she must have been using it as a generic term – and it stuck.'[33] Doremy Vernon, the paper added, had interviewed 225 Tiller Girls, 'and not one remembers her'.

Ms Vernon, a Tiller in the 60s herself, reopened her inquiry for this biography, talking to the girls who worked circa 1947. 'Of course, no joy about remembering her,' she told the author. 'They split into two groups: "Oh, I don't think she would lie about having been a Tiller if she hadn't worked as one!"; and the other set: "I think she just said it to get on!"'[34] Most of the Tiller Girls she talked to agreed that if Betty had aired any political viewpoint she would have been thought very strange. To the best of their recollection, any talk of politics was forbidden.

The *Evening Standard*'s stablemate, the *Daily Mail* (edited then by Sir David English, whose wife definitely was a Tiller Girl), found a live witness to Betty's claims. Scoop! Under the headline MY HIGH-KICKING DAYS WITH MADAM SPEAKER, Vera Norwood, of Stow-on-the-Wold, said, 'Betty had a pretty face and long legs – you had to be pretty to be a Tiller Girl – but it was her name that stuck out. I remember thinking then how unusual it was.' The *Mail* reported that the two met 'in rehearsal rooms in London in 1949', but had never appeared in a show together. 'There would be two or three troupes rehearsing at once. I met her when we were getting our costumes fitted. We went to some of the classes that the Tiller School provided, then we all used to have coffee at the Moo Cow Milk Bar in Cambridge Circus.'

Perhaps there was more than milk in the coffee at the Moo Cow, because the dates do not add up. By her own admission, Betty quit the chorus line within a year, after starting in 1947. And in a telephone interview with the author, Miss Norwood changed her mind. 'I didn't work with her. I said that, but there was a girl in rehearsals called Betty and I thought it was her. I was fed up with all the reporters at the time. When she was made Speaker, I had reporters telephoning me from everywhere because I do give talks on my life as a Tiller Girl.' She had been asked if she knew Betty, and had said Yes, there was a girl with that name.

However, even if the sighting is now unconfirmed, Miss Norwood stoutly defends Betty's right to call herself a Tiller. 'She has every right to say she was a Tiller Girl if she was chosen as one, and did all the rehearsals and everything. How long she was one is another matter. But if she was signed on to go for the rehearsals and classes, and was in a show or part of a show, then she was a Tiller Girl. She wouldn't lie. If she says she was, she was.'

This evidence probably tells us more about sisterly comradeship than it does about Betty, and though there's nothing wrong in that, Vera has muddied rather than clarified the waters. One other customarily reliable source, back home in Yorkshire, who wishes not to be named, adds, 'No, she did become a Tiller Girl. I know for a fact she wasn't. I don't think Betty has actually lied about this. To be a Tiller Girl you have got to be on the stage before and (have) had a lot of experience. And all the Tiller Girls I knew were six-footers. Now that old photo they put on the screen, well, that's just an old Tiller Girl photograph – long before her time. There was a piece in the paper asking anybody who was in the Tiller troupe with Betty to write and nobody did.' There are yet more inconsistencies here. Tiller Girls did not necessarily need experience – the School was there to teach them. And it is not correct that only six-footers need apply: most Tiller Girls were around five feet eight inches. However, another school friend from those days, Mrs Jean Walshaw of Mirfield, states flatly, 'I don't think Betty was a Tiller Girl.'[35]

Betty herself is not now easily drawn on the subject. Interviewed by Sue Lawley on BBC Radio's 'Desert Island Discs', she chose as her first record the overture to Offenbach's 'Orpheus in the Underworld', saying its zip reminded of Paris. It is, of course, also the Can-Can music, and her choice immediately prompted a question about the

Tiller days. 'You did go south, you did join a dance troupe,' said Mr Lawley interrogatively.

Betty went over the old ground, how she thoroughly enjoyed her dance classes, and added, 'I wanted to be a professional, and my mother took me to the Tiller school where I was accepted. All you had to do was high kicks and splits and smile at the same time, and I was in pantomime for a short winter season. My father was horrified at the thought of it. It was the first time I had left home. He said, "This is no way for a good working-class girl to earn her living." I enjoyed it, but it was the very bad winter of 1947, cold, not much food around. I had been cosseted at home, and I soon left and went back to York-shire.' Back from the Palladium to Dewsbury? ventured Ms Lawley. 'That's right,' replied Betty. 'I had a nail in my shoe, and I had a very bad foot so it gave me a really marvellous excuse to go home.'[36]

At the risk of overloading the exegesis, this reply could bear two meanings. First, the obvious one, that Betty passed for the Tiller school, was trained in the ordinary way – almost certainly in London – and then hired for a chorus line-up in the West End, which in her case did not last long. Alternatively, it could mean that she was accepted for the school, and appeared in a panto chorus line, though not neces-sarily as a Tiller Girl and in all likelihood not at the Palladium.

Her own written evidence of 'no specific recollection' of appearing at the Palladium indicates that, even if it conflicts directly with her response to Sue Lawley. Yet an impressionable young woman who performs on stage at the Palladium is unlikely to forget it for the rest of her life. And in a pre-recorded radio show, she had ample time to correct herself.

Doremy Vernon comments, 'She is so canny, like most politicians. "I did go south and join a troupe", but doesn't admit to a Tiller troupe. "My mother", she says, "took me to a Tiller school, and I was accepted" – but doesn't say she took up the offer. Sue Lawley says, "You stubbed your foot." She says a nail in her shoe. One ex-Tiller of the time told me, "Well, we all had nails in our shoe. Where was her Dunkirk spirit? *We* carried on.'

It is strange that no witness other than Betty herself has come for-ward to support her story, despite numerous reunions of the 'old Girls'. Nor has she evidently welcomed the attentions of the expert in the field. Doremy Vernon says she approached Betty for her reminiscences whilst collecting for her history of the Tiller Girls. Here was a golden opportunity to set the record straight. But Betty never replied.

She had another chance, in an interview with *Yorkshire Life* in April 1993, when Catherine Kelly asked, 'Can you once and for all explain the "Tiller Girl" connection, and has the much-publicized area of your life ever caused you embarrassment?' Betty replied, 'I was thrilled to be taken on as a member of the Tiller school, but then a number of things – a poisoned foot, the tug of home and realization that I was never going to be a great dancer – caused me to give up ambitions in that field.

'Of course I'm not embarrassed by references to my dancing career. It was part of my life. But I sometimes think too much is made of it. My dancing days are long over. I've had a reasonable sort of career since then. If I'd been an overworked and underpaid social worker, I'm sure there wouldn't have been so many stories about that.' Interestingly, Madam Speaker only owns up to being at the Tiller school, rather than being a member of a panto chorus line. And her wrath at the rash of stories about her dancing career sits ill with the fact that she was the first to identify herself – 'dammit, I was a Tiller Girl' – as a chorus girl.

Elsewhere, Betty has said, 'You will never see a photograph of me as a Tiller Girl. They are under lock and key at home, and that's where they are staying.'[37] And in the absence of any independent verification, there too lies her claim to be a Tiller Girl. Except on her own say-so, it has not been proved, though the circumstantial evidence supporting her claim at least to have trained in the Tiller school is undoubtedly strong.

Equally, nobody has disproved her claims, and one wonders what profit or virtue there would be in so doing. The dancing episode scarcely ranks alongside her real achievements. Betty has so long and so publicly insisted that she was a Tiller Girl that it now makes little odds whether she was or not. It is part of the Betty mystique, and none the worse for that. But she has demonstrated her integrity beyond peradventure in the half century since she hobbled off the boards and took the train back home to Dewsbury, to her family and her hated 'satanic mills'.

There is a doleful footnote to the Tiller saga. On 12 July 1994, Betty agreed to be the guest celebrity opening the summer sale at Harrods, the 'top people's shop' in the West End of London. She followed an illustrious line-up of Hollywood stars – Charlton Heston, Burt Reynolds and Richard Gere had done it before her. And this charity bash enabled Betty to nominate two projects for Harrods' £50,000 annual donation. She chose the appeal for victims of the civil war in Rwanda, and the Care for Crisis fund in Britain.

But unbeknown to her, the store had hired three models got up to look like Tiller Girls to pose with Madam Speaker for pictures. The photographs show Betty looking rather askance at the supposed 'Tillers'. She does not look impressed. Nor was the public. The *Daily Express* reported that veteran sales-goers said it was the worst turn-out for years, with only a handful of people gathered round the main door at 7.30 a.m. 'I don't think a lot of people know who Betty Boothroyd is, to be honest,' said Iris Hindley, aged forty-nine, of Dedham, Essex. 'Richard Gere brought huge crowds.'

CHAPTER IV

POLITICS BECKON

ETTY WAS GOING BACK to the bosom of a close-knit family, but it was still a wrench to bid goodbye to the glamour of the London stage and return to the small world of Dewsbury. It was an admission of failure, hurtful for an ambitious young woman. She put a good face on her homecoming, but inside she hated it. She had let The Big Prize slip from her grasp. Perhaps she expected too much of herself. Not many seventeen-year-old girls from the back streets of a northern textile town – not even a graduate of the Vivienne School of Dancing – could make it in the raffish post-war West End.

But apart from a poisoned foot and the realization that she was never going to be a great dancer, there was another, deeply private reason for going home. Her father Archie, never a particularly robust man – the image that has come down the years is 'a little fellow in a cap' – was seriously ill. He had been a powerful influence on her, more so, it sometimes seemed than her mother, though Betty was later to acknowledge her huge debt to her mother.

Like many others in the labour movement in west Yorkshire, he had been victimized, though the circumstances are not clear. Life had been a succession of jobs, and though he was by no means old – he was in his early sixties – he was a sick man. The family had by this time moved to 19 East Parade, still in the 'inner-city' quarter of Eastborough, but a more commodious house than the Marriott Street back-to-back. He was still only a rag warehouseman.

Archie died on 25 March 1948, at home. Dr S. H. Hammerton recorded the causes of death as hypostatic pneumonia, degenerative myocarditis and arterio-sclerosis.[1] In other words, heart failure. His wife was present at the end. For Mary Boothroyd, still only in her mid-forties, it was not only a private heartbreak but also an economic disaster. Henceforth, she had to provide for herself. The tragedy etched itself on Betty's memory. 'My father died when I was eighteen. We were very good friends. I missed him very much. There was no other income, so my mother had to work. She worked all her life, from the age of thirteen when she left school to the age when she retired, sixty-five or six. She had to.'[2]

Though she later confessed 'in some ways I have never recovered from that loss',[3] Betty did not despair. She threw herself back into work and Labour Party activity. She got a 'very dreary job as secretary for the Road Haulage Association', which was a far cry from the provincial gentility of Bickers store. 'I was the only female in the office, so I was a dogsbody, a "go'n" – "Go'n do this, go'n do that." '[4] Her contemporaries remember it rather differently. Rather than the RHA – the private enterprise body representing independent road hauliers (which cannot today turn up any record of her) – it was British Road Services, the newly nationalized lorry industry. Harry Manning, of West Town, Dewsbury, worked there as a driver at the same time. 'BRS was formed immediately after the war. Instead of having hundreds of small haulage firms, the government nationalized them all,' he said.[5] The state hauliers were based in an old tram shed in Bradford Road, Carlinghow, Batley. 'Betty was a teenager there, and one of the office girls,' recalls Manning. 'Her job was to pay the drivers their expenses before they went on long-distance trips.' A far cry indeed from the footlights. But she made the best of it. 'Betty was the type of girl who was friendly with everybody,' said the driver. 'She liked to be involved in the social side of things.'

That was also true of her politics. She may have quit the stage, but she was still a trouper. Mrs Jean Megahy, who met her husband Tom when he was debating against Betty in the finals of a public-speaking competition in Leeds, recalls how the future Speaker got involved in her branch of the Labour League of Youth in nearby Mirfield. 'We were highly political. We helped greatly with elections,' she says. 'We used to have a lot of money-raising efforts, and we used to have a concert party. That's where Betty was involved a lot because, as she was a dancer, she did all the choreography. And she designed the costumes and helped make them. It sounds strange nowadays to hear that young people were involved in all this, but we had a really good concert party and we used to go all over giving this show. We gave shows for charity, and went to patients at Storthes Hall [a mental hospital near Huddersfield, now closed] and gave a show for the patients there. We did a lot for children in the community. We gave a Christmas party at the children's home at the bottom of Kitson Hill, Mirfield.'[6]

Betty was an enthusiastic part of this microcosm of a different kind of Britain, one in the grip of a political euphoria, 'the feeling of being part of a great movement'. They were less cynical, less worldly times. There was a feeling that the democratic process would deliver a better society. 'It was like a youth group, but we definitely were political. That was the time when the LLY was flourishing, when young people were political. Mirfield branch had seventy or eighty members who met on Sunday nights at the Labour Rooms in Newgate. There wasn't much to do in Mirfield and the League of Youth was a big attraction. It seems ridiculous to think that we were fighting for the things that have been destroyed under Thatcher. We saw the National Health Service come in, and we saw all the industries being nationalized – gas, electricity, and coal. At the time all those things would be important to us. It seems strange to think that all these have been destroyed, and the Health Service is in the process of being destroyed.'

But these were also the dying days of the post-war Labour government, in which so much hope had been invested. In the General Election of February 1950, Clement Attlee went to the polls, and was returned with a hugely reduced overall majority of only seven in the Commons. His government was weary and riven by faction, and at constant risk of ambush by a Tory Parliamentary Party rejuvenated by an influx of new blood. Barbara Castle noted, 'Since another general election could not be far away, it was clear that they would redouble their attack.'[7] The doughty fighter from Bradford, who was, ere long, to become Betty's employer, was not surprised at the public's restiveness. The war to save civilization had been over for five years, but under Labour food was still rationed. Housewives had to make do with three ounces of cheese per head a week, and the meat ration was still only eightpence (just under 3p) a week. Nylon stockings for women were a rare luxury.

The old generation of Cabinet ministers was worn out. Some were near to death. Stafford Cripps, the Chancellor of the Exchequer, was forced out of office by ill health in October 1950, and was replaced by Hugh Gaitskell, to the fury of Nye Bevan, the Health Secretary and charismatic icon of the Labour Left. Five months later, Ernest Bevin, the tough ex-boss of the Transport Workers' Union who had been a brilliant Foreign Secretary, was compelled to retire and died a month later. He was replaced by Herbert Morrison, 'the Tammany Hall boss of London, 'an appointment which by common consent was disastrous'.[8] Unrest was building up within the parliamentary party about the scale of British rearmament, and when Gaitskell announced charges for false teeth and spectacles in his Budget on 21 April 1951, the dam burst.

Bevan resigned from the government, Harold Wilson, President of the Board of Trade, followed suit and they were joined by John Freeman, a junior minister at Supply and later editor of the *New Statesman* and a formidable television interviewer. Henceforth, Bevan dominated the Keep Left group of left-wing Labour MPs – into whose orbit Betty was soon to be drawn, if only fitfully – and they were now known as the Bevanites. They made up 'a party within a party', opposing the government from an avowedly socialist perspective. The prospect was of an open power struggle between Attlee and the Bevanites at the Labour Party conference in Scarborough in October 1951. But in mid-September, Attlee decided to go to the country and his divided government fell. Winston Churchill was back in Downing Street, and Labour was in Opposition once more. Much had been achieved in six years, but the dream of a socialist Utopia cherished by so many in the Labour League of Youth began to recede.

Betty was by now on the national consultative committee of the League, attending meetings several times a year at Transport House, Smith Square, which was then the powerhouse of the labour movement. On its six floors were housed the Transport Workers' Union, the Labour Party and the Trades Union Congress. Transport House was something of a political Mecca for the Left, particularly the young. The party was out of office, but the struggle for the soul of socialism, and to regain power at Westminster, was pursued passionately here. Chained to her desk at the road hauliers in Dewsbury, Betty looked enviously at her comrades working at Transport House on her regular visits to London. This was the place to be. Here, she could fulfil the ambitions of her father and mother, not to mention her own.

But first she tried to enter politics in Dewsbury. It seems to have been a half-hearted bid, on Labour's part, if not hers. In the borough council election of 1952, Betty was given the unwinnable Trinity North Ward to contest. Her opponent in this staunchly Conservative ward, with its millowners' mansions and streets of owner-occupiers, was the retiring councillor, Ernest Harrison, a chartered accountant standing as an 'Independent'. Dewsbury was one of the many places in northern England where the Tories stood under false colours, knowing that identifying themselves as Conservatives could be electorally counter-productive. Sometimes they were Ratepayers' candidates, at others Independents. Sir Marcus Fox, Tory MP for Shipley who was at school with Betty, first got on Dewsbury council as a representative of the 'Municipal Association'.

Whatever their flag of convenience, the Tories were in control of Dewsbury. Labour was challenging all nine seats up for election in the May 1952 poll, including one in the mining area of Thornhill, where Alderman Matthew Scargill was elected unopposed. All the other contests were straight fights between Labour and 'Independents'. Betty, described as a private secretary of 19 East Parade, Dewsbury, was taking on the second safest Tory seat.

She used the opportunity to denounce the new Conservative government's 'redistribution' Budget, which cut subsidies on essentials and put up the bank rate. Taking issue with the writer of the 'As It Seems To Me' column in the *Batley Reporter*, Betty wrote to the editor, 'As a member of the lower income group, I cannot agree with your statement relating to the Budget. Millions of people in my own class not only heard a bomb, but will surely feel the effect of one, taking both the long and short term view into consideration. One fact is quite true, it is a redistribution Budget. Redistributive of the country's income in such a way as, on the whole, the rich are made richer and the poor poorer.' Her letter, the lead item in Readers' Opinions, continued, 'This is no incentive Budget as sections of the Press acclaim it, or as the Chancellor would like us to believe, at any rate not for the textile workers. Slackness of trade in the whole of the textile industry makes it impossible to guarantee an employee a full week's work, let alone any incentive overtime. Thus, although their weekly income is either stationary or slightly reduced, they are faced with a further increase in the cost of living.'[9]

On polling day, 8 May, turnout was slow, which the *Dewsbury District News and Chronicle* attributed to torrential rain. Polling picked up in the evening and the booths were busy. In Trinity North, the turnout increased on the 1950 poll to almost two thousand. But Betty's first excursion into politics at the age of twenty-two was not a success. Her seat was not among the four gains Labour made from the Independents. Betty failed by 200 votes, polling 863 votes to her opponent's 1063. Remarkable as it would be today, the *News and Chronicle* reported that about two hundred people gathered at the foot of the Town Hall steps to hear the results; from supporters of the two sides 'there were some sharp retorts to the remarks of the candidates'.[10]

It was Betty's second taste of failure. She had not made the grade as a professional dancer, and had fallen at the first hurdle in politics. Perhaps it was a blessing in disguise. As Alf Ramsden observed, 'Had she been successful, she might never have gone further afield. She might have decided to be a councillor, and stay in Dewsbury. She might have got interested in the mundane ways of life of a council, providing new houses, new schools, new nurseries and new homes for the aged.'[11]

It hardly seems likely. For by now, Betty was becoming known as a competent and strong-minded public speaker. And the uncanny way in which her political career was to become entwined with the Speakership also began to make itself felt. After the October 1951 general election, Churchill decided that he did not want the retiring Speaker, Douglas Clifton Brown, a Tory, to be replaced by his Deputy, Major Milner, the Labour MP for South-East Leeds. So Milner was given a peerage in compensation, and a young Transport House apparatchik – the party's international secretary Denis Healey – was chosen to fight his seat in a by-election in early 1952. 'My by-election was memorable only for two events which had nothing to do with it,' he later wrote.[12] 'I took an afternoon off to judge a speaking contest for young socialists, and chose as winner a bonny lass from Dewsbury who danced as a Tiller Girl in the chorus of the local pantomimes: her name was Betty Boothroyd and she later became a Labour MP herself. She is now the Deputy Speaker of the House of Commons.'

Healey was judging the final of the annual national speaking competition run by the League of Youth and the *Daily Herald*, the 'bible of the Labour Party'. Sarah Barker, the party's women's organizer was another judge. These competitions were taken seriously. A three-member team – best speaker, chairman and mover – was chosen in each constituency, and contenders competed first at branch, then regional and finally national level. The Leeds finals in late February were a hangover from the previous year, when the General Election interrupted the normal timetable. Yorkshire's team came second, but Betty was judged the best individual speaker overall.

Molly Walton, a Kirklees councillor of Crossland Moor, Hudders-field, recalls her style. 'Betty's opening lines were typical of how she spoke. She had learned how to speak in public, and how to attract the audience's attention. She didn't do any preamble. She went straight to the body of the speech. "The two evils in the world today are poverty and the fear of nuclear war . . ." Her speech was on social issues. She mentioned education, and referred to Ellen Wilkinson (firebrand socialist MP for Jarrow during Hunger Marches of the 30s, and first woman Labour Education Minister under Attlee who died in 1947), who, she said, she greatly admired. 'As always, Betty's mother was with her.'[13] 'She went everywhere with her. She was very proud of Betty – but would never say so to Betty.'

Later in 1952, Betty landed a coveted secretarial job at Transport House, and was beginning to become known in wider political circles. That same year, the Labour League of Youth took over Butlins at Filey, on the Yorkshire coast, for a week-long national rally, and Betty was in her element. She spoke at various 'fringe' meetings, and even had her picture taken by the newspapers. 'We had just been at a fringe meeting, and when we came out a reporter came up to her and asked if he could take a photograph,' said Molly Walton. 'It was the way she did it, not like you or me. There was an empty wooden beer crate and she tipped it up and stood on it. She had her hands out and mouth open, as if she were in full flow.' Shades of John Major and his electoral soap box forty years later.

Contemporary accounts of that week in Filey sound like echoes from a vanished age. Labour's lads and lasses lived separately in chalets. They had saved for months to go there, to see and hear the big names of the party: Harold Wilson, Barbara Castle, Ian Mikardo and Tom Driberg. They took part in sports. They had mock elections, a beauty contest and a fancy dress competition. Jean Megahy remembers sewing spangles on an outfit for a young man appearing as Carmen Miranda. 'And he actually won the contest. It was absolutely great fun.' There was no alcohol – 'it just never bothered us'. One night, as the young socialists were singing 'The Red Flag' in the Regency Ballroom instead of 'goodnight campers', one of Butlins Redcoats put on a record of 'There'll Always Be an England', regarded as a Tory anthem by the Left. In response, Mikardo and Barbara Castle marched hundreds of LLY enthusiasts round the camp, singing 'We'll make Anthony Eden wear a fifty shilling suit when the red revolution comes' to tune of 'John Brown's Body'.

Betty used to go back home at weekends to see her mother, but inevitably her focus shifted towards London. Betty had been a local agent for the party in Dewsbury in the 1951 General Election, and had come to prominence through her public speaking. But initially her sights were not set on being a politician herself. 'I was then in my early twenties and not thinking of becoming an MP. I always saw myself as the secretary or the agent – the power behind the throne – because I was a woman and I thought that was the be-all and end-all for women.'[14] 'Then I heard of a secretarial job going at Transport House in the research department . . . I hated leaving my mother, but she never stood in my way. She knew that it was very much in my blood, and that I was hemmed in in a small town.'

Despite Labour's loss of office, indeed perhaps because of it, Transport House was then the political hub of the party. Its hopes and visions were undimmed and, for young people, working there was an exhilarating privilege. Pearl Crisp, a secretary there at the same time as Betty, said, 'We just loved it. I used to look forward to going to work on Monday morning. I couldn't wait for the weekends to finish. It was spiritual. You really felt you were with people who believed in the same things as you did. Everyone was very keen. Everyone was in their local party, and very active. They came from a mixed social background, mostly upper working class and middle class. They were just a great bunch of people. Everyone got on extremely well together.'[15] Not everybody took this view. Marcia Williams (now Lady Falkender), quit her job as typist for Morgan Phillips, the party's General Secretary, and went to work for Harold Wilson 'because she was fed up with the right-wing stodginess of Transport House'.[16]

Accounts differ as to how long Betty worked there. Pearl Crisp thought she was there 'hardly a year', but Betty has told an interviewer it was much longer. 'I thoroughly enjoyed London,' she said. 'I loved the people I worked with. I was doing a full-time job for the Labour Party, which I loved, and meeting people who were very like-minded. I had a great time. I was there for three or four years, and then I applied for a job at the House of Commons, and got it.'[17] She started work for two MPs: Barbara Castle, MP for Blackburn and fast becoming a leading Left-winger on Labour's national executive, and Geoffrey de Freitas, MP for Lincoln, a handsome, intellectual lawyer who was to become a political mentor and close life-long friend. In the mid 1950s, MPs did not receive secretarial allowances, and wages were poor. To make ends meet, Westminster secretaries would work for two or even three MPs. Betty's weekly pay packet was 'the magnificent sum' of seven pounds ten shillings a week (£7.50).

Working at Westminster had been 'beyond my wildest dreams', but here she was, in her mid twenties, treading the corridors of power. It was a long way from Marriott Street – demolished at just about this time, in 1954, to make way for an undistinguished council estate – and the small town politics of Dewsbury. In the Commons, Betty was right in the political hothouse. She had her own, basic, direct Labour beliefs. As her letter to the *News and Chronicle* showed, she still thought in class terms, of 'us' and 'them'. Working in Parliament disarmed some of these simple tenets of faith. Labour was still divided between the Bevanite Left and the Atlanticist Right. Working for these two MPs, she was pulled in different ideological directions. Her involvement in their political initiatives exhibited what may be termed an ideological derivativeness. Betty has tended to take her political cue from the strongest influences around her. That is not to say she was not capable of thinking for herself, but her evident willingness to follow where others lead became apparent over the years. She would not pretend to

being an original political thinker. There is no such thing as
Boothroydism.

Barbara Castle was a leading light in Labour's Keep Left group,
named after a policy pamphlet so titled, written by Michael Foot, Ian
Mikardo and Richard Crossman in 1947. It attracted little attention
until the resignations of Bevan, Wilson and Freeman in 1951, who
then naturally gravitated to the group, bringing numerous other MPs
with them. By the early 50s, Keep Left counted among its membership
forty-seven MPs and two peers, including five former ministers.[18] They
met regularly, in the House, in Dick Crossman's London home, and at
a 'modest' restaurant in Soho. Sometimes they would go into weekend
retreat at Crossman's cottage in the Chilterns. Jo Richardson, Ian
Mikardo's secretary, was the secretary to the group. She was also Betty's
flatmate, and Betty soon found herself roped into this curious political
menage. Barbara Castle said Betty 'a jolly, plumpish Yorkshire lass'
helped Keep Left 'occasionally' with the secretarial work.[19]

Betty cheerfully concedes that she 'learned a great deal' from both
her MP employers. 'Barbara was a very determined lady, extremely
dedicated to socialism and a very good person to work for,' she said
later.[20] 'She was a hard task master, very hard, but I never had any
complaints. She was tremendously efficient.' Betty thought her a good
role model to follow. Barbara took everything in her stride: her constituency, the NEC, and running a home.

But she was not destined to be the critical social and political influence on Betty's subsequent life and career, despite having many things
in common – not least being a woman in a man's world. That role
fell to Geoffrey de Freitas, the debonair haute-bourgeois barrister and
diplomat. Yet the two could scarcely have come from more different
backgrounds. Six foot four in height, he was an ex-Haileybury public
school boy who joined the Labour Party while still at school 'moved
by a belief in Christian Socialism and by the misery of the working
class after the Depression'.[21]

He was born on the island of St Lucia (much later to figure signifi-
cantly in Betty's life) in the West Indies, where his father was Attorney-
General, in April 1913. After Haileybury, he went up to Clare College,
Cambridge. He won an athletics blue and became President of the
Union, the debating society where he saw 'quiet little Clem Attlee'

triumph over the bombastic oratory of Oswald Mosley. He was a Cholmeley Scholar at Lincoln's Inn, and was called to the Bar in 1936. He spent two years in the USA studying international law as a Mellon Scholar at Yale University, and on the return ship journey met his wife-to-be Helen Graham Bell, daughter of an anglophile Chicago lawyer. She was also to become Betty's life-long friend, sharing some of her adventurous holidays.

He ended an uneventful war as Squadron-Leader Geoffrey de Freitas, and while still in uniform was elected MP for Nottingham Central in the July 1945 election. 'Now he was to become attached to that greatest of institutions – the House of Commons. "I'll love that place until I die," he said,' in an autobiography completed by his widow and published after his death.[22] 'Everything about it . . . suited him: the gregariousness, the unpredictability, the challenges, the chance to put Labour Party beliefs into practice; all these contributed to the euphoria of those years.' Change the sex, and the mixture of enthusiasm and awe sounds just like Betty. De Freitas was asked by Clem Attlee to be his Parliamentary Private Secretary, his eyes and ears in the Commons. Attlee thought very highly of de Freitas, and shocked his Downing Street staff by showing his young PPS papers above his station saying: 'Study these well. You will never have another opportunity like this.'[23]

In 1946, Attlee made him Under-Secretary for Air, and four years later promoted him to Under-Secretary at the Home Office where he handled much of the departmental work because the Home Secretary was also Leader of the House. When Labour went into Opposition after the 1951 election, he had a safe seat, having switched from Nottingham Central to Lincoln. He was spokesman on Housing in Labour's front-bench team until 1954, when he was switched to air affairs. Hugh Gaitskell moved him in 1959 to agriculture, of which he had practical experience. Financially secure, partly as a result of his wife's fortune, de Freitas had bought a 150-acre dairy farm in Cambridgeshire, not far from the country cottage that has been Betty's home for the past three decades.

Returned with an increased majority at Lincoln in 1955, a year or so after Betty became his secretary, de Freitas became deeply involved in European and foreign affairs. He had been on the UK delegation to the United Nations in 1949, and for three years up to 1954 he was a UK delegate to the Counsultative Assembly of the Council of Europe, of which he was later president. Now, he helped found the NATO Parliamentarians' conference, and was the organization's treasurer until 1960. He was also prominent in the British council of the European Movement, the all-party pressure group for the EEC (as it then was).

Parliamentary biographer Andrew Roth says, 'He was strongly pro-NATO and pro-American in defence affairs . . . but he was far from an American stooge.'[24]. He attacked the Conservative government's decision to station 'Thor' missiles in Britain, condemned air patrols carrying nuclear weapons as unnecessarily provocative and opposed the siting of Fylingdales Early Warning Station in the North Yorkshire Moors National Park, even though he was joint treasurer of the British American Parliamentary Group at the time. These close contacts with the United States – he had been in forty-nine of the fifty states – inevitably brought Betty into close contact with American congressmen and senators and their aides, and the pro-Europe establishment in Britain. These contacts substantially shaped her views. If she had ever been 'of the Left', in her links with Keep Left, which is debatable, she certainly began to move into the Atlanticist-European Right-wing of the Labour Party during these years.

But uppermost in her mind was Parliament itself. Initially, she was content to be 'the power behind the throne', doing things for other people, making their job a little less difficult. She enjoyed that very much. But she also looked around the talent on the Commons backbenches, and came to the conclusion that she could do the job as well as most of them and quite a lot better than many. She thought, ' "Well, I could do this job too." I wasn't in awe, I knew that I too could help to make changes. However, at that time it was terribly difficult for a woman to get selected.'[25]

She spoke the truth. Getting a seat was a daunting task for a woman in her mid twenties. 'In the mid 1950s, I was told by the then National Party Agent that I was too young and needed "to get some age on my shoulders." '[26] Betty checked the average age on the Labour benches, and found it to be near the pensionable age of sixty-five – compared to the 'deliberate intake' of younger Tories. Furthermore, the Labour Party was still dominated by trade union worthies, particularly in her home territory in the north of England. Dewsbury, for example, was a fiefdom of the National Union of Mineworkers, as was much else of west and south Yorkshire. And she had no union sponsorship, although she was a member of the old Clerical and Administrative Workers' Union (now part of the general union GMB) and was chairman of Parliamentary Staffs trade unions from 1955 to 1960.

Harold Sims, Labour Party organizer in Leeds after the war, remembers Betty 'searching around for a parliamentary seat' after 'getting the flavour' of the Commons.[27] 'She did come into Yorkshire looking for a seat. But it was unfortunate that the idea of women becoming MPs – even in the Labour Party – was very difficult at that time. Most of the seats in Yorkshire were union-sponsored, and that ruled out Betty. I am sure she would have liked a seat up here, but it was not to be.'

But she persevered, and in the summer of 1956 was adopted as prospective parliamentary candidate for the safe Conservative seat of Leicester South-East. This was the stamping ground of 'Gunboat Charlie' – Captain Charles Waterhouse MP, leader of the Tory Suez Group, the home of the Quorn hunt, and Tory to its roots. Gunboat Charlie had a majority of 11,541 at the General Election, which Betty later exaggerated somewhat. In her 1982 *Times* article it was 15,000.[28] By 1993, she was telling Glenys Kinnock and Fiona Millar, 'I was the only person who thought I could win that seat with a 21,000 majority!'[29]

Being a prospective candidate gave Betty some clout in party circles, if not much. As an ex-officio delegate to the annual conference, she was called to speak in a debate on pensions and national insurance. Conference was discussing an NEC document on the issue, which proposed a national superannuation fund costing £424 million a year by 1980. Betty said she did not under-estimate the tremendous cost, but urged: 'Let us not forget that in the early stages of this scheme we shall have in power a Labour Government. I would hope that in the initial important stages we would also have simultaneously an intelligent policy of disarmament. Would I be Utopian in asking whether or not with a Labour government carrying out a gradual policy of disarmament the saving here would help to implement this superannuation scheme?'[30] She added: 'The people of my generation do not ask for security now. They ask for opportunity, and for social justice. The time will come all too soon when we want comfort and security.' To her mind, a national superannuation scheme was 'the greatest instrument for social justice which we can bring to this country'.

It was a commendable performance, but it did not seem to increase her stock with the party hierarchy. Shortly afterwards, Captain Waterhouse resigned his seat to take up a directorship with Tanganyika Concessions. A by-election was called for 28 November 1957. Years later, when she was being given an honorary law doctorate by Leicester University, she disclosed: 'Fighting that by-election . . . was my idea alone. The then general secretary of the Labour Party did not share my enthusiasm for becoming a candidate. In fact, he thought I was much too young. This city was where my parliamentary career really began, where I graduated in campaigning. Leicester provided my first real political fight. I was young and believed that anything was possible.'[31]

The announcement of a by-election was front-page news back home in Dewsbury. 'HOPING TO BE AN MP' was the headline in a short story in the *Dewsbury Reporter*, which recalled her unsuccessful bid to win election to the borough council. The item also recorded, 'In recent years she has travelled extensively.' This may have been in part a veiled reference to her controversial six-week trip to a number of Communist countries beginning in April 1957. She acted as secretary to a group of Labour MPs who undertook an unofficial tour of China and North Vietnam, via Moscow. It was an eventful trip, which was to cause her some diplomatic problems a few years later when she went to the United States, by then embroiled in war with Ho Chi Minh's north Vietnamese army.

The only record of this journey is in a series of reports by Ian Mikardo MP to *Tribune*, the Left-wing weekly. In the 10 May edition, he complained of being woken up by rehearsals for the May Day Communist Parade in Red Square, which indicates that they were official guests in one of the few decent hotels in the very heart of the Soviet capital. He urged the British Left not to underestimate Soviet party boss Nikita Khrushchev, who was pursuing a path of 'controlled liberalization'. The party watched a Tajik ensemble at the Bolshoi,

Ben Archibald Boothroyd, Betty's father, taken in 1925, four years before she was born.

Betty's mother, Mary, supporting her in the Nelson and Colne by-election in 1968. Mum was always there when Betty needed her.

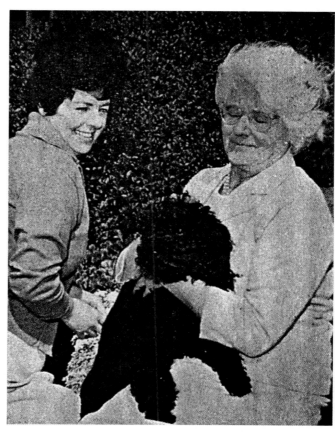

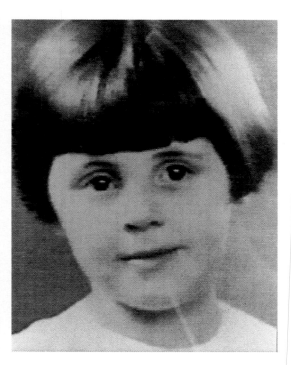

The only child: straight-haired Betty in her primary school days.

Battye Street, where Betty lived with her parents for a time.

Scenes from Betty's home town of
Dewsbury in the mid-war years.

Above: The cast of *Cinderella* in 1942; Betty is Prince Charming *(to the left of the producer in the centre of the back row)*

Above: Betty *(middle row, second from left)* did not always say no to a wig: here she was appearing in *Robin Hood* in 1941.

The Dewsbury Empire, where Betty played in panto as a child.

under the gaze of 'a boxful of VVIPs, including Khrushchev, Malenkov and Molotov, "characteristically hiding behind a curtain". A week later, Mikardo is reporting from the Peking–Hanchow express, arguing that the Chinese treat Marxism 'as a background wash, and not a blueprint.'

There was no mention of any of the other visiting MPs – until the third week, when a third epistle from Mikardo, headlined THE LAST OF THE REVOLUTIONARIES, is topped by a photograph of the British delegation taking breakfast tea with the Communist leadership of north Vietnam: Ho Chi Minh himself, and his Prime Minister, a smiling Pham Van Dong. The caption identifies Harold Davies MP, a favourite of Harold Wilson's, Lena Jeger MP, stalwart of the Left and Ian Mikardo. The fourth guest, a western woman with a fine head of hair, large ear-rings, and wearing a long flower-patterned dress is not named, but it is unmistakably Betty. Mikardo is fulsome about the Vietnamese. 'You don't talk for long to Ho Chi Minh without realizing that he is one of the very great men,' he gushes. 'Indeed, he may be (unless South Africa one day produces a Negro Lenin) the last of all the classic revolutionaries.' It is hard to believe that Betty actually regrets anything she has done, but the Asian saga is certainly one she has tended to leave out of more recent potted biographies.

Strongly encouraged by Geoffrey de Freitas, Betty threw herself into the fray at Leicester South-East with characteristic verve. The *Daily Express* called her 'the girl with the ideal boss', but predicted that her Tory rival, John Peel, a forty-five-year-old former colonial administrator, would win. *Tribune*, evidently unaware of her appearance in its pages a few months earlier, was more upbeat. Under a headline THE OLD PEOPLE ARE BACKING BETTY, its reporter enthused that she was setting the pace for the Tories. 'Every morning, at half-past seven, the Labour loudspeaker van pulls up outside one or another of the factories in the constituency, and the candidate, attractive 27-year-old (author's note: she was 28) Betty Boothroyd, begins her day with a short meeting for the workers as they clock on.'[32] At one such gathering one voter was heard saying to another that 'that fellow Peel' would not be out of bed yet. He may well have been right. By-elections were much less frenetic before television discovered they made good situation comedy.

Labour's *Daily Herald* agreed that Betty was setting the pace, and said she 'has her opponent on the defensive'. The Tories wheeled in some of their big guns, including Lord Kilmuir, the Lord Chancellor, who had spoken in a by-election at Tonbridge the previous year. He did not appear to have helped much there; the government's majority went down from more than 10,000 to only 1600. Betty hoped she could repeat – even better – that performance. She passionately condemned the government's financial policy, which had forced the city council to stop new housing projects except for slum clearance, a move which rattled her opponent. 'There are still about 8000 families on the council's housing list. What hope for the future do they have?' she said on the hustings. Betty excoriated the government's Suez debacle, which had 'lost Britain the moral leadership of the world'. And she sharply criticized ministerial attempts to hold down pay while allowing prices to rip free. In this, she had the support of her party leader Hugh Gaitskell, who sent her the traditional leader's message a few days before polling day. 'They blame their own failure to stop price rises on the unions, although it is clear that the government's action in directly increasing living costs through cutting food subsidies, imposing higher health charges and driving up rents has itself caused a great deal of trouble,' he said.[33]

This was uninspiring stuff, but Betty struggled gamely on, bringing the windy rhetoric of Westminster down to earth in the back street of Leicester. In an area of Victorian terraces known as Poet's Corner – Pope Street, Lord Byron Street, Cowper Street and Wordsworth Houses – voters complained that the Tory Rent Act was doubling their rents. At the Co-op shoe factory in the neighbourhood, she promised to be 'an MP who's in touch with your lives and wishes at last'. Men and women workers applauded.

Just forty-eight hours before polling day, an 'issue' suddenly made its appearance. An excited John Peel, who had swapped the colonial service for something in the cement trade, called in the press to read out an extract from a letter from Betty sent by Labour's Chief Whip, Herbert Bowden. 'I have known her since she came to work in the House of Commons some four years ago, and the experience that she has thus gained in Parliament will be invaluable to her as a Member.'

Peel, his face a mask of earnestness, said the use of the phrase 'in Parliament' might lead electors to believe that Miss Boothroyd had sat in the House as an MP. This was 'most misleading'. He added, 'I might have been misled myself if I had not known exactly what her experience was. I do not think that the phrase was deliberately used, but certainly the sentence is strangely expressed – particularly as it was written by the Labour Chief Whip, who ought to know the situation.' Peel thought Labour should have used the expression '*of* Parliament' rather than '*in* Parliament'. The matter had been raised by some Conservative canvassers, he added lamely.

Under the headline A PREPOSITION STIRS THE CALM OF SE LEICESTER, the *Manchester Guardian* reported that the polite calm of a dull by-election had been broken by a squabble about a preposition.[34] The paper reported that some local Conservative activists were trying to whip up a scandal, and there were mutterings about the question of a possible breach of privilege 'but these have not been loud'. What was loud, however, was Betty's reaction to the Tory squib. Taking the phrase 'in Parliament' out of context was ridiculous and an insult to the Leicester electorate, she declared. Bowden's letter was on her election address sent out two weeks earlier, and the leaflet clearly stated her position as an MP's secretary. There could not be possibly be any mistake. 'She was – perhaps for the first time in the campaign – "almost speechless",' said the *Guardian*. Apart from the arrival of Betty's mother at the railway station that day, said the *MG*, this had been the only drama of the last seven days. Meetings had been small and silent, leaving scarcely a mark on the surface of a calm, prosperous constituency. But Betty had made her mark. On one small estate, almost everyone had recognized her. Her determination had been noted, even in a constituency that had been described as 'too comfortable to bother'.

On polling day, 28 November, the turnout was low, fifty-six per cent, compared with more than seventy-eight per cent at the General Election. Both parties suffered a fall in votes, but Betty secured a respectable swing to Labour of 3.8 per cent. She polled 11,541 votes (exactly the same as figure as Gunboat Charlie's majority at the 1955 election) to Peel's 18,023. Betty said, 'I want to make it clear that the percentage swing in favour of Labour in this election shows a sign of no confidence in the Tory government.' Peel, once Our Man in Brunei and Resident Commissioner in the Gilbert and Ellice Islands from

1949 to 1951, called the virtual halving of his party's majority 'a magnificent victory'. Politically speaking, he was never heard of again.

The voters of the East Midlands, however, had not seen or heard
the last of Betty Boothroyd. She licked her wounds and went back to
Westminster, biding her time for the next opportunity. It came sooner
than she might have expected. Tory premier Harold Macmillan, the
'Supermac' of the cartoonists, was not obliged to go to the country
until the spring of 1960, but with the economy moving strongly in the
right direction during 1959, he judged it right to call a snap election
in the autumn.

Some local Labour parties were caught on the hop. One such was
Peterborough, a solid, middle of the road constituency with a strong
power base in a small cathedral city with good Labour roots in the
railways and engineering works that dominated the local economy.
Unfortunately, the seat was actually Peterborough and North
Northants, and included eighty-seven villages and hamlets north of
the city where voting habits were still deeply deferential. That had not
stopped Labour from winning the seat in 1945, and it was only lost
in 1950 by 144 votes.

This time, the Peterborough party was embarrassed by the unexpected resignation of its prospective candidate, Patrick Hopwood, a Wor-
cestershire farmer who decided that the political commuting from
Pershore had become tiresome. He quit in the early summer, only
four months before Macmillan called the General Election. The party
was stunned. Vic Phillips, who had assisted in the Leicester SE by-
election eight months previously, was the party's full-time agent in the
city. He began to cast around for nominations. 'Then one day, Betty
Boothroyd walked into my office. Someone had told her we were
looking for a candidate. I should imagine it was Jim Cattermole [Betty's
by-election agent in Leicester, and a keen pro-European]. I thought
my prayers had been answered.'[35]

Within days, Betty had been nominated, and she sailed through
the selection process, winning it on the first ballot. There was some
controversy over her sudden emergence on to the political scene. Local
girl Phyllis Stedman was a disappointed loser who quit the party, and
later became an SDP peer. 'Some people said I rigged it for Betty, but
that was absolute nonsense,' said Phillips. 'Apart from getting her

nominated I didn't see much of her. And when she got on the platform – I can picture it now – there was no chance for anybody else when she started speaking.'

She was the first woman to stand for the Peterborough seat, and created a considerable stir. 'She was young, and very attractive,' recalls Phillips. Extraordinarily, a number of young railway workers all asked to take their annual leave to work for her. Charlie Swift, a train driver in the city and president of the local party, whose mother had gone to school with Betty, said, 'There was one young lad who drove her everywhere. They gave up their holidays, because some of them were really attracted to her.'[36] Perhaps it was wise that they did not breakfast with the Swifts, in whose house Betty stayed some of the time. 'We were brought up stiff and starched,' said Charlie. 'Betty came to stay, and the first day she came downstairs out of the bedroom with one of those blinking negligee, see-through nighties on. Both of us were so prim and proper, we didn't know where to put ourselves. You could see right through. Everything she had got you could see. But you got used to it. That was Betty. She was very broad-minded.'

At her adoption meeting on 12 September, Betty promised supporters 'the fight of our lives. I'm going to enjoy every minute of it. This is our hour of destiny as it never was before.' She lambasted 'the Tory record of mess, misery and miscalculations'.[37] She insisted international affairs would play a large part in the election 'because in this jet age the world has, so to speak, shrunk and we are living much closer together than ever before. I want to see a Labour government so that we can put forward the plans we have for stopping the spread of nuclear armaments. I want to see a Labour Foreign Secretary negotiating our plan for disengagement in central Europe.' She also promised to scrap NHS prescription charges, and spend as much on the Health Service as Mr Fraser spent on taking over Harrods. The local paper noted that she went canvassing in Wittering with Geoffrey de Freitas.

Her rival at Peterborough was the hugely popular Harmar Nicholls, whose career was in some ways uncannily the mirror image of her own. The son of working-class parents, he was born in Darlaston, Staffordshire, close to Betty's own constituency today. He went to elementary school and Queen Mary's School, Walsall, trained as a surveyor and stood successfully for his local council at the age of twenty-six. Like Betty, he won a national speaking competition at the age of twenty-two, although in his case it was the 'young reactionaries' – the Junior Imperial League. And, as Betty was to be, he was an unsuccessful candidate at Nelson and Colne before getting into Parliament. In his election address, he returned to the theme of prosperity – Macmillan's 'You've never had it so good' slogan that was to dog Labour throughout the election. He also had his adoption speech taped so that any member of the public could ring up to hear it. Few are thought to have taken the trouble.

Betty put her all into the campaign. This time she was going to win. She toured the agricultural hamlets where some farmworkers still voted as their employers told them, and spoke on the green when the squire refused to allow Labour use of the village hall. Women's guilds, old folks' homes, factory gates, street corners: a gruelling eighteen-hour day. Even the adoring footplatemen tired of her energy. Harold Wilson, then Shadow Chancellor, came to lend his support, but the meeting in Thrapston market place did not last long. Wilson reminded the fifty onlookers that Betty was from the same county as him and could be relied on to show the toughness that was usually associated with Yorkshire people. Then the loudspeaker failed, and the two tykes were reduced to one-to-one conversations with the voters. But he did leave her with a £100 cheque from the Derbyshire miners for her fighting fund.

At a 'meet the Press', she volunteered the thought that people were more interested in the election than at any time since 1945. For the last week of the campaign Betty's mother joined her in the campaign. Labour switched tack somewhat to point out that they were the only party offering votes at eighteen (instead of twenty-one). Young people were now much more mature than twenty years previously, she told a city meeting on 21 September. If they were old enough to drive a car and fight for their country, they were old enough to decide what type of government they should have. Unfortunately, it was scant consolation for such young people – deprived of the vote for another decade until the law was changed. They could not vote in Peterborough, and the 2.9 per cent swing she was seeking began to look more and more elusive.

The *Daily Herald* saluted the house-to-house barnstorming campaign of a 'vivacious brown-eyed lass' (a term that would now bring untold wrath on the head of the luckless reporter), but admitted that finding the lost labour votes 'had never been done before in placid Peterborough, where there is prosperity and little unemployment'.[38] Vic Phillips talked the campaign up, telling reporters, 'Every day that goes by our hopes grow stronger. We are now more optimistic than we were in 1955. I've a bet on that there's going to be a recount – with someone who thinks that Miss Boothroyd will get in even without one.' Even he had to admit, 'I think she'll get in, but I always was a bit cautious.'[39] The Tories said the 'Socialist temperature' was low, and they had detected no evidence of a much talked-of swing to Labour. All parties talk like that during elections, but the Tories' assessment sounds more convincing.

Both the government and Labour regarded Peterborough as highly marginal, and treated it accordingly. Apart from Harold Wilson, Labour sent George Brown, then shadow Defence Secretary, and the party leader Hugh Gaitskell also went to the city. John Boyd-Carpenter, Minister of Pensions and National Insurance, played John the Baptist to his Prime Minister. At his appearance on 26 September , Gaitskell argued that old-age and widows' pensions should be raised by ten shillings (50p) a week, and tackled the 'never had it so good' Tories head-on. 'We hear of prosperity, but it is not what it should be if you really want a government which planned expansion in this country. The fact remains that millions of our fellow citizens are still living under conditions of hardship and poverty which the rest of us ought not to tolerate any longer.'[40]

After the leader's high-flown prose came the future deputy leader's 'incident'. There was always a George Brown incident of some kind. This time it was over posters of Harmar Nicholls in the Bull Hotel, Westgate, where Betty had been staying since the campaign got under way. On Saturday night, she arrived back at the hotel at 11 30 p.m. to find Brown and his wife Sophie quitting the premises. He had insisted to the manager, a Mr W. Callard, that the Tory posters be taken down, or similar ones of Betty put up alongside. Not to be out-Browned, Callard retorted that he didn't like being spoken to in that way, and the hotel was not only his living but also his home. Brown had become 'very unreasonable, shouting and shaking his fist'.

He then refused to stay any longer and gave orders to depart for Grantham, where he had another election appointment the next day.

Hapless Betty had no real option but to follow suit, and move out to the Great Northern, a Victorian pile by the station. She had not originally complained about the posters in the Bull, but she now said, 'I feel that this is not the usual courtesy which should be extended by a commercial organization to patrons of the hotel. Therefore I am compelled to withdraw my patronage.'[41] Naturally, the Conservatives seized on the incident with glee, even though Betty had not been directly involved. Nicholls blustered that when Britishers began allowing themselves to be brow-beaten by bad-tempered politicians as to which banner they should fly, parliamentary government would be at an end. Mercilessly over the top as this was, it did the Tories no harm.

Six days before polling day, the *Peterborough Citizen and Advertiser* headlined its front page: NICHOLLS IS TIPPED — BY A SHORT HEAD. The paper estimated that the government would hold the seat with a reduced majority of around 2900. The story was based on the return of postal votes, which usually favour the Tories because of their better organization in the field. The paper gave both candidates space to answer the question 'Why do you think you will win?' Betty replied, 'It's neck and neck, say the statisticians. The gap has closed and so it should. It has become obvious to me over the last few weeks that there is a moral upsurge against the Conservatives after their mismanagement abroad and their callousness on the question of social progress at home.' She concluded, 'The spirit is there, the votes are there – and we have the will to win.' With those giveaway words 'we have the will to win', Betty was in danger of appearing to concede the fight to Nicholls, who simply repeated the party line on prosperity and accused the Labour Party of irresponsibility.

Polling day was Betty's thirtieth birthday, and the turnout was high – eighty-three per cent. The count in the Town Hall began the next day at 11 a.m., when the two candidates met face to face for the first time. Betty's mother was at her side. The result was announced to a waiting crowd some 500 strong at 12.23 p.m. It was a bitter disappointment for Betty. Nicholls had not only retained the seat, but increased his majority by more than 1300 to 4584. His own vote had gone up by almost 1100, and Labour's had gone down by 250. It was Labour's worst performance in the constituency since 1935. Betty put a brave face on it, promising her successful rival, 'I shall be breathing down your neck in the House of Commons during the next few years.'[42] In turn, Nicholls was gallant, but patronizing, 'She has proved to be a bonny fighter. She has done her job well, but I think it is true to say that on this occasion our case was the stronger one.'

Betty's personal tragedy was mirrored in the electoral calamity that swamped Labour nationally. Under Gaitskell, Labour had largely healed its internal wounds, but it could still not convince the electorate that it could manage the economy as well as the Conservatives. Macmillan's simple appeal – 'Life's Better With the Conservatives – Don't Let Labour Ruin It' – had struck a ready chord with the electorate. Macmillan bounded back with his Commons majority increased to 100, while Labour was left to a self-devouring inquest as to why the party's vote had fallen by 2.7 per cent.

For Betty, it was back to Westminster, but back to her secretary's desk. Her employer, friend and loyal supporter Geoffrey de Freitas had had a bit of a scare. He got back at Lincoln with his majority slashed by nearly 1000 to 4389. Though he did not know it then, it would be the fourth and last time he would fight the seat. His career was on the verge of radical change. So was Betty's, though in her case by her own initiative.

There was no pressure on her to quit her position, quite the contrary. As Lady Helen de Freitas noted in the posthumous memoir of her husband, 'The linchpin of his activities in those days was Betty Boothroyd. She had emigrated from Yorkshire, served an apprenticeship with Barbara Castle, and then swept in to become indispensable to Geoffrey. She shared his views on most subjects, and therefore was not only efficient but supportive. She saw him through the 50s and when at the end of 1961 he left the House of Commons she branched out on her own . . .'[43]

De Freitas astonished his political friends by accepting from the Macmillan government in 1961 the post of British High Commissioner in Ghana, complete with accompanying knighthood. He privately told Hugh Gaitskell he did not want a life peerage, because he intended to re-enter the Commons at a future date.

Linchpin or no, Betty did not want to go with him. Instead of being 'stuck out in Africa', she 'did a flit', as they would have said in her native Dewsbury. Frustrated with the double setback at Leicester and Peterborough, and exasperated at Labour's stick-in-the-mud commitment to trade union time-servers in the safe northern seats, she began to look enviously across the Atlantic, at the vibrant, youthful politics of John Kennedy, who seemed poised to usher in a new world of opportunity for people like her. She had already had some contact with American politics, working behind the scenes for the NATO Parliamentarians' Conference that de Freitas helped set up in 1955. He was the body's treasurer until 1960, and took Betty with him as amanuensis to its conferences, including one in Paris, where it was initially based before moving to Brussels after France's break with NATO. So she was building up contacts as well as an interest in the USA.

Betty's own version is romantic. 'By that time, I'd seen quite a lot of the world. I'd seen the Far East: I knew a lot of Europe. The one place I hadn't seen was America. I was very fed up with the old men of Europe in 1960 – de Gaulle, Adenauer, Macmillan – I wanted to see how things worked in America.'[44] So she went to the US Embassy in Grosvenor Square, got a visa and caught the plane. 'I flew into New York, with a return ticket in my sweaty paw to come back if things didn't work out.'

When she was standing for Rossendale in the General Election of 1970, the local *Free Press* printed her curriculum vitae from a publicity hand-out on its front page, recording that 'on leave of absence from Sir Geoffrey de Freitas, and independent of any organization, she travelled as an observer with the Kennedy election team during the campaign.'[45] This has been a recurrent theme in her reminiscences: that she helped get Kennedy elected to the US presidency (typically, 'she campaigned in America for the late President Kennedy'[46]), or at any rate, travelled with the campaign team as an observer. The Kennedy Library has no record of her involvement, and the Democrat Party records of campaign volunteers do not go so far back. Pearl Crisp, who succeeded her as de Freitas's secretary, thinks she was 'probably just helping out, a general dogsbody. They need lots of people, like we do here.'[47]

The plain facts of how she came to be with the Kennedy roadshow appeared at the time in her local paper. On 9 September, the *Yorkshire Evening Post* reported that a 'young Dewsbury woman' who had made two unsuccessful attempts to become an MP was flying to America in two weeks' time 'to study the way the Americans conduct their presidential election campaigns'. Speaking at her mother's home in Moorcroft Road, Dewsbury, she said she had obtained six months' leave from Geoffrey de Freitas, 'Socialist' MP for Lincoln (this was the period when the *YEP* was owned by Yorkshire Conservative Newspapers: anything Labour was Socialist), to travel across America with the campaign teams of Democratic candidate John F. Kennedy and Lyndon Johnson.

'I don't think we could adopt anything like the American campaign system here,' she said. 'But I shall be looking for pointers and ideas which we might be able to use in future campaigns.' Following her tour, which would only take in the last two months of the exhausting two-year US presidential campaign, she would spend the rest of her leave working as personal assistant to an American senator.

The Kennedy campaign trail is Betty's first recorded foray into journalism. Only a fortnight after arriving, she filed a despatch from Pittsburgh, Pennsylvania, to the *Evening Post* in Leeds, headlined KENNEDY IS THE ONE COOL MAN. By-lined with her own name in capitals, the article is a mixture of youthful excitement mixed with a powerful desire to impress. She began her story, the second of two despatches, 'As I begin to write this I looked up and asked a man, "What day is it?" He was a middle-aged man, one of John Kennedy's aides who had been with the election team from the start. He replied, "Never mind the day – what month is it, September, October or November?"

Betty wrote that travelling through America with one of the most exhausting shows on the road, the days and the months ran into one another and, providing the light held good, time had little or no meaning. 'My watch means little or nothing to me at the moment.

'This 1960 presidential campaign has everything: drama, comedy, exhaustion, triumph, and colourfully clashing personalities. Its changes of atmosphere are as unpredictable as the conditions surrounding a thunderstorm. The only person who appears to remain cool is John Kennedy himself. Electioneering American-style is an ordeal made up of fatigue, occasional hunger and thirst and almost constant noise and hullabaloo. Oversleep by half an hour and there is nothing for it but to miss breakfast. When the Kennedy procession is running an hour late at noon, you skip lunch – and arrive in the afternoon to start the first big rally of the day only to find that all the hot dogs have already been eaten by the waiting crowd.'

The bus she travelled in carried no drinking water, and by mid afternoon their 'leather-lined throats' were croaking for water. In one town she became so desperate that as the motorcade arrived in the main square she jumped out and ran two blocks to the nearest bar – Jim's – and asked for his biggest container to be filled with water. The astonished barman gave his English customer an enormous jar filled with water and ice cubes, and would not take a cent. Back at the bus, they drank straight from the jar even though it tasted slightly of relish, which is what it had previously contained.

'Back in New York, Kennedy was hailed by a milling mass. It had a purpose, this quest for votes among New York's millions. In this race for the steps to the White House Kennedy must have the 45 electoral votes which New York has to confer and the presidential candidate acted as though his life depended on it,' she wrote. 'Judging by the shrieking crowds and the side comments of top politicians, he must now feel fairly confident that he is well on the way to getting them.'

There followed some graphic, I-have-seen-it stuff, a pastiche of *Time* or *Newsweek*, but fresh for a British reader. 'The people in the crowd certainly gave the impression they were for Kennedy. "Vee luff heem – hees so vigorous," said a shawl-clad old lady in the garment workers' district. "I think he will be the greatest next to Roosevelt," said another. Nearby was a very sprightly old woman wearing an enormous button on which she had printed: "If I were 21, I'd vote for Kennedy." As the motorcade made its way out of New York, two waitresses and a chef handed the candidate two boxes. One contained clams, the other a fried chicken. Another admirer had already tossed him a salami sandwich and a still more enthusiastic type poured whisky over him.'

Their excitement comes through Betty's breathless prose. She had no training as a journalist, but she sought and enjoyed the company of journalists almost from the time she came to London. The desire to communicate and be taken seriously is clear. She wrote that she was never tired, finding the enthusiasm of cheering, jumping, laughing crowds infectious. 'I find the endless sea of faces enthralling. They are a complete cross-section of America.

'At first, the faces are expectant. When Kennedy waves and smiles, they light up and become radiant with affection and the cries ring out. Call it mass hysteria if you will, but I think it has a deeper significance. In my opinion it reinforces the inner spirit of the candidate for the most arduous task in the West today. Whether the next President be Nixon or Kennedy, he will always have with him the memory of those faces. If ambition should ever tempt him to deviate from the path of duty and compassion, these faces of America, raised in hope and faith, will inevitably strengthen the next occupant of the White House for his fearsome responsibilities.'

Reading between these faintly apocalyptic last lines, Betty's awe and enthusiasm are plain to see. How different to beating round the villages of rural Leicestershire, trying to persuade farm workers to vote against the squire's wishes! Or shaking the apathetic burghers of Peterborough from their 'never had it so good' political daze. America was more to her liking. By April 1961, when she should have been on her way back across the Atlantic, the gossip columnists were disclosing that she had extended her leave of absence to twelve months, and would stay in Washington until the end of the Congressional session. But her sights were still set on Westminster. 'I would like to run again as a Labour candidate, she said, 'even though I have lost twice before.'[48]

The interesting aspect of Betty's long-standing insistence that she was somehow part of the Kennedy campaign is not that she was in any way prominent, but that she felt compelled to state (perhaps even overstate) it so often: as if the cachet of being involved with the powerful and the successful was some kind of talisman that would impress the folks back home and bring her political good fortune.

Yet she was quite a success in her own right in the USA. She had met a few Congressmen through the NATO parliamentary link, and she worked her contacts on Capitol Hill to such effect that she soon landed a job. She was hired as a legislative assistant to Congressman Silvio Conte, a Republican from Massachusetts, a rare bird indeed: the state was customarily thought of as solid Democrat territory. But

Conte was no ordinary Republican. A first-generation American, he came from a poor Italian migrant family, and during the war served in the Pacific theatre where he built airstrips. He married a navy nurse, and came back to the USA after the war to study law. He was elected to the state legislature in his late twenties and became a Congressman at the age of thirty-five. He was politically active – particularly in the environmental field – until his death from cancer in 1991.

His widow Karen remembers her husband hiring Betty some time in 1961, probably not long after President Kennedy's inauguration. 'Betty came over to work for JFK, and when he was elected, there was no one who would give her a job because she was from Britain. They just couldn't see it. Silvio said, "You come in and let me see what your 'work is like. I'll keep you until you have enough money to go home." But she stayed for two years, even though she had plenty of money to go home. She was very active in the office. She was one of the best secretaries – she could type faster than any machine they have today.'[49]

Betty was elated. She worked in Suite 245 of the Longworth Building in Washington, with a first-floor view of the Capitol. 'Silvio was a very super individual to work for and he gave me a lot of opportunities,' she recalled.[50] 'He rather liked my British accent, so I answered the telephone, and then I used to send out literature to his constituents.' Conte was meticulous in this respect. Betty used to go through the papers, and if one of his potential voters had a baby, she would write a letter of congratulations for the Congressman to sign, and send off a copy of the Baby Book, on how to bring up baby. Similar letters followed the marriage announcements, this time with a copy of the Cook Book. A new chairman of the Lions Club got his congratulations and a book on civics.

'Then I graduated and began writing speeches for him. I was there for a couple of years and thoroughly loved the job. I liked American people, liked the standard of living: I was earning far more than a British Member of Parliament, and I was the most junior in the office. And what a contrast to the facilities and the support system that an MP has! We had electronic typewriters, even in those days.'

Betty became a firm friend of the family, travelling up to the Conte home in the Berkshires, the mountain country in west Massachusetts where the Congressman had his electoral base. 'Betty was very well liked,' remembers Mrs Conte. 'My children just loved her. Every day they came home from school they would call her to talk on the telephone. She would come to our house for dinner, and we really enjoyed her. She was a wonderful girl. She had the most beautiful face and hair. She had a very pleasant personality. Everyone who met her liked her. We were very happy when she went back and decided to run for the Labour Party.'

She also made many friends among the expatriate British community in the US capital, particularly the journalists. Ian Aitken, political columnist of the *Guardian* who was out there as Washington correspondent of the *Daily Express*, recalled, 'I think the first time she went out to dinner was at our dinner table. She met a lot of people and they all fell for her, and from then on she was round the dinner tables of Washington. She was very much in demand; she was a decoration at the political dinner tables while she was there. She burst upon us as a fresh, brash young northern girl that the Americans found they could relate to immediately. This was remarkable because political Washington was Democratic, and she was secretary to a Republican congressman from the Democratic state of Massachusetts. Very weird.'[51]

The company round those expatriate dinner tables would often have included *The Times*'s distinguished Washington correspondent, the late Louis Heren; Tony Howard, then the *Guardian*'s man, there on a Harkness Fellowship; perhaps Bruce Rothwell initially of the *News Chronicle* and later the *Daily Mail*; or Alan Watkins, political columnist of the *Independent on Sunday* but then New York correspondent of the *Sunday Express*; from the White House, Spokesman Pierre Salinger's number two; and a diplomat from the British Embassy.

Aitken's home at 2218 Cleveland Avenue – Beaverbrook's 'ambassadorial' outpost in the USA – was the scene of 'quite big' dinner parties. It was certainly a step up from her own basement apartment, nicely furnished as it was. Here, Betty could rub shoulders, if not with the rich, famous and powerful, at least with those who did rub shoulders with them. After working for the well-connected de Freitas, mixing with NATO parliamentarians and the denizens of Capitol Hill, Betty was developing a taste for the high life which was to find freer rein later, and never to leave her.

But that nail was agitating in her shoe again, if only figuratively. She had not seen her mother for so long, and in any event, America could only ever be a sideshow, politically speaking. The lure of home reasserted itself. 'Europe is my home and I'm European and I wanted to come back here, although I loved the States,' she confessed.[52] 'Perhaps if I'd met somebody who'd asked me to marry them, maybe I would've stayed. But, again, there was my mother here, on her own. She didn't put any obstacles in the way of my going, but I'm an only child, and I always felt the tug of her being on her own. But over and above everything else, I felt very much a European. So I came back and started looking for a job.'

CHAPTER V

THE GIRL MOST UNLIKELY
TO SUCCEED

B ETTY RETURNED to an early 60s London that was seething
with political ferment. The Conservatives were losing ground
to the ersatz glamour of Harold Wilson's 'technological revolution', and slowly being sucked under by a succession of ministerial
sex scandals that sapped the government's authority to govern. Coming
back from the apparently brave new world of John Kennedy, it must
have felt even more sleazy than it was, though history has restored the
moral balance. Ever the self-sufficient, Betty's first task was to find a
job. She did not seek to go back to Westminster, at least, not directly.
Sir Geoffrey de Freitas was still in Africa, having slipped unobtrusively
from Ghana to Kenya, where he was to become High Commissioner
of the planned East African Federation. So, though they were still
friends, there could be no advancement there.

Then, quite out of the blue, indeed from St Lucia in the Caribbean
Ocean, came an opening. Harry, Lord Walston, socialist millionaire, life
peer, art connoisseur, Europhile, cultured and extraordinarily well-
connected in the upper reaches of the Labour Party, was looking for a
secretary. His redoubtable Mrs Doris Young, a starchy lady from Tunbridge Wells, was retiring. She was given the task of finding a successor.
Betty, fresh back from the States where everything was always worth a
try, applied. Mrs Young (as she was always known) interviewed her, and
wrote to Walston on his banana plantation in the West Indies that Betty
was 'the best person to hire'. But, noting her lack of Tunbridge Wells-
ness in several departments, she added, 'You will not like her. She will
not last.' Back came the reply, 'Hire her anyway!'

And so she was. When Walston returned to his lavish flat in the Albany, just off Piccadilly, haunt of the artistic wealthy, his Right-wing friends in the Labour Party warned him, 'Betty Boothroyd is far too Left-wing. She is one of them, not one of us.' Oliver Walston, the peer's son, notes, 'She started with a less than perfect political pedigree.'[1] Fortunately for her, Labour's princes were out of date. They were talking about the Betty who had taken notes for the Keep Left group, fraternized with the socialists of Hornsey Labour Party and made sandwiches for the Aldermaston anti-nuclear marchers. Walston had employed the woman who called herself a European and accepted the necessity of NATO. The partnership was to endure twelve years, and blossom into a family friendship.

Walston was a fascinating, superficially contradictory man, part visionary, part scientist; part metropolitan lunch lizard, part farmer. He was then nearing fifty, having been born in 1912, the son of archaeologist Sir Charles Walston. Educated at Eton and King's College, Cambridge, he was Research Fellow in Bacteriology at Harvard University in the US, where he met and married Catherine Macdonald Crompton, a beautiful American society belle who subsequently conducted a long, passionately indiscreet affair with novelist Graham Greene. Catherine and Betty shared a love of fine clothes.

Walston inherited the 100-acre Thriplow Farm, south of Cambridge, from his father, and by careful buying during the agricultural depression built up an estate of 3000 acres. In 1957, when Betty was hobnobbing with Ho Chi Minh and desperately trying to persuade the rural voters of Leicestershire to support her, he bought a 3000-acre banana and coconut estate on St Lucia – birthplace of de Freitas – and holidayed there for six weeks every year.

The scientist-farmer used to say, 'I see nothing to be ashamed of in having been born rich or in having made money. For the life of me, I cannot see why, just because one has money, one is forced to be a member of the Conservative Party.' Like Betty, he had, in his younger days, set his heart on the green benches of Westminster, though he was in some confusion about which party he should represent. In the Labour landslide election of 1945, he contested the Tory bastion of Huntingdon as a Liberal. He stood unsuccessfully for Labour in Cambridgeshire in the General Elections of 1951 and 1955, and for

Gainsborough in a by-election in 1957 and the General Election of 1959. He was a close confidant of George Brown, and high-ranking Labour politicians often came down to Newton Hall, his stately home, for the weekend. Hugh Gaitskell made him one of Labour's first life peers in 1961, not long before he hired Betty.

It was not, however, an exclusively political salon. George VI and the Queen had been guests there, and so had Bob Hope and James Cagney. In 1948, Evelyn Waugh wrote to Nancy Mitford of his visit to 'an extraordinary house', which showed him 'a side of life I never saw before – very rich, Cambridge, Jewish, socialist, high brow, scientific farming. There were Picassos on sliding panels and when you pushed them back plate glass and a stable with a stallion looking at one.' Walston was often unpredictable, berating conservationists one minute and proposing a form of land nationalization the next. He took up Nelson Mandela's cause in the 60s, long before it was fashionable, argued against a South African cricket tour and later became Chairman of the Institute of Race Relations.

This was the milieu of money and social brilliance into which Betty was launched in 1962. She loved it. 'She liked rich men,' observes Tony Howard.[2] The work was less predictable than Westminster can be. 'She was very largely a social secretary,' recalls Oliver Walston. She would write letters to Walston's political buddies, and even to his children. 'She would arrange his lunches, which were sacred. He was one of the world's great lunchers. He *was* a legend in his own lunch. That was his secret love. He was one of the great fixers, on the Gait-skellite wing of the party. He would put A and B together over lunch or dinner. They all used to charge along to Albany.' In later years, much of the plotting to establish the breakaway Social Democratic Party was done round Watson's dinner table.

Betty's job was 'not the most onerous or politically demanding' one, says Oliver Walston. 'On the contrary, I would have thought it was very unonerous. Her problem would have been how to occupy her day. I think he and Betty spent a great deal of time getting to know each other. He was a Gaitskellite. In those days, she had no political ambitions, or at least, she kept them fairly well hidden.

'She was a political woman, no question about it. She had a political past, but did not look to any of us as if she had any political future in those early days. Of course, as the years progressed, it did.' As did Walston's influence. 'He had a formative influence, without either of them realizing it at the time. There was no outward and visible sign of Betty changing her tune. It was something that happened gradually without either of them knowing it. She was mixing with a predominantly Right-wing, European group.' Of course, she could have quit the job if she couldn't take the politics. But she stayed, and increasingly took on the views of the Walston circle: pro-Europe, to the Right of the party, Atlanticist.

Somewhat to the surprise of the Walstons, *père et fils*, Catherine Walston took a particular shine to Betty. 'Mother was a strong-willed woman who didn't like other women. She was an American, and to everybody's amazement Betty got on quite as well with my mother as with father – possibly better,' said Oliver. 'They were two strong-willed woman. One would have thought they would have locked antlers. But they got on exceptionally well, and did so right until my mother died.'

Betty was not so surprised, observing subsequently, 'He had a big family and I became very much involved in the family. I used to go off with them to the West Indies for six weeks of the year. That's how it is if you work with somebody like that, they take you to their hearts. I do enjoy being in the bosom of a family. I loved the de Freitas family, and the Walstons likewise. I do enjoy having a family around me.'[3]

The extended Walston family, including Betty, went out to St Lucia every winter, where they took over what had been a quarantine station on a small island called Rat Island offshore from the capital, Castries. There, among the palm trees, they would party with their chums. Friends from the upper reaches of politics vied for an invitation: Hugh Gaitskell was there when Nye Bevan died. Walston's plantation manager and his friends would also turn up. The former quarantine station was an old colonial building, with a veranda and about ten rooms almost like monks' cells off a central corridor. 'Betty became very enamoured of St Lucia, of the island, of the people and the locals,' remembers Oliver Walston. 'She made a huge number of friends there. For years after she stopped working for my father, she would still go there and visit friends and lie on the beach and have a nice time.'

Eventually, Betty's job expanded to become almost a 'family secretary'. She spent more and more weekends on the family estate in Cambridgeshire, and though the post remained primarily secretary to Lord Walston, she also became a vital companion to Catherine Walston 'who was becoming sicker and sicker, due to the ravages of alcohol'. She died in 1978. By that time, Betty had been given a 'grace and favour' house on the Thriplow estate. In the late 60s, Walston sold some land in the village of Thriplow, on which stood a cottage, a listed building with a preservation order on it. The developer was allowing it to fall down, so Walston stepped in, had the three-bedroom cottage dismantled brick by brick and re-erected it on his own land. He then gave Betty a rent-free life tenancy of the property. It is still her weekend retreat, the only place she calls home.

Being in the fulfilling bosom of the Walston family did not, however, dent the hard edge of Betty's political ambition. There is no record of her seeking a seat in the 1964 election – she would have been hard put to find a constituency worth fighting in the months that remained before the election on her return from the USA. But she kept her ear to the ground. Early in 1965, the seat of Plymouth Sutton, nearly won at the General by Dr John Dunwoody – husband of Gwyneth, who was later her seconder for the Speakership – came up for selection.

Betty applied, and got on to the short list. So did Dr David Owen, a debonair but not very well-known young hopeful. On the night of the selection, Dr Owen wrote, 'The strongest challenge came from an extremely attractive candidate, Betty Boothroyd. She spoke far better than I, as many of the general management committee teasingly reminded me over the years.'[4] But he was the local boy. Some of the delegates were even patients of his GP father, and he secured the nomination. Having won the seat, he was, more than a decade later, to be one of the conspirators who gathered in Walston's Albany flat to plot the SDP breakaway.

Her one political success at this time was to win a seat on Hammersmith Council, in the west London borough where she then lived in a flat in Kensington Hall Gardens. Whether this was the flat she took adjoining that of her old friend Jo Richardson, also a Commons secretary who became an MP, is not recorded. What is most certainly the case is that for years the story circulated at Westminster that the two socially active young woman had knocked a door through between the flats so they could come and go as they pleased. Betty won the council seat in Gibbs Green Ward, unseating a Tory by 1347 votes to 1219.

Even this modest achievement made Fleet Street. The *Daily Mirror* reported that a Labour life peer was out knocking on doors. Betty was quoted, 'Lord Walston asked what he could do to help. I suggested door-to-door canvassing, and he thoroughly enjoyed it. He even offered to take people to the polls in his Aston Martin.'[5] Labour had a huge 62–7 majority over the Tories on the council, and a thirty-three-year-old local government novice could not expect much by way of preferment. Nor did she get it. Betty was appointed to the relatively unglamorous Health and Housing Committees, and the Catering Committee, of which she was made vice chairman.

Becoming a councillor was a side-show, not the real thing. Betty's attendance record was only moderate, particularly in the St Lucia season, and when the council elections came round again in 1968, she did not stand. It was a wise decision. The Conservatives romped home, taking all three seats in the Gibbs Green Ward which she had represented. In any event, with Lord Walston having been in the Wilson government since October 1964, first as Parliamentary Under-Secretary at the Foreign Office, and then as Parliamentary Secretary at the Board of Trade until August 1967, her sights were still emphatically set on Westminster, and what looked like her prize opportunity soon presented itself.

In February 1968, Sidney Silverman, the controversial MP for Nelson and Colne whose unrelenting campaign against capital punishment led to the abolition of hanging in Britain, died after a long illness. He had held the seat against all comers since 1935, and his death triggered a by-election in the east Lancashire constituency. This was prime electoral territory for a weaver's daughter. Textiles still dominated these gritty Pennine towns, just over the border from her native Yorkshire. The people were 'her kind', and if anybody could keep the seat for Labour, she could.

But these were difficult days for the Wilson administration, despite Labour's impregnable parliamentary majority of seventy-three. Successive incomes policies, Selective Employment Tax and a host of other unpopular measures had dragged the government down into low public esteem. Nelson and Colne was to be the twentieth by-election since the General Election of March 1966. Of the fourteen defended by Labour, the party had retained only four, losing eight to the Tories and one each to the Scots and Welsh Nationalists. Defending Silverman's 4577 General Election majority would be no easy task.

Wilson refused to call an early by-election. Goaded by local newspapers, which kept up a regular barrage of accusations that Labour was afraid of a fight, he kept the voters waiting for months. Then another by-election was called in the nearby seat of Oldham West, and Labour's Lancashire agent Paul Carmody favoured having them both on the same day – 7 June. This move horrified local party workers. At this low ebb in Labour's fortunes, two polls on the same day in the same county would strain party resources beyond breaking point. Leonard Dole, a party activist in Nelson who had been a full-time agent in Staffordshire, secretly met Harold Davies MP, Wilson's PPS (and a long-standing friend of Betty's), and urged him to get the Prime Minister to change his mind. 'It's not on,' he said. 'We'll be splitting our forces.' Dole, a former textile worker, prevailed. The date was changed to 27 June, and he was made agent for the by-election.

The selection conference was held on 21 April in the Labour Rooms in Every Street, Nelson, where the local textile union, the Nelson Twisters' and Drawers' Association had their headquarters. 'Battling Betty', as the tabloids were already beginning to call her, turned up on the night dressed patriotically in a blue coat, with red and white shoes and scarf, saying, 'It's to support my slogan "I'm Backing Britain – and Betty".' This was a reference to a highly popular but short-lived 'I'm Backing Britain' campaign started by girl typists in a Surrey central heating firm who volunteered to work an extra hour each week without pay to help their firm through economic difficulties. For about six months, the 'I'm Backing Britain' craze swept the country, generating all manner of mildly heroic sacrifices by workpeople in the name of helping the national economy, before it fizzled out.

There were six candidates for the Labour nomination, but Betty won on the first ballot by a clear majority. She spoke last, and took thirty-seven of the sixty votes. One delegate observed, 'She took us by storm. She was full of smiles and what she said made sense. She's another Barbara Castle in the making.' Her victory owed much to trade union spadework. Impressed by her textile background, and unfazed by the fact that she would be the first woman candidate in the history of the constituency, the Nelson Weavers, easily the biggest affiliate with ten seats on the general management committee, voted for her en bloc. 'It was the textile workers who put her in,' recalls Dole.[6] 'There was no question about that. In textiles, both men and women had to work to exist. So there was no women's lib question at all. They were both on a level playing field when they got married. They both had to work to get a little house.'

Betty was now thirty-eight, a member of Hammersmith Borough Council and a veteran fighter – and loser – of two by-election campaigns. She set to with a vigour, insisting, 'I am looking forward to the by-election. I don't know when it will be, but whenever it is we will win.' She told the old, Odhams-owned broadsheet *Sun*, 'The northern people can stem the tide which has been running against the government. Local issues will play a big part in my campaigning. The area has been left to decay, especially under the Tories. In the years 1950 to 1960, the industrial growth rate was well below the national average.' Then she added, rather ambiguously, 'Although the late Mr Silverman had a small majority at the last election, it must be remembered that capital punishment played a part in his campaigning.' Whether she meant that hanging would not figure as an issue in this contest, or that there would not be an anti-capital punishment candidate as there had been in 1966, was unclear. What was certainly clear was the interest aroused by her candidacy. The *Sun* headlined their story WOMAN TO FIGHT THE NELSON 'MARGINAL', and the *Daily Mail* said LABOUR WOMAN CHOSEN.

Nelson and Colne, with a population of around 60,000, of whom 46,000 were on the electoral roll, looks like archetypal Labour territory. Long stone terraces of two-up, two-down weavers' cottages cling to one another up and down the hillsides as if seeking shelter from the constant rain. Yet owner occupancy, at sixty per cent, was much higher than the national average. Nelson's chief claim to fame in modern times was the welcome that local people gave to Sir Learie Constantine, the great West Indian cricketer who became professional for the town's Lancashire League team in the 1930s. Sir Learie declined Mr Jeremy Thorpe's invitation to stand as the Liberal bearer, this dubious honour going to a Blackpool master plumber, David Chadwick, the party's first candidate in the constituency since 1924. The local Labour party was 4000 strong, nominally at any rate, and the constituency had been won by the Tories only once – between 1931 and 1935 – since 1902.

So, although they had only three months in which to make an impact, Labour's stalwarts launched into the electoral fray in good heart. Betty was quickly identified in the local press as 'a far cry from the old-school socialism of Sidney Silverman'.[7] 'I may be Left-wing in some policies, but not in others,' she said. 'I don't like classifying Labour supporters into camps. I am a card-holding member of the Party, and that's classification enough for me.' At the time, this was the classic self-description of the party's Right-wing. She added, 'I suppose you could describe me as a radical, but I certainly wouldn't join that group of Labour members which describes itself as Left-wing, although I disagree with some party policies at the moment and no doubt will do in the future.'

Perhaps unwisely, she also vouchsafed that if elected she would continue to live in Hammersmith, where she was chairman of one of the borough council's welfare committees. 'I don't think it's necessary for an MP to live in the constituency,' she told the *Evening Star*. 'After all, the work is in London, and I can't live in a number of places. Of course, I would visit Nelson and Colne frequently.' When she finally did get elected five years later, she was as good as her word in one respect: she did not live in her constituency. She did, however, manage to live 'in a number of places'.

Betty's election address was a professional product. On the front cover was a serious but attractive portrait, her thick dark hair cut short and piled quite high in the fashion of the day. Inside was a long, by contemporary standards, address to the electorate couched in the form of a 'Dear Friends' letter. She accepted that local people had a right to know why they should choose her 'to try to fill the vacuum left by the courageous Sydney Silverman'. And she gave her reason: 'My upbringing the other side of the Pennines gave me a background that made me aware early in life how much our whole setting could be improved. Recurring – and at times prolonged – unemployment; the problems of housing and worries of old age; lack of opportunities in education and the shadow of war. To me the Labour Party was the instrument that could help to get the changes that were needed.

'Since my teens I have been active in the Labour movement. Of course I have sometimes been disappointed because change has not been fast enough. But I have never succumbed to disillusion and cynicism. Those are still the enemies of progress.'[8]

The rest of her election address was in the same kind of personal, even folksy, style, with Betty admitting that the Wilson government had met with setbacks that bred grumbles and discontent. 'Frankly, I have been among the grumblers, too,' she confessed. But Labour, with its determination to put the country on a sound economic footing was still preferable to 'a free-for-all which had cruel results for Lancashire'.

By-elections inevitably shine a more powerful spotlight on the candidate than general elections, and there is always pressure to produce the right 'family' image. As a single woman, Betty could not pose with husband and children. So the address was completed by a charming picture of her with her mother, and the family's black poodle, Banda. Mrs Boothroyd, by then aged sixty-six and white-haired, had her own mini-manifesto: one former mill girl talking to other mill girls. 'I've seen a lot of changes in my time. I started work as a weaver when I was thirteen years old and it's not long since I retired. I'm glad that's all changed, and today young people have the chance of a good education before they start their working lives.

'But the greatest changes have come about in the last few years when our Labour government set about providing reasonable standards for older people like me, and for others too. When I hear people complaining today, I remember the time when there was really something to complain about – though prices were low we were often out of a job. We then had real problems in making ends meet and buying the essentials for a decent family life. People who want opportunities for the young, employment for the bread-winner and security for the elderly have only one vote – that's for Betty.'

Labour was more prepared for the by-election, because the government had control of the timing. By contrast, the Tories were in disarray. Their local selection committee had chosen an 'out of towner', David Penfold, a thirty-three-year-old salesman from Burton-on-

Trent. But wiser heads among the Conservatives decided he was not the man to beat Betty. On the night that Penfold was due to be endorsed, there was a behind-the-scenes coup. Party officials picked up the telephone and summoned to the stormy meeting at Tory HQ in Cross Street, Nelson, a local barrister, David Waddington, aged thirty-eight, who had not even been on the original short list. Waddington was very much a local man. He lived with his wife and two children in the nearby rural village of Sabden. He was also a director of two local cotton mills founded by his grandfather.

When the dust settled that night, a 'very disappointed' Penfold had 'withdrawn' from the contest, and Waddington – better known these days as Lord Waddington, governor of Bermuda – was the Conservative parliamentary candidate for the constituency. Not only was he known locally, Waddington was well connected. His father-in-law had been Financial Secretary to the Treasury in the previous Conservative government. More to the point, he had stood for Nelson and Colne in 1964, cutting Silverman's majority to little more than 2600. He was the man to beat 'Battling Betty', and he was duly grateful to his party, saying, 'I am very gratified at being called in at the last minute. Mr Penfold has taken this very sportingly.' He had no other choice.

The Tories' double-shuffle was bad news for Betty. Instead of facing an inexperienced 'off cum'd 'un', she must now battle it out with a local man who had fought and nearly won the seat once before. Nor was her nomination universally popular in her own party. A Labour supporter wrote to the *Nelson Times* on 3 May, accusing 'London bureaucrats' of foisting on local people 'a strong supporter of Wilson policies – presumably including that of neglect of north-east Lancashire'. He suggested that Labour supporters should register a protest against 'local party hacks' and the Wilson government by abstaining from voting or by writing in the name of a 'more befitting candidate'.

Similar doubts were expressed elsewhere by another correspondent to the *Nelson Times* calling himself 'Lancastria', who went to a May Day rally to hear Betty expound her policies. 'Although Miss Boothroyd came across as a charming and attractive personality, her speech merely rubber-stamped the official policies and held out no hope of her putting up a full-blooded fight on behalf of this area for new industries,' the writer lamented. 'Her contrived reference to the

sheep on Haworth moor was one of the few local references she made
– and that, Sir, was so much Yorkshire pudding in the sky.' Replying
to her 'folksy' allusions to hard times in Lancashire, he reminded her
that spinners and weavers in the 1860s starved for their principles and
refused to use cotton produced by slave labour. 'We are a proud people
here, and rightly so.' Paying tribute to Sidney Silverman – 'our tawny
owl' – he said, 'We are used to having doughty campaigners on our
behalf, and supporting them, come what may.' Only if she showed 'the
vital spark which Sidney had' and was not 'merely concerned with
getting into Parliament on the Labour Party ticket' could she succeed.
These were alarming straws in the wind. Fighting a national swing
against Labour and inheriting such a small majority, Betty could not
afford defections among Labour's ranks.

Superficially, that May Day rally had been a success. Next day, the
story was the front page splash in the local evening paper. Labour's
Deputy Leader George Brown had promised voters that the government would not let north-east Lancashire 'wither away'. He said, 'We
have an obligation to see that new industries come to the area as the
old ones contract. Everybody has the right to a job, but not necessarily
the same job with the same firm forever.' But firms must go to where
conditions were best for them; in other words, to development areas.
And although the Hunt Committee was at this very time investigating
the prospect of making north-east Lancashire a 'grey' or intermediate
area, making it eligible for government grants, he could not make any
firm pledges.

'Priorities of unemployment must be taken into account in the setting up of development areas, and in this respect East Lancashire is
not as badly off as other areas.' At present, the region only had 'fear of
problems that may occur, not of actual problems'. These discouraging
words did nothing for Labour's chances. Nor did the fact that Brown
had taken a job with 'the bosses'. Soon after his exotic resignation
from the Foreign Secretaryship in March of that year, he had accepted
a lucrative part-time post of adviser to Courtaulds, the biggest textile
firm in the country with many mills in Lancashire. Some of these were
now closing, and one Labour loyalist said of this period, 'His name
stank in every street in the constituency, for the simple reason that
people associated him with redundancies.'[9] Betty herself cannot have

made many friends with her characteristically blunt insistence at the outset of the campaign that north-east Lancashire should not be awarded the prize status it wished. 'I don't think it should be classified as a development area. The whole idea of these areas would be lost if there were too many of them.'[10]

By now, it was becoming clear that Labour could lose. A note of desperation appeared in Betty's speech to the constituency Labour Party's annual meeting on 10 May, when she criticized Labour voters who had stayed away in droves in local council elections a few days earlier. 'The people who stayed away are mainly our voters, and it is up to us between now and the by-election to give them enough confidence so that they will come out and cast their votes in our favour,' she said. 'I believe this is possible.' Complaining of 'a great deal of apathy', she warned that they had a hard fight on their hands. 'But I am a hard fighter, and I am very determined that we shall have the best result.'

Though accompanied by a battle cry to go back to their party sections, unions and ward parties, this is already beginning to sound more like political bravura than genuine confidence. 'The party needs rejuvenating. This is the time where we are going to start the fight back,' she maintained. Nationally, the party was in trouble with Cecil King, powerful Chairman of IPC which owned the Labour-supporting *Daily Mirror*, then at the height of its influence and selling nearly five million copies daily. That same day, King had published a Gallup Poll which rated Wilson as the most unpopular Prime Minister for a generation, and a signed leading article calling on Labour MPs to get rid of their Prime Minister. King's staggering hubris soon boomeranged on him, and he was sacked. But at Nelson and Colne's annual party meeting, a gloomy-sounding Betty blamed Cecil King for trying to find a scapegoat 'for the very sad situation in the Labour Party'.[11]

She thought the megalomaniac press baron was trying to get back at Wilson because he had passed over King for the job of chief press officer at 10 Downing Street. This was as unlikely an explanation as the truth: that Cecil King had in fact tried to plot with Lord Mountbatten and others to form an emergency government that would be led by the Queen's uncle. Betty would also have been anxious had she known that Wilson, who benefited politically from the farcical coup attempt, had instructed the whips to give him a list of the seventy-seven Labour backbenchers who had refused to sign a parliamentary motion condemning King. Among the usual list of suspects was her former employer and close friend, Sir Geoffrey de Freitas, who spent some time in Nelson supporting her candidature.[12]

The Tory camp was optimistic, but not complacent. At a fund-raising garden party in the grounds of his country mansion, Whins House, Waddington said the people of Nelson would 'speak for Britain', adding, 'They will give this government notice to quit.' He was only indulging in normal by-election rhetoric, but the Conservatives had good reason to feel buoyant. Labour has just reported 'a bad decline in membership' in the constituency. A textile mill had partly closed, and Nelson Engineering also shut down. Talks of a new town at Leyland in central Lancashire did not help an area that was already suffering depopulation. By later standards, however, unemployment was low – 2.7 per cent across the constituency, fewer than 750 in total.

When nominations for the by-election closed, the three main parties had unexpectedly been joined by a fourth candidate, night-club owner Brian Tattersall, standing as an 'English Nationalist'. His far-Right, 'bring back the rope' platform revived echoes of the General Election, when Patrick Downey, uncle of one of the child victims of the gruesome Moors Murders, picked up 5117 votes when he stood as an Independent seeking the restoration of capital punishment. His votes were thought to have come more from the Tories than Labour, but only marginally so. The far-Right's intervention was not expected to be anything like so important this time.

Waddington, fluent and persuasive, scored points with his insistence that he had never sought election anywhere but his native Lancashire, where he would continue to live if returned on 27 June. He heaped scorn on the local Labour MPs 'none of whom has done anything for the area. I couldn't possible do worse, if they've done nothing.' And he ridiculed Betty's proposal that north-east Lancashire should become a tourist centre. The idea was too far ahead of its time, and had attracted some amusement locally. It has certainly come true in recent years, but Waddington riposted then, 'Nelson and Colne needs new industry. We don't want Miss Boothroyd's idea of a fancy tourist trap. All we want is a fair crack of the whip. This is a nice place to live and work. We have the expertise and the factory space, and it could be a flourishing industrial area once again.'[13]

George Brown paid another visit to the constituency on 11 June. But it was in his Courtaulds advisory capacity, and therefore 'non-political', explained local party officials lamely. He would not be meeting the candidate. The fatuity of Labour's deputy leader paying a business call to the town's biggest mill in the middle of a critical by-election dawned overnight, however. Brown interrupted his mill visit to pose for photographers with Betty, blustering, 'There was no question of my coming to the constituency without meeting Miss Boothroyd.' He promised to return.

All the candidates were asked to provide a personal manifesto for a local paper, responding to set questions ranging from 'Have you any associations with this area?' to 'Should capital punishment be restored as an essential deterrent?' The questions were breathtakingly loaded in favour of the Tory candidate. But Betty stood her ground, particularly on immigration and race relations. 'Immigration is curbed. To suppose otherwise is to ignore the facts.' She favoured cuts on arms spending rather than the axing of teacher training or reduction of pensions. But she was 'not opposed to stricter law enforcement if it will curb waves of violence'. And she havered on the question of hanging, pointing out that the Silverman-inspired legislation which ended capital punishment was up for review the following year. 'I would examine the question purely on its merits at that time and when all the evidence had been submitted.'

On the question of local roots – posed as 'Do you think an MP should have a home in *his* [my italics] constituency, and play an active part in its life when *he* is not engaged at Westminster?' she replied, 'In order to be effective, an MP needs to spend a good deal of time in the constituency. A home here is no guarantee of that. I already have one close by and one in London.' Close by? Dewsbury? In fact, a good fifty miles by winding roads over the Pennines. As a further slap-down, she could not resist saying, 'If it became essential to live in one's constituency we would be aping the Americans – not an ideal example.'

The clearest hint of trouble ahead came on 14 June, two weeks before polling day, when the Tories captured the Labour stronghold of Oldham West for the first time, on a swing of seventeen per cent. Betty refused to betray any apprehension. 'The Tories gained Oldham by riding on the backs of Labour voters,' she said. 'It was the stay-at-home Labour voters who let them in.' This was her private nightmare: Labour apathy. In the municipal elections, the turnout in Nelson and Colne was only fifty-two per cent. But she brazened it out in public. There would be a seventy per cent turnout, and Labour would hold the seat. 'Nelson and Colne has made history before, and will do it again. This by-election will bring the best out of our workers and we will win.' But her tone on the hustings became more hesitant, querulous even. 'Don't reject us when we are putting the country right,' she pleaded at a meeting in Colne on 16 June. 'This is a time to create, not to destroy. I ask you to give me the support that you gave to Sidney Silverman for more than thirty years, and make Nelson and Colne constituency the place where the fightback starts.' She disclosed that she had made private representations to a member of the Hunt Committee on regional development for more help for the area – while repeating the old mantra: 'Development area status is not necessarily the answer.'

Things were not going well. *The Times* reported on 17 June that Waddington had been spontaneously applauded by factory workers at the end of 'one of his earthy little ten minutes speeches' – on the same spot where he had been booed and shouted down in 1964. 'By contrast,' said the *Times* man, 'I heard a group of millworkers shout: "What's Labour done for Nelson? Nowt!" when Miss Boothroyd's van passed them.' In the sexist parlance of the day, the reporter added gratuitously: 'However, Miss Boothroyd, aged 38, with considerable charm and other more visible attractions to go with it, must not be underestimated.'[14]

With only nine days to polling day, her former boss and close friend Sir Geoffrey de Freitas turned up to support her. He told a press conference, 'Betty has had a great deal of international experience, including working at the NATO headquarters in Paris. I have also seen her fight a by-election and a general election, and even in this campaign two MPs who have already visited the constituency have said what a fine fight she is putting up.' Sir Geoffrey's presence must have been a comfort. As he disclosed, he had helped her when she stood in the by-election in Leicester South-West in 1957, and again in the General Election of 1959 when she fought Peterborough and North Northants.

Rather less helpful was George Brown's self-pitying speech when he returned a few days later. He insisted that the prices and incomes policy was 'harsh but inescapable', and justified his job at Courtaulds by saying that a failed Tory minister would have collected twenty directorships within a week. 'I didn't fail, I walked out,' he whined. With admirable chop-logic, he claimed that the Oldham swing 'wasn't against us. We just didn't get our votes out.' In line with political custom, the Prime Minister did not pay the constituency a visit, and his eve-of-poll letter, dull and self-serving, did nothing to improve her chances. Betty was probably happier to receive a good-luck telegram from Doris Speed, the actress who played Annie Walker, no-nonsense landlady of the Rovers' Return in Granada TV's soap opera 'Coronation Street'. Wilson's letter struggled to find anything positive to say, beyond promising to deliver 'whatever action the Hunt Committee recommend when their report is published in the autumn'. This would not pull very many votes, and no one was very surprised when seven students of Mansfield Secondary Modern School conducted a street poll in the four main urban areas of the constituency and found the Tories with a clear lead.

By now, Betty must have privately resigned herself to losing the seat. Talking to the *Daily Mirror* four days before the poll, she was reduced to amiable chatter about her clothes. 'I haven't a lot of money to buy clothes, nor a lot of time to go shopping, but it is good for my clothes and good for me to have constant changes,' she said, confessing that she was saving her best dress for the election count. But even the Labour-supporting *Mirror*, which two weeks previously had tried to oust Harold Wilson, thought 'the political dice are loaded heavily against her'. At 6.2 per cent, the swing required to deliver the seat to the Tories was only a third of their worst swing over the previous six months. While Betty was sending out last-minute broadsheets headed, 'DON'T LOSE YOUR NERVE,' Labour was sufficiently rattled to threaten an action for defamation against Waddington for his attacks on her election address. Regional organizer Paul Carmody accused her Tory rival of suggesting that she had deliberately lied, and demanded an apology. Waddington dismissed the matter as 'a red herring', but duly apologized.

The government's announcement of a new motorway for north-east Lancashire only hours before voters went to the polls 'delighted' Betty, though the eccentric timing may have puzzled her. More worrying for Labour was the torrential rain that pelted down on the morning of polling day: bad weather is traditionally held to benefit the Tories. Polling stations closed at 9 p.m., and the result was declared shortly before midnight from the steps of Nelson Town Hall.

Betty had indeed got most of her voters out. Turnout was high, at 74.2 per cent. But it was not enough. Waddington was in with a majority of 3522. He polled 16,466 to Betty's 12,944. The Tory vote was up 2000, Labour's down by nearly 5500. The other two candidates lost their deposits. The swing against the government was 11.4 per cent, easily the lowest for many months, but still practically double the figure needed by the Tories. If repeated in a General Election across the country, Edward Heath would be in Downing Street with a 250-seat majority.

Betty took her third parliamentary defeat calmly, making as much political capital as she could from the reduced swing. 'This is where the fight begins. This is the best result we have had for many a month. I am proud of the people of Nelson and Colne and in the Labour government. I say that the Tories will not hold this seat for very long. The radicals of Nelson and Colne will take it back from you next time.' In fact, Nelson and Colne never did return to the fold, and it was to be 1992 before the redrawn seat of Pendle came back to Labour, ironically to a party official who had been a Hammersmith borough councillor.

Betty's own campaign won much sympathy and praise in the national press, though often tinged with patronizing remarks about her being a woman. *The Times*'s verdict was typical: 'She has been an impressive candidate, sparkling and in many other ways effective. On another occasion, in a different political climate, she might make the grade.' Her agent, Len Dole, recalls, 'She fought a hard fight. She had to. I would not accept excuses from her. Even if she had a bit of a cold, there was no way she was getting a night off. She worked hard. She was a good speaker, and a good candidate. She was so full of verve.'[15]

He thought she would be back, to make good her promise to unseat the hugely self-satisfied Waddington, for whom personal victory was 'notice to quit' for the Wilson government. Dole was wrong. The party activists of Nelson – the place they once called 'little Moscow' because the citizens refused to celebrate the King's Silver Jubilee – never saw her again.

'We were looking forward to having her as Labour candidate in the general election,' said Dole. 'There wouldn't have been any question about her being candidate. She would have been endorsed again, and I'm sure she would have won it. But she was anxious to get into the House of Commons. That's her own business. It wasn't mine. But it was mine to look after the constituency. When we were looking forward to the general election, she gave me a ring. She said she was on a short list somewhere else with a good chance. I said to Betty, "Please yourself, but I tell you this, if you go for an interview, that is the end of your candidature here because I know this constituency." And it was the end of her. My workers were so enthused by the fact that she had put up such a good fight, so certain that she would have been, without question, endorsed again as candidate for the parliamentary election that the immediate reaction was "she has ratted on us".'

There was a postscript to the Nelson and Colne episode. Labour's election expenses totalled £726 9s 6d (just under £726.50). The local party was around £500 short to meet the bills, so Dole, knowing that Betty's employer Lord Walston was a rich man, travelled down to London to make an appeal for funds. He met the socialist peer, in his exclusive Albany flat, furnished with fine antiques. 'A cheque was on the doormat when I got home,' he remembers.

The word was that in her indefatigable search for a winnable parliamentary seat, Betty's eye had alighted on Farnworth, in Greater Manchester. So few were more surprised than her supporters in Nelson and Colne when she reappeared practically next door, in the very similar textile-cum-Pennine seat of Rossendale, Lancashire, in the General Election of 1970.

This was the election that Harold Wilson thought he could win by playing it as a presidential contest against Edward Heath, who was trailing by twenty points in the popularity polls. Labour was now 'the

natural party of government'. The economy was coming right. Six
years of hard labour would now be rewarded by a grateful electorate
giving Wilson an unprecedented third term of office. Surely this time
Betty could make it to the Commons? Rossendale had been left
stranded only weeks before the election by the abrupt departure of
Anthony Greenwood, son of a Labour Minister of Health, a Cabinet
minister in his own right and scion of the Bevanite Left, who quit to
join the board of the Commonwealth Development Corporation.

Greenwood, suave, handsome and something of a playboy, had quite
a strong personal following in his constituency, even though he never
had a very large majority at election times. Local activists called him
'the mill girls' pin-up'. He had come to Rossendale in the 50s, and
with other MPs in the region who had clout, especially Barbara Castle
in nearby Blackburn, had always been credited with getting the best
deal for east Lancashire when Labour was in power. Sometimes his
alliances were unusual. He had good links with the Free Churches in
the area, for example.

His unexpected disappearance from the political scene devastated
his local party. 'We only had three weeks' notice of his telling us he
was not in a position to become a candidate,' remembers Joe Connolly,
president of the constituency Labour Party at the time. 'It was a great
shock for us because he was so very well respected. He would have
won that seat for as long as he wanted to, albeit with not a very large
majority.'[16]

Rossendale was in many ways similar to Nelson and Colne, though
slightly larger and containing a higher proportion of middle-class voters because of its proximity to Manchester. The constituency in those
days (it has since been redrawn) was a compact area of Lancashire
valleys. From the textile town of Rawtenstall at the centre, they ran
west to the strongly Tory village of Haslingden, east to Bacup, which
at one time had the only Liberal council in the country, south to
Ramsbottom and north towards Burnley.

The seat had been held by Labour for twenty-five years. A local
train driver, George Walker, won it in 1945, and held it until 1950.
Anthony Greenwood followed in his footsteps that year, and hung on
until quitting politics in 1970. Similar topography to Nelson dictated
similar industry. The strong, clear streams rushing down from the

Pennine tops encouraged the manufacturing of felt in these valleys, and by extension blankets – but especially slippers. This was the home of the Slipper Workers' Union.

Into this political turmoil stepped Betty, looking for her fourth opportunity to enter Parliament. This time, there was more high-profile competition from an ex-MP, Trevor Park, a schoolteacher who appeared to have become jaundiced with the reality of Labour in government. One of a regular band of Left-wing rebels against the Wilson style of government, he gave up his seat – and a 5496 majority – in Derbyshire South-East, but then had second thoughts. He began canvassing for Rossendale, in his native Lancashire, but reckoned without Betty's organizational skills.

Appearing yet again from over the Pennines with her mother, Betty set about marshalling the critical trade union vote. In Rossendale, she had to win the backing of the textile workers, the slipper workers, the Transport and General Workers' Union, the shop-workers' union USDAW, and several smaller unions. Her spirited performance at Nelson and Colne had not been forgotten by the textile workers. Their seven votes were in the bag, and others followed. The selection took place on 28 May 1970, with less than three full weeks to polling day on 18 June. The short-list had been whittled down to three, and Betty was the only woman contender. She spoke first, and won by a substantial margin on the first ballot.

The *Rossendale Free Press* headlined her victory: YORKSHIRE WOMAN IS CHOSEN FOR THE CONTEST, perhaps not the most obvious passport to success. Though there were many women workers in the mills and factories, this was the first time Labour had fielded a woman candidate, and the stress laid on her tyke origins might also have offended some. Remember the 'Yorkshire pie in the sky' taunt in Nelson? The *Free Press* described her as living in 360 Latymer Court, Hammersmith, though having a home in Dewsbury where her mother still lived. It also said she had been a trade unionist since 1946 (not an aspect of her political development made much of hitherto) and stated that she was a member of the TGWU. This could prove useful. There was a large corporation bus garage in the constituency.

Rather more startlingly – and this could only have come from her camp – the paper solemnly recorded that 'in the Nelson and Colne by-election, which aroused a good deal of national publicity, the swing against the government was reduced in two weeks from 25 per cent to 11 per cent'. This is fair enough in the context of political struggle, but it makes merry with the facts. Betty's instant biography also said that she had just returned from the United States after completing a three-week lecture tour of American universities at the invitation of the US Bureau of Higher Education. She spoke on 'The Wilson Administration' and 'Race Relations in Britain'.

The contest was a straight fight between Labour and Conservative. In a similar fight in 1966, there had been an eighty-per-cent turnout, and Greenwood commanded 55.4 per cent of the vote, a majority of 4109 – a career best for him. The personal following of even a very popular MP is not normally calculated at more than 2000 votes. But once allowance had been made for the absence of 'the Greenwood Factor', and Labour's continuing unpopularity (disguised at the start of the campaign by misleading polls), Rossendale was always going to be the sort of uphill struggle upon which Betty seemed to thrive, relying on her Yorkshire grit to see her through. However, as her abandonment of Nelson and Colne had only just shown, even she was tiring of magnificent failure. The consolation of having played a great game is not counted very highly in her native county.

Betty's opponent in the election was Ronald Bray, aged forty-eight, but looking in his publicity photographs much older. He was scarcely a local boy. A former pupil of Latymer Upper School in London, and at one time a member of Woking Urban Council, he was now a farmer and Lloyds underwriter. Indeed he owned one of the largest cattle and sheep farms in Buckden, high in Wharfedale, Yorkshire, and had previously contested Stockton-on-Tees unsuccessfully.

There was one unknown factor in this contest. 1970 was the first general election in which eighteen-year-olds had the vote. This reform increased the electoral roll from 47,357 in 1996 to 50,186, and the margin represented a substantial but unknown swathe of voters whose verdict could determine the outcome in a tight finish. Betty, by now aged forty, brought some of the elements of an American-style campaign to Rossendale in the hope of injecting a certain *joie de vivre* into the campaign.

Initially, the more traditional locals including those in her own party were taken aback by the open-top car (despite it being a genuinely flaming June), the balloons, and the full-size blown-up facial posters of the candidate. 'She brought lessons over here that she had learned in the USA,' recalls Connolly. 'There was a certain amount of razzmatazz that she created. People here didn't create it. Greenwood had never used that sort of thing. She came over like a film star. She was at home in a theatrical setting, and she used it to the full.' There was also the woman factor. Once again, she was the first woman to seek election to Parliament from the constituency. Before Betty, no woman had even ventured to fight, much less expect to win.

But aside from the showbiz dimension, it was for her a deadly serious campaign. Delivering her adoption speech, dressed in a short-sleeved summer frock, at the Rawtenstall OAP centre, she revived her basic 'I'm one of you' theme heard so often in Nelson almost exactly two years previously. 'I know what the mills around here look like,' she said. 'I don't come from an agricultural area to represent you. I know what industrial people want. I know what it is like to live among dark satanic mills and I know the people who made the wealth of this nation.'

She appealed to voters not to be fooled by the Conservatives' 'mouth-watering promises' and entreated them to look at what Labour had done for industry. Textiles had 'certainly had its problems', but aided by the government it now had some of the best machinery in the world. Lancashire's boot and shoe trade had hoisted its export sales by seventy-two per cent. 'Don't let the Tories come here and talk to me about stagnation and unemployment, or I won't half give it to them,' she said, lapsing into the vernacular.

It was not an easy speech to make. On the one hand, she had to argue Labour's record, on the other to persuade voters that things would get better. Harold Wilson had brought 'this great country' from an £800 million deficit to a £550 million surplus, 'and that was not bad management'. On 18 June, Rossendale would contribute to the resounding victory that would return the winning team more years to make Britain a great nation to live in. Politicians feel obliged to say these things at such times. The faithful Sir Geoffrey de Freitas was on hand to supplement her encomium to Harold Wilson that evening.

Out in the workaday world of the slipper factories, the street-corner meetings and bus depot early morning calls, it was a good deal more basic. Betty visited lovely, but isolated, Summerseat and insisted that the Bury–Rawtenstall railway line slated for closure be kept open at least until alternative bus services could be provided. She spotted potential sites for new factories, that might halt the depopulation of the valleys. She took the message to mill girls sitting in their curlers in the noonday heat and, though she did not dismiss the eighteen- to twenty-one-year-old new voters, she did not exactly pander to them either. She told a press conference that she had not gone out of her way to court them into voting Labour. But on balance she felt they were progressive-minded people and not Conservative in that sense. They would vote for the candidate who was nearest what they wanted. She lambasted the Tories with another American borrowing: 'I will make a bargain with my opponents. If they will stop telling lies about me, I will stop telling the truth about them.' She added, 'I don't say we have solved all our problems. Of course we haven't. But there is no immediate crisis – the Tories are the only crisis this nation faces as far as we are concerned.'

But there was a crisis. Like the pollsters, the political commentators and the Wizard of Huddersfield himself in Downing Street, party workers in Rossendale believed they had it in the bag. 'We did expect to win,' admits Joe Connolly. 'The impact of her campaign was really good.' Betty knew otherwise. In the last few days of the overheated campaign, she noticed a strange shift in the response of people in the street. 'They have started to look past me, not at me,' she confided to her campaign team. Call it woman's intuition, or the sensitive antennae of a politician, or a mixture of both, but she was right. It was slipping away, not just in the Pennine valleys but right across the country. She knew she was going to lose, and the Wilson administration with her. The best chance she had in a thirteen-year-long campaign to get into Parliament was escaping.

The end of her hopes came quickly enough, at 12.35 a.m. on Friday 19 June. Returning Officer Ted Dugdale, Mayor of Rawtenstall, announced that in a turnout slightly up at eighty-two per cent, pipe-smoking Ronald Bray had won the seat for the Conservatives for the first time in a quarter of a century. He polled 20,448 votes to Betty's 18,568, a Tory majority of 1880. Labour's share of the vote had slipped almost eight points to 47.5 per cent. If the young people had turned out for her, their votes had been more than compensated for by older voters. Labour was out of office, and Edward Heath entered Downing Street at the head of a Conservative Government with an overall majority of thirty.

Betty congratulated her rival on ending twenty-five years of Labour hegemony in the Valleys, and went out on her usual song. 'We shall be back again, I promise you.' Labour would be back, but, as was now becoming the pattern, it would not be Betty shouldering the flag. A superstitious dread of repeating defeat in the same place appeared to have taken hold of her.

CHAPTER VI

PARLIAMENT AT LAST

I T WAS HEARTBREAKING to be a four-times loser. Betty had proved her worth and her staying power in a series of contests that had not gone her way more by bad luck than by bad judgment. She had been the right woman in the wrong place at the wrong time. Even so, Rossendale was a particularly bad blow. Right up to the last week of the General Election, it appeared that Labour might just pull off its third victory in a row. Opinion polls on the Sunday before polling day gave Harold Wilson a lead of between two and twelve per cent. 'So our defeat four days later was as big a surprise for the Conservatives as it was for us,' wrote Denis Healey later. 'There is no doubt that the 1970 election was lost by the government rather than won by the Opposition. The Wilson government of 1966 to 1970 was not regarded as a success even by the Labour movement. It can now be seen as the turning point which started a long decline in the Labour Party's fortunes.'[1]

In defeat, Wilson retired to his study to write his memoirs, sold to the *Sunday Times* for a sum approaching a quarter of a million pounds, and the party drifted listlessly to the Left. Trade union leaders, most notably Jack Jones of the Transport Workers, and Hugh Scanlon of the engineers, who wielded the dominant block votes at party conference, encouraged the trend, which was reinforced by disappointed socialist activists in the constituency parties. Stimulated by their victory in 1969 over Barbara Castle's 'In Place of Strife' package aimed at curbing their power, the unions pushed for greater state intervention in industry and commerce, articulated a hostile line on European integration and increasingly backed anti-NATO, pro-Campaign for Nuclear Disarmament policies. The party followed willy-nilly, much to the dismay of middle-of-the-road, pro-Market supporters of the Atlantic Alliance like Betty.

But dismay did not turn to disillusion. Betty has always been one to stand and fight rather than to run away from a political confrontation. As the party slid uneasily into a more hard-line posture, she redoubled her efforts to find a winnable constituency – always more difficult when the party has just lost office and with it a substantial number of seats. Little more than a year after Harold Wilson's disastrous gamble with the electorate, her persistence was rewarded. However, the road to the green benches of Westminster finally began not in her native Pennines, but in the sprawling industrial megalopolis of the Black Country.

In late 1971, the Labour Party in West Bromwich began to cast around for a candidate for the next general election. Under a complicated revision of parliamentary boundaries, several constituencies were abolished and new ones created. West Bromwich East, marginal but definitely winnable, came up for grabs. Though this was geographically not really her territory, Betty moved quickly, mobilizing her contacts in the party hierarchy and the trade unions. Friar Park Community Centre, Wednesbury, in the middle of a blizzard on an overcast Sunday afternoon in January 1972 was the right place to be. While a miners' strike gripped the nation, the constituency party was busy choosing its candidate for the next election. It was so cold in the community centre that the candidates were allowed to sit in a member's house close by to keep warm. Betty had been nominated by a local branch of the Fire Brigades' Union – traditionally a Left-wing union which was later to oppose her ambitions to win a place on Labour's national executive. But in this area, the firemen were more supportive of her brand of politics. Other influential unions – the engineers, foundryworkers, Transport and General – moderate rather than militant in this region, were in her camp. The tiny Musicians' Union also had a delegate, and though it is not recorded how he voted, in all probability it was for his fellow stage artiste. In any event, she impressed the stolid Labour burghers of the Black Country enough to collect the candidacy.

From that date, she began to cultivate the fledgling constituency, which as yet only existed on paper. It was a labour of politics, rather than of love. West Bromwich was a lusty son of the industrial revolution. In 1828, Pigot's Directory of Staffordshire described it as 'a populous and widely spread village in the hundred of Offlow South, situated in a county abounding with inexhaustible mines of iron and coal, that run in all directions beneath the parish, affording by their produce and workings materials for flourishing manufactures, and employment to a great population'. Only a few years previously, it had been a rural heath 'in which rabbits burrowed in great numbers'.

By 1882, the population had quintupled, and industry had grown accordingly. If the Black Country was the workshop of Britain, West Bromwich was its heartland, making everything from roasting jacks to the finest spring balances. A local works football team was known as The Strollers, more easily recognized today as West Bromwich Albion. There have been few famous sons and daughters of West Bromwich: Francis Asbury, the Methodist preacher, the Victorian writer David Christie Murray and William Henley, 'the English Paganini' born in 1874. Perhaps the nearest to Betty Boothroyd was the film star Madeleine Carroll, born locally but a star in Hollywood in the 1930s and 40s in films such as *The 39 Steps* and *The Prisoner of Zenda*. Since 1918, the seat has been Labour apart from a brief, four-year Tory interregnum after 1931.

By the mid-1970s, when Betty arrived on the scene, the collieries and ironworks had gone, but there remained a flourishing foundry trade, and engineering was still in its heyday, along with steel-tube manufacture, motor components and the traditional nut and bolt industry. This was strong, traditional Right-wing Labour territory for the unions: ideal terrain for Betty. The constituency had a keen, young new agent, Peter Killeen, who had been appointed during Betty's selection process. He was very pleased with his constituency's acquisition. 'She had, as she has now, a strong personality,' he recalled later. 'She was extremely popular with all types of elector, of all political persuasions. She is one of those people who gets on with everyone.'[2]

But before her campaign of nursing the marginal seat could come to fruition, one of those rare strokes of political good fortune came her way. Not before time, she may well have mused. In late 1972, Maurice Foley, the incumbent Labour member for the old seat of West Bromwich, which was due to disappear under the boundary changes, decided to quit. Foley, a junior minister in the previous Wilson government, and an ardent Europhile, had been lured to a high-flying job with the European Commission in Brussels. His departure meant a by-election.

There was a prospective double-bonus here, too. Earlier, under the normal rules of party protocol, Foley had been given the opportunity to decide which seat – West Bromwich West or West Bromwich East – he wished to fight when his existing constituency disappeared. Naturally, he chose West Bromwich West, by far the safer seat. It was therefore virtually guaranteed that his successor, assuming he or she could hang on to the moribund West Bromwich constituency, would inherit a lifetime passport to Parliament.

Betty's prospects did not go unnoticed among the astute political commentators of Fleet Street. Cross-Bencher in the *Sunday Express* noted that a by-election was due in the seat of Europe-bound Mr Foley. 'But if any Labour hopefuls are casting an interested eye in that direction, I must warn them there is already a dainty foot in the door,' he revealed. 'It belongs to Miss Betty Boothroyd, a dark and buxom forty-three-year-old, who is the prospective candidate for the new seat of West Bromwich East, which will include about seventy per cent of the present constituency. And you may be sure that she regards herself as the lady in possession.'

Just so. But the uncharitable columnist warned that Betty's performance at her last two outings bore an uncanny resemblance to the challenge she was now contemplating. At both Nelson and Colne, and Rossendale, she had been defending a Labour majority of just over 4000, and she had lost both. At West Bromwich, Foley's majority in a straight fight with the Conservatives had been very similar: 4436. The comrades might hesitate, thought Cross-Bencher.

But here his political sagacity had deserted him. The circumstances were different. In 1968, Betty was desperately trying to stem the tide against an increasingly unpopular Labour government, which finally brought down the Wilson administration two years later. This time, she could count on a political current running in her favour, against the statutory prices and incomes policy of Edward Heath's Tory government. In her second selection process in just over a year, Betty beat off two local candidates, Councillor Tony Salter, a member of

West Bromwich Borough Council, and Dr Hiron Roy, a local GP, to land the nomination on 18 March, 1973. Polling day was fixed for 24 May, the same day as another by-election in the safe Labour seat of Westhoughton, Lancashire.

Betty, who had been spending one day a week in West Bromwich for more than a year, sitting in on Foley's regular 'surgeries', quickly identified with the industrial constituency and her electorate. 'I appreciate the problems of an area like this. I was brought up in an industrial area,' she told the regional morning paper.[3] 'What appeals to me here is the same kind of dogged determination to overcome disadvantages like industrial pollution and the scars on the landscape. You can see it in the work that has already been done.' This kind of talk went down well with Labour veterans such as the constituency chairman Roley Vernon, who still says candidly, 'She's no shrinking violet. The character of Black Country people is something similar to Yorkshire. They don't make friends quickly, but when they do, they get established. Betty has established herself with the people of the Black Country.'[4]

Though there seemed little doubt about the outcome of the by-election, Labour was in no mood to take chances. Ted Castle, the veteran former Mirror Group journalist and husband of Betty's former employer Barbara Castle, was despatched to handle the media. In the absence of committee rooms on the High Street (reputed to be the longest in Britain, and certainly among the dullest), the party made its base in a disused police station at Hilltop on the fringe of the constituency.

Betty might have wished for more worthy opponents. The Tory candidate, David Bell, was an estate agent and former city councillor from Birmingham, who, like her, had been prospective candidate for the new constituency of West Bromwich East. He had achieved a swing of more than eight per cent against Labour in the Birmingham Northfields division in the 1970 General Election. Bell, aged forty-seven and born in Dublin, was well to the Right of his party, a self-confessed admirer of Enoch Powell. The *Observer* described him as 'plump, engagingly expansive, with silver hair and a mysteriously celebratory air as if he were constantly about to hand around a box of cigars'.[5] Peter Paterson, later the entertaining biographer of George

Brown but then a young turk reporting for the *New Statesman*, found the Conservative 'a nervous automaton who believes in repatriating immigrants and in hanging'.[6]

There was also a gadfly candidate, a former Labour Lord Mayor of West Bromwich, Joshua Churchman, who bore an uncanny resemblance to Enoch Powell. He drew out his savings and stood on a platform of opposition to the forced amalgamation of West Bromwich and Warley to form the new metropolitan district of Sandwell – still perhaps the least-loved of Sir Keith Joseph's phoney cities. But worse, far worse, was the arrival on the political scene of the National Front, in the burly shape of Martin Webster, its thirty-year-old national organizer. Webster, a self-declared racialist, was seeking to capitalize on the upsurge of anti-immigrant sentiment in the wake of General Idi Amin's expulsion of 40,000 Kenyan Asians to Britain the previous autumn. From scoring only three or four per cent in the General Election, the NF was now able to notch up sixteen, eighteen and even twenty-three per cent in council by-elections in cities with a large black population.

Not surprisingly for a heavy-industry area with low unemployment – only 1.8 per cent – West Bromwich had attracted quite substantial numbers of immigrants since the 1950s. Local community relations officers put the number of people of Indian-subcontinent or West-Indian origin in the borough at about 7000, or 5.5 per cent of the total. Webster claimed the figure was actually three times higher, and tried to smear the incomers with charges of causing an increase in violent crime. Police said violence was showing steady decline.

Webster certainly appeared to have plenty of money. He hired the old Army and Navy stores in the High Street and decked it out with Union flags. He boasted five loudspeaker systems and enough money to deliver two leaflets to every household. He toured the housing areas in a white estate car demanding that 'not one coloured immigrant' should be housed ahead of white Britons. The *Yorkshire Post* found his campaign 'the most vigorous and certainly the most eye-catching . . . it is very difficult to move very far without coming face to face with one of its [NF] posters.'[7] Michael Foot could only attract about fifty to a public meeting. The NF drew 400 to theirs. It seemed a bad omen.

Working from her own instincts but perhaps also guided by her media 'minder' Ted Castle (described in the *New Statesman* as 'the dominant influence'), Betty based her campaign on prices and inflation. 'This is what people are really bothered about,' she told the *Sunday Times*.[8] The newspapers praised her 'impressive homework' in the High Street. The Co-op provided her with a list of prices of various staple items when Heath came to power, and those charged less than three years before. A pound of New Zealand Cheddar cheese cost 16p under Harold Wilson. Now, despite statutory pay restraint, it cost 30p. English rump steak had virtually doubled from 57½p to 95p.

This straightforward comparison struck a ready chord in the electorate, but her real problem was voter apathy. Labour had always had a loyal, rather than a mass, party in West Bromwich, enjoying sometimes tenuous support from the large working-class vote. On the traditionally solid Greets Green council estate, only one in eight voters had turned out for the local elections that month. Even at the General Election, the turnout was only sixty-two per cent.

Betty tackled the issue head on. The *New Statesman* noted her 'slightly desperate enthusiasm for the democratic process', as she lectured, cajoled and pleaded with the voters to get out and vote. 'You may be forgiven if you feel, you have had a basinful of elections lately,' she said. 'And now here I am asking you to vote again.'[9] But she promised voters: 'Next Thursday is the last one.' She was tireless. No old folks' home was too insignificant, no factory gate too trifling. She had failed too often to fail again, and the fear of losing pushed her to the limits. Some analysts caught her edgy lack of confidence, which had appeared before and would appear again and again in her political career. Peter Paterson, who believed that 'Miss Boothroyd' would win, nonetheless observed, 'I was just a little alarmed by the haunting memory, as I left West Bromwich, of those vulnerable, anxious eyes.'[10] Some of her party workers found that down the years she was 'a very pessimistic candidate, always expecting the worst'.[11]

But the Tories, desperately clinging to the theme of 'Booming Britain', and aware that they were being outflanked on the right by the National Front (Enoch Powell had humiliated Bell by refusing to appear on his platform), did their best to inject a bit of showbiz into their lacklustre campaign. They paraded a bikini-clad Young

Conservative through the streets ringing a bell, and she attracted rather more attention than Betty's counter-attraction – actress Doris Speed, better known to voters as Mrs Annie Walker, prim landlady of the Rovers' Return pressed into service again. 'Annie', reported the *Daily Telegraph*, passed largely unnoticed except by those she approached in the street.

In the party leader's traditional eve-of-poll message to the candidate, Wilson hammered home the theme of the Heath government's failure to deliver on its price-restraint policy. 'Food, housing, fares, clothing – all the things which were to be reduced in price, or whose rate of increase was to be slowed down, have risen catastrophically for the ordinary family. In three short years, the Conservatives have doubled the rise in the cost of living.'[12] The by-election could not, in itself, remove the Conservative government, 'but it could tell them once again that the electorate are impatient to be rid of them and it could help bring that day about'. Labour piled in its Shadow Cabinet – Foot, Roy Jenkins, Barbara Castle. The ever-loyal Geoffrey de Freitas turned up, and Betty mother's travelled down for the climax of the campaign.

As it turned out, she need not have worried. Despite the very low poll – only 43.6 per cent – Betty retained the seat for Labour with a swing against the government of more than nine per cent. The Tory vote collapsed , tumbling from 18,976 to 7582, while Labour virtually doubled its majority to 8325. The intervention of the former Lord Mayor had made no impact, while the National Front had evidently taken most of its worryingly high poll of 4789 votes from the Conservatives. Betty condemned the NF's anti-immigration vote.

Reporter Laura Gillan watched the election count for the *Wolverhampton Express and Star*, and described Betty 'exultantly clutching a wilted four-leaf clover' as the returning officer declared the victory that made her the twenty-seventh woman among 650 MPs. 'As I watched her at the vote counting, I thought that she could easily have been mistaken for a typical Tory woman,' she wrote.[13] 'Her immaculately coiffured hair, careful make-up and almost midi-length mauve silk coat belied her working-class background.' But Betty revived the quip she always used for such occasions, swearing that her roots were 'there under my finger-nails'. At her moment of victory, said the *Express and Star*, there was her mother, 'a grand little Yorkshire woman who said with an accent you could cut with a knife, "I'm proud of her."'

The *Daily Telegraph*'s political correspondent, H. B. Boyne, a wise, dry old Scot, was tempted to think in his despatch that the ministerial resignations over a call-girl affair had induced some habitual Conservatives to vent their disapproval by abstaining. Lord Lambton, Under-Secretary for the RAF, had just been forced to resign after photographs of him with a prostitute, Norma Levy, were offered to the Fleet Street tabloids. And when Edward Heath asked his ministers if their was anything they had to hide, Trade Minister Earl Jellicoe owned up to 'casual affairs' with call girls and quit, too. The inference that these ministerial shenanigans had anything to do with the result, thought Boyne, was 'rather simplistic. The news broke too late in the campaign to have much influence. Nor is there any reason to assume that the electors of West Bromwich are particularly prudish.' The *Telegraph* man put Betty's good result down to the more realistic assumption that the economic boom being acclaimed by Mr Heath and his colleagues had failed, as yet, to impress the Midlands.

Betty contented herself with calling it 'a tremendous victory for Labour', and the well-satisfied party team repaired to the Flash Harry pub for a 'magnificent celebration' that went on until two in the morning. The police then turned up to end the partying, only to find a considerable number of their colleagues already in the bar.

Betty's victory at the age of forty-three and the return of Roger Stott at Westhoughton the same day – also with an increased majority, though with a lower swing against the government – came as a tonic to Harold Wilson, whose star was once again in the ascendancy. He was celebrating ten years as party leader, confirmed as the four-to-one favourite of the rank and file against his old rival Roy Jenkins. His carefully leaked *Programme for Britain* was a politically cautious document, omitting any further nationalization. Labour was ahead in the polls, but by sometimes no more than a nose – three per cent the month before the West Bromwich by-election. Enoch Powell was busily hinting that he might advise his followers to plump for Wilson at the next election, because Labour alone offered an opportunity to vote against the Common Market. One way and another, it was a good time to return to the House where Betty had worked so long as an MP's secretary as the Honourable Member in her own right.

She took her seat on 11 June, though not without incident. The *Daily Telegraph*'s Peterborough gossip column reported that she was 'a most noticeable figure in a yellow frock', but had been a shade unlucky in her introduction to the Commons.[14] Paraded with her sponsors at the Bar of the House well before the appointed hour of 3.30 p.m., she then had to stand for twenty minutes while MPs grilled Maurice Macmillan, the Employment Secretary, about the finer points of an industrial dispute at Chrysler's motor manufacturing plant in Coventry. 'Thoroughly instructive,' sniffed Peterborough, 'but no way to treat a lady.'

In fact, Betty would probably have been able to tell Macmillan's critics a thing or two about trade unionism. During her secretarial days, she had chaired the Commons Trade Union Committee, and exhibited no problem in supporting the party line of total repeal of Ted Heath's hated and ill-starred 1971 Industrial Relations Act, which sought to bring the unions to heel. Despite their lurch to the Left, the unions had proved, and would prove again, to be her power base.

The House did not have to wait long before hearing from the new member. Only five weeks later, Betty was on her feet, making her maiden speech immediately the Prime Minister had sat down in a debate on inflation. Her name was called by Speaker Selwyn Lloyd at 5.47 p.m., and she asked the House to be tolerant with her. She first paid tribute to her predecessor Maurice Foley, and then introduced herself. 'My roots are working class and I have earned my living since the age of seventeen. Therefore I claim to be able at any rate to speak for ordinary working people... This, reinforced by recent support of the electorate might, I hope, help to balance in some way my lack of parliamentary experience.'[15]

She recited a litany of praise for the voters of West Bromwich – 'people who earn their living in industry – in foundries, rolling mills, in factories, making components for motor cars and aircraft and a variety of engineering products – industries which secured for Britain her former industrial power and which today ensure her economic survival.' Politicians and parties must give a lead, Betty admitted, 'but they must also turn a sensitive ear to the views of constituents'. She asked MPs to listen to just two major issues concerning her constituents: inflation, and 'a strong feeling they have about injustice in our national life today'.

She complained bitterly that land and house prices had doubled in the Midlands since the Tories came to power in 1970. She recalled her by-election survey of prices on West Bromwich High Street, which revealed the cost of essential items going up every week. 'No wonder the cost of living was the talking point. No wonder I was constantly asked, "When will something be done about it?"' She wanted new local consumer centres proposed by the government to have teeth, powers to protect as well as advise the consumer. 'Honourable Members will recall, as I do, that nationally organized band of woman known as the Housewives League. They campaigned dutifully in the late 1940s objecting because ration books were still required for essential foods. Where are the daughters of the consumer revolution now that we have rationing by purse?'

She excoriated the Chancellor for failing to increase family allowances, and demanded that Phase Three of his pay policy must be linked to the cost of food and other essentials. She called for reform of the Common Agricultural Policy, to end the glut of dairy products and meet the growing demand for beef and pigmeat. She was scathing about the plight of pensioners: 'In far too many cases they do not have a life, but a struggle for existence against the odds.' She said the October pension increase had already been overtaken by prices, treating MPs to some homespun Yorkshire wisdom that must have puzzled some: 'In my family we would say in such circumstances, "It has got its coat and hat on before it is over the doorstep."' She demanded a pension rise in August.

And finally, she turned to 'the question of our national life'. The firm impression she carried from West Bromwich was the dissatisfaction of people, the feeling that society was unjust and unfair, that people lived by the rule of law but that there was one law for the well-off and another for those who are not so well off. It was difficult for her to articulate their feelings, 'but I shall try'. Had the government any right to expect wage restraint when company profits were rapidly increasing? Why should people listen to the government when rents were being deliberately increased and property speculators were elevated to the top of society? Why should hard-hit families listen to a government that rejected measures to protect their interests?

'The government were not elected constantly to explain away the problems of world conditions, world prices or the actions of primary producers. They were elected to find the answers. There can be no real progress until everyone realizes that we have a two-tier society and that until practical steps are taken to alleviate its injustices people everywhere will feel badly about this government which were elected on false promises.' She thanked the House for listening tolerantly and sat down at 6 p.m., having filled four columns of *Hansard* in thirteen minutes.

Betty's maiden speech may not have been so newsworthy, or notorious, as say Bernadette Devlin's, but it was clearly a *tour de force*. It marked out her territory as the housewives' champion, and a principled fighter against social injustice. And it rang true. Echoes of her parents' struggle abounded. Not even a decade of working for the rich Lord Walston in his opulent Albany flat, rubbing shoulders with the high and mighty, it seems, had dulled her sense of outrage about the 'two-tier society'.

When she had got to her feet, Betty had feared it might be 'particularly difficult' to follow the Prime Minister. It could not have been easy to follow her. The task fell to one of the Tory party's old buffers, Sir Henry d'Avigdor-Goldsmid, fellow Black Country MP for the adjoining constituency of Walsall South. He did his best. 'There used to be a tradition, which I am glad to see is disappearing', he bumbled, 'that maiden speeches were non-controversial. It was an unhealthy tradition and I am glad to see that the Honourable Member would have no part in it.'

D'Avigdor-Goldsmid begged her forgiveness for not taking up 'too closely' the points she had made, and then referred to a story the previous week in the *Evening Standard* Londoner's Diary. 'I understand . .. that she announced her return to these corridors which she has for so long decorated by saying that she had been permitted to enter the executive loo.' He paid her what would now be regarded as a ham-fisted, sexist compliment: 'I can assure her that we should like to see her in all the executive seats, including the Front Bench.'[16] Betty had confessed to the *Standard* that, while working as a secretary in the House, she was restricted to the public lavatories. But after her landslide by-election win, she was now entitled to the more convenient amenities and elegant surroundings of the Lady Members' Room. Betty commented, 'Can't get used to the idea that I can now use the executive loos,' though admitted that as often as not she still patronized her usual haunts.

Outside Westminster, the Heath Conservative government itself was going into terminal decline. In the autumn, the Yom Kippur War in the Middle East triggered massive cutbacks in oil supplies just as the miners were beginning a nationwide overtime ban in pursuit of a pay policy wildly in excess of the Chancellor's statutory wage-rise limits. On 13 December 1973, Heath announced a three-day week for industry to reduce energy consumption. The IRA exploded in London, and the balance-of-payments crisis got worse. As the pits disruption moved towards an all-out miners' strike, there was constant talk of a general election. Heath was assailed by conflicting advice from within his Cabinet, but bowed to the inevitable on 7 February 1974, more than a year before he was obliged to seek a fresh mandate. With the miners slowly strangling the economy, he announced a General Election on 28 February on the theme of 'Who Governs Britain?'

Harold Wilson sensibly refused to allow the campaign to be confined to the ground of Heath's choosing. The election, he insisted, was not about the miners, not about the power of the militants, not even about the powers of the unions. 'It is about the disastrous failure of three and a half years of Conservative government which has turned Britain from the path to prosperity to the road to ruin.' Nor did the voters necessarily blame Labour for the strike – and perhaps not even the miners themselves. Moreover, they had not forgotten Heath's ill-judged promise to cut prices 'at a stroke'.

In moving the battle away from the single, controversial issue of the coal strike to the state of the economy, Wilson knocked the main prop from under Heath. For Betty, of course, this was home territory: prices and social justice. Labour was winning ground on its 'social contract' governing wages and social policy with the TUC, and also made substantial progress on the issue of the Common Market, particularly after Enoch Powell revealed he had cast his postal vote for Labour.[17]

Betty went back to West Bromwich early in February 1974 to fight her second election campaign in only nine months. It was a whirlwind affair, but, almost certainly because of 'the Powell factor', Labour performed particularly well in the West Midlands. Standing in her new seat for the first time, she crushed the Conservative, P. M. Smith, winning with a majority of 13,431. Betty could feel well satisfied, having taken 62.9 per cent of all the votes cast. The National Front collected just over 3000 votes, and was never to be a serious threat again.

Nationally, the picture was less sharply defined. The voters could not quite make up their minds. They had lost faith with Ted Heath, but were unable to bring themselves wholeheartedly to embrace Harold Wilson once again. In the early hours of 29 February, the political landscape was clarified. Britain had voted for the first hung parliament since 1929. Labour polled fewer votes than the Tories – fewer, indeed than at any time since 1931. The Liberals and the nationalist parties gained at the expense of the two main parties. But, critically, Wilson had four more seats than the Conservatives, and was able to form a minority government after coalition talks between Heath and the Liberals, who held the balance with their fourteen seats, came to nothing.

Wilson dealt with the miners simply. He appointed Michael Foot as Employment Secretary with a brief to buy them off with a generous pay rise sanctioned by the Pay Board, a creature of the Heath statutory incomes policy. The colliers went back to work, with their general secretary Lawrence Daly, promising to abide by a Labour–TUC voluntary pay restraint deal. The three-day week ended quickly, and the public began to heave a sigh of relief that the much-vaunted 'social contract' might, after all, deliver a quiet life, free from strikes and social upset. An 'independent' industrial relations conciliation service, ACAS, was set up.

It was not a particularly busy parliament for Betty. On 25 March 1974, she was on her feet asking the Trade and Industry Secretary what means there were for identifying the origin of steel imported into the UK. Steel counted in the Black Country. There was, she said, great concern about British steel being exported and then imported back again at a higher foreign price. To Labour cheers, she demanded ministerial action, with Customs and Excise and our EEC partners, 'to find a method of identifying steel so that this unscrupulous practice can be stopped?' A month later, she intervened in a debate on consumer protection, arguing against exemption for small neighbourhood shops, on the grounds that those of limited mobility would be hit.

But it was a phoney period in politics. For seven months, Wilson played a waiting game with the enervated Tories, before calling an election on 10 October. As if to point up the contrast with Heath's 'at a stroke' albatross pledge yet again, he chose the slogan 'Labour Keeps its Promises'. It was a short campaign, conducted against a background of misleading opinion polls, not unlike 1970. Labour won again, but it was agonizingly close. Early predictions of a thirty-seat majority for Labour dwindled overnight to an actuality of just three, but Wilson insisted his administration was viable, and would endure.

In West Bromwich, Betty improved on her near-impregnability. Her majority over the Tory N. Bridges-Adams was 14,799, a swing to the government of 2.9 per cent. The National Front continued its slide, to just over 2000 votes. From being the girl most unlikely to succeed, she had become the invulnerable woman.

That was not all. A late but welcome forty-fifth birthday present landed two weeks after polling day. On 25 October 1974, Betty was appointed to her first job in government, in the Whip's Office. She was the first woman to become a Labour whip while the party was in power, and had responsibility for keeping West Midlands MPs in line, getting them through the voting lobbies and helping to push Bills through their various stages. She was now also assisting with the organization of the work of the House, watching the operation of the mysterious 'usual channels' between government and opposition at close quarters. This was her first glimpse of power and the behind-the-scenes machinations of the House of Commons. It was to have a profound effect on her political career.

Betty was thrilled. Normally, the first rung of the governmental ladder is to be an unpaid Parliamentary Private Secretary acting as the eyes and ears of a minister in the House. She had jumped that hurdle to become a paid member of the government. 'When I was offered the job, the chief whip Bob Mellish said he knew I was a very feminine woman, but he knew I could be tough enough for the job. I told him

I could be so tough that I chewed tobacco for breakfast,' she said.[18]

As a former Leader of the House, John Biffen has pointed out that the Whip's Office has a misleadingly sinister name.[19] 'In fact, it is primarily concerned with managing affairs so that parliamentary business can be done, not with coercion or the trampling underfoot of tender consciences.' However, few MPs would deny that coercion does sometimes happen. There have even been allegations of MPs – Tories – being reduced to tears by whips threatening to inform a member's wife of his peccadilloes if he did not vote for the government. The whips, being the disciplinarians, usually 'know where all the bodies are buried' and can exert pressure at sensitive points. The term whip derives from the hunt, where whippers-in keep the hounds running in a tight pack, and that is their main role. But parliamentary whips also act as a sounding board of back-bench opinion for the government, a role for which Betty's maiden speech suggested she was admirably suited.

Nonetheless, promotion came early. Her local paper pointed out that she had only been in Parliament sixteen months, and it was unusual to be offered the post of regional whip after such a short parliamentary career. But senior Labour members had seen her as a 'tireless worker' and decided to harness some of her enthusiasm in the tough job of keeping the three-vote majority government afloat.

There were drawbacks to the job, which paid £7000 a year – £2750 more than a normal MP's salary. 'As a whip, I will not be allowed to speak in Parliamentary debates, and this is obviously a blow,' she said. The first casualty of this self-denying ordinance was a Commons speech she was preparing on equal-rights legislation for women. It would also be virtually impossible for her to undertake constituency engagements while the House was sitting. With such a tight majority, the government had to guard against Tory ambushes, and sittings often went on until the small hours. Columnist Cross-Bencher was at his most impish when her appointment was announced from Downing Street. The 'cheery, competent' Miss Boothroyd would soon be greeting erring Labour members 'in the West Bromwich MP's characteristic style "And where were you last night, luvvie?"' He also thought she might invite the policemen on duty in the Lobby for late-night tea and biscuits in the Whips' quarters, as a predecessor had done.[20]

These were days of unaccustomed silence for Betty. But on one remarkable scandal she felt it her duty to speak out. John Stonehouse, Labour MP for the next-door Black Country constituency of Walsall North, and once a rising star in the Wilson firmament, disappeared suddenly while on a visit to the USA. His clothes were found on a beach in Florida in circumstances suggesting suicide. Weeks later, he was traced to Melbourne, south Australia, where he had fled with a false passport under the name of a dead constituent. He was hoping to start a new life 'down under' with his Commons secretary, Sheila Buckley. Stonehouse refused to return to Britain. He was one of Betty's parliamentary charges and, in January 1975, she sent him a telegram in Melbourne saying: 'Your responsibilities to Walsall make immediate resignation imperative.' It was, she added, time he stopped trying to justify his actions and considered the people of Walsall instead. Perhaps as fearful of Betty's wrath as he was of British justice, Stonehouse stayed put. He was eventually extradited home, and jailed for seven years on a range of fraud and forgery offences. On his release, he married Ms Buckley but died in 1989.

Despite her evident pleasure at getting so far so quickly, Betty's stint in the Whip's Office was destined to be a short one. After only eight months working for hard-man Mellish, she took the chance of becoming a member of Labour's delegation to the European Parliament. Her name appeared in the list of twelve MPs and six members of the House of Lords approved by the Parliamentary Labour Party on 26 June 1975. Also on the list were her two most influential employers: Sir Geoffrey de Freitas, back in the Commons as MP for Kettering Northants, and Lord Walston.

Europe was to prove congenial rather than controversial. But Labour's first delegation to the unelected parliament was divided by an internal row even before they got on the plane. The brothers and sisters could not decide whether or not to join the Socialist Group of Euro MPs at Strasbourg. Betty's friend and ally (whose devotion to the cause of European unity had earned him the affectionate nickname of Sir Geoffrey de Strasbourg) urged joining. He was, reported the *Guardian*, 'vigorously supported by Miss Betty Boothroyd, the Labour Whip on the parliamentary delegation'.

She declared that members of the European Socialist Group would be 'deeply offended, if not insulted' should the Britons not link up with the European confreres. John Prescott, the former seafarer who was now MP for Hull East, was sceptical and counselled caution. The argument petered out in classic Labour manner, when the delegation's booking on the Commons Committee room ran out of time, and the meeting had to close. A subcommittee was set up 'to travel to the continent' and make inquiries about the obligations involved. Once they realized that membership committed them to virtually nothing, Labour soon signed up.

Happily, there was more to the European Parliament than matters of political procedure. On the MPs' first charter flight out, *The Times* diarist, PHS, travelled with them to Strasbourg to see for himself how Labour was settling in. He found that life was more agreeable than at Westminster. The delegates were entitled to an allowance of French francs equivalent to £35 a day, out of which they had to find their bed and board. *The Times* man found prices 'less exorbitant than feared', and had a decent dinner for £2, with a bottle of the 'lovely local white wine' for the same price. The Labour Group, he discovered, were staying at the newly opened Holiday Inn, though hardly any of them ate there on the first night, except their leader Michael Stewart, who dined frugally, alone with a book, on a cheeseburger and half a bottle of Perrier.

His troops were more adventurous. With characteristic insouciance, Betty declared, 'I can eat at a Holiday Inn in Birmingham,' and went off to look for something better. Around midnight, reported PHS, the delegates got back to the hotel bar with excited tales of gastronomic triumphs at little bistros that served the finest onion tart. *The Times* described Betty's whipping duties as a responsibility to get them all back to Westminster if their votes were needed in a division, adding that this was none too easy because of the paucity of direct flights to London. 'I keep the times of all the planes in my handbag,' she confided. Betty was also the group's 'unofficial housemother', and had led the hunt for Lord (formerly Patrick) Gordon-Walker's spectacles. They were eventually found by Sir Geoffrey de Freitas in a restaurant.

Betty was not appointed to any of the top European Parliament committees, which covered political affairs, budgets, economic and monetary affairs, regional policy and the like. From 6 March 1976 she

sat on the Committee on Environment, Public Health and Consumer
Protection – a particular personal interest – with six other British
representatives, including the Labour MP John Evans, who was later
to work closely with her on Labour's National Executive in the battle
against the Militant Tendency. At the same time, she was also
appointed a member of the Committee on Development and
Co-operation, with Lord Walston and Sir Geoffrey de Freitas, an
amiable arrangement. From 12 May of that year, the happy trio sat
on an EEC/African, Caribbean Pacific joint committee, where their
personal experience of the Third World was invaluable.

Her first six months in the parliament were not exactly onerous.
She asked four oral questions, chiefly on farm prices and consumer
protection. This activity earned her the generous title of 'the housewives' champion of Europe' from the *Wolverhampton Express and Star*.
Her local paper breathlessly reported that 'after only a few months as
a British representative, Miss Boothroyd stirred up a hornets' nest on
consumer affairs'.[21] First, she told the parliament, sitting in Luxem-
bourg on this occasion, that the housewife must be protected in Community planning on food, prompting German Socialist leader Ludwig
Fellermainer to demand a full debate on the issue. Betty was described
by a young European politician as 'a fine parliamentarian – frank and
enthusiastic. We like those qualities over here.'

In the debate that followed, Betty declared that the Commission
could no longer 'drag its feet' on giving housewives a voice in taking
part in decision-making on consumer affairs. Consumer involvement,
she argued, was no longer limited to questions of food, quality and
hygiene. Britain's Consumer Affairs Secretary, Mrs Shirley Williams,
had just made her first appearance at a meeting of Europe's agriculture
ministers. 'I hope it will not be the last and that other member states
will also appoint secretaries of state dealing with consumer affairs who
will also discuss with agricultural ministers, because the largest single
item in the Community budget goes to agriculture,' declared Betty.

Housewives met the cost of farm prices, and as consumers had a
right to be involved in decisions concerning food production, the cost
of the policy, the disposal of surpluses and storage policy. With greater
planning, there would still inevitably be surpluses, but she would prefer
them to be 'manageable molehills rather than immovable mountains'.

Food surpluses and farm prices continued to dog the EC down the years long after Betty had left Strasbourg. At the time, hers was a voice in the wilderness, ahead of its time, perhaps, and certainly well intentioned – but doomed to failure.

In 1976, she asked four more oral questions, on issues as diverse as freedom of movement within the Community and the award of public works contracts. She also took part in drawing up a Development Committee report on the import of beef and veal from African, Caribbean and Pacific countries. There were interventions in half a dozen debates and in January 1977 she presented reports on a directive on dangerous substances as deputy rapporteur. Betty also asked more questions on farm prices and consumer protection. And she continued to be the delegation Whip.

Back at Westminster, the Cabinet was discussing direct elections for the European Assembly, instead of the existing system of appointment by the parties. The rest of Europe wanted a directly elected parliament by 1978, and Betty supported this move. She also thought a first-past-the-post electoral system was 'the only practical and sensible one to be used in the early years'.[22] The European Parliament would win only limited powers in time, and at the expense of the Commission and the EC Council of Ministers rather than Westminster. The British people should have closer democratic control over the so-called faceless men of Brussels. It was a judgment not borne out by events.

In the world outside the hothouse of the Commons and Strasbourg, politics were becoming more unpleasant. The government's 'social contract' with the TUC was under increasing strain because the unions could not control their pay militants. And there was scandal. Jeremy Thorpe, leader of the Liberal Party, was implicated in an affair with Norman Scott, with whom he was accused of having a homosexual relationship. Betty's fellow woman MP Joan Lestor quit her government post in the Department of Education and Science over draconian spending cuts imposed by the Chancellor, Denis Healey, who dismissed his Left-wing critics in the PLP as 'silly billies'.

Then, on 16 March – only a week after Betty took up her first European committee seat – came the real bombshell. Harold Wilson announced to a thunderstruck Cabinet that he was resigning as Prime

Minister, and would stay on only long enough for the party to find a new leader. He was motivated, he said, by the record-breaking length of his term as Prime Minister, by a desire to allow others to contest for the post, by the necessity to give his successor time to settle in before the next election, and by the need for a new approach. These four reasons were 'the total explanation' of his decision, he insisted to a sceptical world. Some suspected a personal scandal, particularly after his resignation honours list rewarded some quite exotic people. But, as Denis Healey later pointed out, 'There is now too much evidence that he had planned it years earlier, to make that credible.'

Three weeks later, in the last leadership ballot to be conducted solely among Labour MPs, James Callaghan – who had been tipped off about the resignation four months previously – beat Michael Foot for the leadership. On 5 April 1976, he entered Number 10, and sacked a number of ministers including Barbara Castle, Betty's former employer, and Chief Whip Bob Mellish, who had nurtured her parliamentary career. With its shoestring majority kept alive by Michael Foot, Leader of the House, the government was battered by another financial crisis in July 1976. The pound was under heavy pressure, and Denis Healey brought in a further round of spending cuts of more than £1 billion, plus a two per cent rise in employers' national insurance contributions which would bring in almost as much. These measures failed to convince the markets, and after hoisting interest rates to thirteen per cent and spending $100 million dollars in a fruitless bid to prop up sterling, the Chancellor caved in and applied for a conditional loan from the IMF.

As this crisis accelerated, the Labour Party began their conference in Blackpool. There, on the first day, with the pound crashing to record lows against the dollar, the TUC-Government social contract was the focal point of debate. Hugh Scanlon, the engineering workers' leader long presumed to be a hostile Left-winger but in fact most often a critical supporter of the government, moved a motion expressing deep concern and disapproval at the level of unemployment, then running at one and a half million. 'Unemployment', he said, 'is an obscenity which violates every principle and aspect of our social creed.' He demanded import controls and government action on investment in industry.[23]

Betty was not in the habit of wading into these annual tests of strength between the trade unions and the Labour government. In that, she was typical of most back-bench MPs, whose appearance at conference was tolerated rather than welcomed by the party activists and the trade union barons who controlled the votes. MPs were usually corralled in a pen of their own, left talk to each other, do the crossword or buy drinks in the many bars of the gothic Winter Gardens complex. They were certainly not encouraged to go to the rostrum and speak. On this occasion, however, Betty was determined to address conference, financial crisis or no. The social-contract debate was on the eve of her first bid to get elected to the party's ruling national executive, and she wanted to be seen by the people who had the votes.

She was the second speaker in the debate, and began by tilting her bonnet at the trade unions – the power brokers. 'The TUC has certainly in recent months demonstrated that if the economy is dependent on the social contract, then that contract means what it says and it has been made to stick. They deserve praise for an achievement beyond the wildest dreams of our competitors.'[24] Jim Slater, general secretary of the National Union of Seamen who had just pulled his members back from the brink of an international strike over pay, 'and his crew' deserved a pat on the back.

In the West Midlands, complained Betty, quality jobs were vanishing, while 'Jim the pirate' – City tycoon Jim Slater – and his ilk threw other people's millions around like confetti while industry was starved of capital. The argument that the economy must be restarted gradually to avoid a run on the pound was wearing thin. 'Every Labour government has sacrificed half its goodwill and half its programme defending the pound.' The TUC had made its contribution on the wages front, yet the CBI – the employers – had failed to deliver on the investment front.

'We now look to the government to see that a substantial proportion of the profits in the private sector are withheld for investment purposes. Let us not fool ourselves that such an investment fund [author's note: £1 billion a year] as we talk about can be achieved voluntarily . . . We have to look to our government to acquire those extra powers to make the reserve fund mandatory, because only then will it do and will we be satisfied.'

Betty conceded that the measures she was proposing 'will make the financiers panic, and they will sell sterling short'. But she urged 'let us keep our cool. Let us keep our nerve a little bit . . . Let us say to the government, "Throw off the stale advice of the City. Of course the value of the pound abroad is important, but so are the industrial talents of our people at home, and they must not be abused."' The conference report records 'applause'. She went on, 'Let us say to the nation from this conference that the Labour Movement is actively demonstrating its contribution to Britain's future prosperity. We now look to the other side of industry to demonstrate that same responsibility to Britain.'

She sat down to more applause. It had been vintage Betty, a tough intervention, all the more welcome to her potential electorate because she was by now firmly identified with the Europhile, Right-wing strand of the party. The *Birmingham Post* reported that she 'surprised many delegates by taking a distinctly Left-wing approach in the public-spending debate.'[25] In fact, her speech could easily have been delivered by Hugh Scanlon. It did not ring exactly true, and it failed to get her a coveted place on the platform. Not because she said the wrong things, but because she had not said them earlier, in different places, and to a more carefully selected audience. She was standing in the Women's Section of the NEC, whose members were elected by the trade unions. Five women were chasing eleven seats. She was standing against veteran party figures, mainly on the Left: Mrs Judith Hart, a former junior minister; Mrs Lena Jeger, Labour MP for Camden who was soon to become chair of the party, and who Betty had accompanied to Vietnam nearly twenty years previously; Mrs Shirley Williams, a member of the Cabinet; veteran left-of-centre figure Mrs Renee Short; and Miss Joan Maynard, hard-Left MP for Sheffield Brightside.

Although this was her first outing, Betty performed remarkably well, polling 2,462,000 votes and coming second runner-up to Dr Shirley Summerskill. Another 980,000 votes – that is, the support of a few two middle-ranking unions – and she would have made it. The reason for her good showing was that the general union GMB – then the General and Municipal Workers' Union – had talent-spotted her as a useful prospective addition to the ranks of the Callaghan-loyalist moderates on the NEC, whose ranks desperately needed strengthen-

In pantomime again at the Dewsbury
Empire in 1943. Betty is standing in the
back row, ninth from left.

Swing days: teenage Betty in silk bodice
and split skirt, performing centre stage
with the Swing Stars band in wartime
Britain.

Betty's first shot at becoming an
MP was in 1957, in the Leicester
South-East by-election.

Betty on the platform with
Harold Wilson at Dewsbury
Town Hall.

Meeting Ho: Betty on a
tour of Russia, China and
Vietnam met Vietcong
leader Ho Chi Minh in
1957. To their left is
Harold Davies MP.

Betty appearing with party leader Hugh Gaiskell while fighting Peterborough in the 1959 General Election.

Frontier girl: disillusioned with British politics, Betty went to Washington and worked in John F. Kennedy's presidential election campaign, and then for Republican Senator Silvio Conte until the early 1960s.

The third bid for Parliament: she stood in the by-election for Nelson and Colne in 1968 but failed to hold the seat for Labour.

Winner at last: Betty finally got to Parliament at a by-election in the Black Country seat of West Bromwich in 1973. She has been MP for the town ever since.

ing. With her thorough grounding in the old loyalist bastions of the Right in the Black Country – the engineers, the GMB, and the foundryworkers – Betty was ideal material. Her problem now was how to break the Left-wing hegemony on the national executive, but at least it was a problem shared with powerful trade union friends.

However, she also had other problems on her mind. With the government's majority diminished to vanishing point, she was too ill to attend for critical Commons votes on the extension of the dock labour scheme and measures to phase out pay beds in the NHS. Labour's business managers had to bring in Helen Hayman, MP for Welwyn and Hatfield, who was breastfeeding her fourteen-day-old son Benjamin, to make up the numbers, while Betty was 'paired' with a sick Tory. She told her local paper, 'I went into hospital a couple of weeks ago for a minor operation and unfortunately I caught a kidney infection. The doctors told me to stay in bed. I was determined to try to get to the Commons to vote for the government. Indeed, I even laid on an ambulance to take me to the Palace of Westminster.'[26] But she would have had to stay in the ambulance for eight hours for a series of votes, and even the hard-nosed Tory business managers relented.

Although she was officially listed as a member of her various European Parliament committees as late as 13 December 1976, it is clear that her illness was making Betty have second thoughts about the constant trekking back and forth to Strasbourg. She complained about feeling unwell with a recurrence of the symptoms that had led to an internal operation the previous autumn. Her specialist advised an 'emergency operation', believed to be an appendectomy, carried out successfully at Westminster hospital in late January 1977. Certainly, the *Express and Star* had in previous months reported her as suffering from appendicitis.

On 1 February her local paper announced 'MP STEPS OUT OF MARKET JOB'.[27] After the 'super hectic life' of the last two years, she was returning to the Commons full time. She thought it important that as many MPs were exposed as soon as possible to the workings of the Common Market. 'I am stepping down to make room for other MPs to take a look at the Market,' she added. Her resignation was officially recorded on 7 March 1977. Her former boss Lord Walston

quit at the same time. It had not been a long stint as a Euro MP –
barely eighteen months – nor had it achieved very much, though that
could be said of virtually all the other members. But it did confirm
Betty's Euro-credentials, and confirmed her as a prominent 'moderate'
in the party's political pantheon. This was a time when enthusiasm for
Europe was very much a Conservative trait. When Heath took Britain
into Europe in 1972, Labour, particularly the Left, was deeply suspicious of 'the capitalist club' of the EEC. The National Executive
had opposed going into Europe, and the Shadow Cabinet had
instructed MPs to oppose the principle of entry – though sixty-nine
defied the whip and voted with the Conservatives. But that had been
in Opposition. Now, they were in government, and could not afford
to ignore the institutions of Europe. Labour's hostility did not quite
disappear, however, and resurfaced disastrously in the 1983 General
Election to Betty's dismay.

Betty was still too ill to attend Parliament in mid March,[28] but she
was back on her feet in May, sponsoring a parliamentary Bill to give
local authorities powers to investigate price rises of goods in the shops.
Her Bill was introduced under the ten-minute rule, which allows backbenchers to move a private Bill on a subject of their choice. The
chances of such a Bill becoming law are negligible, but the procedure
(introduced in 1950 against the wishes of the Attlee government) does
give backbenchers an opportunity to air their grievances. The House
allows one private member's Bill to be introduced each Tuesday and
Wednesday, and limits the MP to a ten-minute introductory speech.
If there is a speech against, this too cannot go on for longer than ten
minutes. There is occasionally a vote, but it is very rare for a ten-
minute Bill to gain further parliamentary time and become law. All
backbenchers – more than 500 at any given time – can avail themselves
of this privilege, which allows them to bring to public attention an
issue close to their hearts. It is a popular avenue of parliamentary
protest. Pressure on the time available for ten-minute bills is so great
that MPs have been known to camp all night outside the Public Bill
office to get their issue debated.

In her role as the housewives' champion, Betty introduced a Consumer Protection Bill that would make a practical contribution to
fighting inflation. It would give trading standards officers powers to

make on-the-spot investigations into 'unnecessary' price rises. House-wives were often fed up and felt 'conned' by unjustifiable price rises, she told the Commons on 24 May. Nicholas Ridley, the hard-line free-market Tory MP for Cirencester and Tewkesbury (and later a senior minister in Mrs Thatcher's Cabinet) accused her of wanting a new rope to beat the backs of small shopkeepers. She believed the high price of pork was due to excess profits, but 'she could not tell the difference between pigmeat and a scapegoat'. Despite his ungallant remarks, Betty's Bill got a first reading by 192 votes to 179. She cele-brated her fourth anniversary as an MP in style, and told her electorate that if her measure was further approved in future readings, 'the attack on inflation can be made more positive and effective – for then the battle will be taken to the High Street itself.'[29] However, due to lack of parliamentary time, nothing further was heard of the Bill. It was something of an embarrassment for the Labour government, anyway, for it brought into the open dissatisfaction with the operation of the Price Commission, which was supposed to hold back price inflation but had a poor record of achievement.

Balked of a parliamentary prize, she turned back to the 'inner front', within the Labour Party. In late July, almost three months before the annual party conference was due, Betty figured in a new plot to dimin-ish the power of the Left in Labour's policy-making machinery. Right-wingers in the party set up a new pressure group, the Campaign for Labour Victory, in February 1977, with Bill Rodgers, MP for Stockton and junior minister at Defence until the previous year. He was later to be one of the infamous 'gang of four' who set up the SDP. In the eyes of some observers, the campaign carried 'none too distant' echoes of the old Campaign for Social Democracy that overthrew the party's commitment to nuclear disarmament in 1960. In Tony Benn's view CLV was no more than 'a cover for a Right-wing organization designed to clear the National Executive of some of its Left-wing members, of the women's section, and so on.'[30]

He was right. With the support of five Cabinet ministers, CLV lobbied fiercely for its list of moderate nominees for the national execu-tive, attacking the dominant Left-wing coalition. Since James Calla-ghan had been forced by the loss of his parliamentary majority into a pact with the Liberals in late March, the NEC was regarded by the

Left as 'of supreme importance because it is the only uncommitted part of the Labour Party'.[31] The government loyalists in CLV argued that a Labour administration with its back to the ropes had had to contend not only with the frontal attacks of the Tories, but also sly jabs from NEC members who were supposed to be in its own corner. In the women's section, the Campaign declared its support for Shirley Williams, Betty Boothroyd and Shirley Summerskill (MP for the adjoining Yorkshire seat of Halifax).

With the support of the moderate General and Municipal Workers' Union – secured by her long-standing friend and fellow tyke, David Warburton, the union's political officer – Betty was in a strong contending position. CLV's newssheet *Labour Victory* promised, 'This is the conference where the great fightback begins. Last year's conference [1976] was a disgrace to the party – a noisy shambles as delegate after delegate launched bitter, wrecking attacks on our Labour government just as it was grappling with a dramatic run on the pound which threatened its life. That crisis of confidence is well behind us now.'[32] The Campaign argued that a fundamental change in the composition of the national executive was essential to revive the party's internal health and strength. It urged support for Betty, 'well known as a party figure and a tough fighter' who was standing for the first time. In this respect, CLV was wrong. She had stood unsuccessfully the year before.

When the delegates cast their votes at Brighton on 4 October, it was the same old story. Apart from Shirley Williams, still in the Cabinet as Education Secretary, the moderates took a drubbing. Betty's vote actually went down on the year before, from 2,462,000 to 2,258,000. Worse, from the CLV's point of view, the Left on the national executive that week pushed through the principle of automatic re-selection of Labour MPs, by a majority of only two. The NEC also decided to propose changes in the election of the party leader, which until then had been the prerogative of the Parliamentary Labour Party. These radical reforms were to bring about a massive internal split and trigger the formation of the SDP. Labour's locust years were just around the corner.

Betty soon had other things on her mind: a storm in a teacup, in fact. A few days before Christmas 1977, she protested to Sir Peter Parker, Chairman of British Railways, that the tea and coffee on

Inter-City trains was 'undrinkable' and appeared to be composed of sweepings-up, 'warm water and grit'.[33] Early in the new year, it was a different kind of drink. In January 1978, she lambasted the government's own Prices Commission for allowing the Distillers Company to put up its wholesale prices by fifty per cent virtually overnight. It was 'unacceptable' that Distillers could bring in such a price hike simply to protect its overseas earnings, she said to cheers from Labour MPs, many of whom were angry about having to pay more for their own 'nippy sweetie'. That same month, she also protested about an 'unwarranted' devaluation of the EEC's Green Pound, the notional currency for agricultural products, brought about by the powerful farmers' lobby. This reform, she claimed, would leave housewives having to pay 2p in the pound more for tea, coffee, whisky and the weekly food basket: Betty was determined to live up to her title of the consumers' champion.

More critically important, she also joined a back-bench rebellion in January 1978, in which thirty-four Labour MPs joined with the Conservatives to vote down proposals for devolution in Scotland tabled by the government. She went into the 'Noes' lobby with all her old political enemies, including those who had defeated her in the national executive elections only four months previously. The effect of the vote was to insert in the devolution Bill a requirement that forty per cent of the Scottish electorate had to vote 'Yes' for the Act to be implemented. Betty's involvement in the 'Cunningham Rebellion' – named after George Cunningham, Labour MP for Islington South and Finsbury who tabled the successful amendment – was a puzzling business, explainable only by an aversion to devolution that she had not hitherto shown – in public, at any rate. Defeat in the Commons in a vote of confidence on this issue was eventually to bring down the Callaghan administration little more than a year later.

There were other diversions, and time for some travel. In the Easter parliamentary recess of 1978, Betty visited Japan and India at the invitation of the United Nations, as part of a new project concerned with the problems of population growth in poor countries. Betty welcomed the government's decision to declare much of her constituency a Derelict Land Clearance Area, qualifying the Black Country for a state-funded facelift. 'The eyesores round the Black Country certainly need to be removed and it is high time the plans were taken off the drawing board and the bulldozers put to work,' she said. 'Coming after this week's announcement that Sandwell is to have special urban programme status, it is a big boost.'[34]

A general election was on the cards for October 1978. Chancellor Denis Healey had got inflation down to seven per cent by June, the economy was in a healthy shape, and he believed he could make a five-per-cent pay norm 'stick' without the formal consent of the TUC. But Callaghan favoured delaying until the spring of 1979, hoping that growth in what is nowadays called 'the feel-good factor' would deliver an overall majority for Labour. He was heartily sick and tired of the squalid parliamentary deals that being the Prime Minister of a minority inevitably entailed. So he decided to soldier on through the winter.

There then followed one of the most clumsy episodes in post-war British politics. Callaghan went to the Trades Union Congress in Brighton that September to rally support for the government. A select band of TUC leaders had already been to see him at his farm in Sussex, and they came away convinced that he would announce his intention to go to the country to Congress, or at least give the unions a nod and a wink that an election was on the way. At the close of his speech, he sang the music-hall song 'There Was I, Waiting at the Church'. The closing lines, 'I can't marry you today, my wife won't let me', brought the house down.

But in the hilarity, most delegates missed the Prime Minister's serious point. With twenty–twenty hindsight, it is clear that Callaghan was actually hinting that he was not ready to go to the country. The unions did not read it like that. Initially, they believed that Callaghan was merely confirming the mistaken impression they had gained at his farmhouse: there would be an election that autumn, before the annual wage bargaining round was really under way, and therefore before the government's tight pay limit was put to the test. This fatal misunderstanding was a recipe for disaster, which duly came in the ensuing 'Winter of Discontent' when Ford workers bust the pay curb with a seventeen-per-cent settlement, opening the way to months of strikes. 'Our hubris in fixing a pay norm of five per cent without any support from the TUC met its nemesis, as inevitably as in any Greek tragedy,' confessed Labour's Chancellor, Denis Healey, later.[35]

The following month, at Labour's annual conference, Betty made her third attempt to gain election to the party's national executive. In what was now becoming an uncomfortable re-run of her attempt to get into parliament, she failed again. Her vote fell marginally, by 6000 to 2,252,000. She endured the Winter of Discontent in a discontent of her own, before the worst came.

In the new year of 1979, strikes by road-haulage and oil-tanker drivers, combined with widespread stoppages by public-service workers, made civilized life – particularly in the cities – well-nigh impossible. Rubbish piled high in the streets, and when grave-diggers stopped work the tabloid press screamed 'NOW WE CAN'T BURY OUR DEAD!' TUC leaders belatedly offered a 'solemn and binding' agreement on the conduct of future strikes, but it was too late. Harried by the Tories, who were increasingly confident and enjoying a consistent lead in the opinion polls under the leadership of Margaret Thatcher, the government staggered from crisis to crisis. By March 1979, recorded Healey, Callaghan was 'exhausted and dispirited'.

The government actually fell on a vote of confidence, the first time this had happened since 1925. Callaghan called a General Election for 3 May. It was a rout. Betty survived at West Bromwich East, with her majority cut from 14,799 to 9468 in a three-cornered fight with the Conservatives and the National Front. Nationally, Labour suffered its worst disaster since 1931. Margaret Thatcher entered Downing Street with a parliamentary majority of forty-one seats over all other parties. Tony Benn noted grimly in his diary, 'A dramatic day in British politics. The most Right-wing Conservative government and leader for fifty years; the first woman prime minister. I cannot absorb it all.'[36]

CHAPTER VII

EYES ON THE PRIZE

O N 9 MAY 1979, taking her seat on the Opposition back-
benches for the first time in more than five years, the newly
returned member for West Bromwich West surveyed a political scene very little to her liking. Across the Chamber, at the head
of a Conservative government committed to rolling back all that
Labour had achieved, Mrs Thatcher revelled in her power: a power
that had, to some degree, been given her on a plate by the forces
within the Labour Party against which Betty had struggled for years.
Around her were the remnants of a defeated government, MPs seemingly incapable of wresting the initiative from the hard-Left, which was
now gathering its strength for a three-pronged constitutional attack
designed to make Labour a truly socialist party ultimately controlled
by its grass roots.

The Left's three objectives were: to strip MPs of their exclusive
rights to choose the party leader, and replace the traditional system
with an electoral college involving the unions and the local parties; to
introduce mandatory re-selection of Labour MPs, so that no one had
a seat for life; and to make the party's national executive alone responsible for drafting the general election manifesto, thereby removing the
leader's veto on policy. The cost of engaging in such a power struggle
was obvious. Denis Healey recalled, 'There followed ten years of
internal fighting which was quite as damaging to the Party as the
decade of struggle with Bevanism after Attlee lost power.'[1]

For one who had exhibited such an interest in 'mixing it' with the
hard-Left, and who might justifiably have looked for a junior, or even
middle-ranking Opposition front-bench posting, the better to pursue
her political instincts, Betty chose an unusual course at this stage in

her career. But it was a choice pregnant with meaning. She allowed her name to go on to the Chairmen's Panel, a select group of around two dozen MPs who take on the unglamorous but vital work of chairing Commons committees. For the most part, ambitious MPs hungry for office and power avoid these jobs, preferring to be even a Shadow Minister's dogsbody to the publicity-free zone of chairing a standing committee.

But these committees have been likened by a former leader of the House, John Biffen MP, to 'a miniature House of Commons'. Flanked by clerks and officials, the chairman sits at one end and has powers similar to those of the Speaker. Getting on to the panel is the first rung on the tortuous ladder to the Speaker's Chair. Bernard (now Lord) Weatherill was the chairman of the Chairmen's panel after the 1979 election. In due course, he was to become Speaker himself. Betty's name appeared on the official list little more than six weeks after polling day, on 20 June 1979. She was one of only two women, and the only Labour woman. The other woman was Miss (now Dame) Janet Fookes, MP for Plymouth Drake, who twelve years later was to be canvassed among Conservative MPs as the only possible woman contender who might halt the Betty bandwagon.

Taking her place on the Chairmen's Panel may have removed her from the hurly-burly of the Commons, but it did not disqualify her from politicking. Betty stood again for the party's national executive in October 1979, but again failed to win a seat, though her vote increased by more than 600,000 to 2,861,000. It must have been slightly galling that the one new female face on the NEC was that of her old friend Jo Richardson, now chairman of the 'soft-Left' Tribune group, who leapfrogged the runners-up to take Barbara Castle's seat, vacated by her transference to the European parliament. The national executive swung even further to the Left at the party conference in Brighton that month, and though the Bennites failed to take control of the manifesto, they did win mandatory re-selection of MPs. Henceforth, Betty would be constantly looking over her shoulder at what was happening in her constituency. West Bromwich West was not a particularly large party – around 200 – and though her standing with the voters was high, her pro-Common Market, tough-Right stance risked a Left-wing backlash.

Back at the Commons, her steady progress brought her membership of the Select Committee on Foreign Affairs, a high-profile body of MPs who scrutinize the foreign policy of the government of the day. She was also a member of its Overseas Development Sub-Committee. Of necessity, because much of her time was taken up chairing parliamentary committees, her interventions in parliamentary debates became less frequent, but her voice was still heard when issues close to her heart were being discussed.

In January 1980, Betty opposed the government's move to close down the Prices Commission, arguing that the simple fact of its existence had often deterred those who wanted to put up prices. In a debate on employment in March, she said the government, by its policies and actions, 'have shown neither concern for the future of Britain as an industrial nation, nor compassion for the people who worked in industry'. In her own area, a new study showed that more than 11,000 school leavers would be coming on to the unemployment register at a time when jobs for unskilled and semi-skilled had 'contracted enormously'.

However, her steady shift to the Right of the party brought sharp criticism from the Left. On Saturday 15 March 1980, Betty appeared at a 'fringe' meeting for the Campaign for Labour Victory at Labour's south–west regional conference in Exeter. To the embarrassment of the platform, Tony Benn was in the audience. He later wrote, 'Betty made an awful speech about how we need a radical policy but we can't be too far ahead of public opinion.'[2]

In what way was it radical? Betty argued that there was a great attraction to private investment in public industry and perhaps Labour should give people a share or 'divvy' in the nationalized industries. Apart from the 'divvy' idea, which was a straight pinch from her experience of the Co-op thirty years previously, this speech now reads like mainstream Labour policy – particularly the private–public investment link-up. The rest of her remarks was similarly prophetic: 'We want to create a society on the basis of a consumer democracy. We have got to strike the right balance between individual and collective rights.'

This was Betty at her instinctual best. She has never invited regard as an original, or even a deep, political thinker, but she has always had a gut feeling of what the ordinary voter wants. Those few lines, reported nowhere but in Benn's diaries, marked out her values and the nature of her appeal at a time when Labour was consumed with internal self-doubt and constitutional wrangling. The speech may well have been written for her by one of the CLV's bright young things, but even so it was Betty who had the nerve to stand up and say it out loud when it was least popular.

It was 'awful' to Tony Benn, and unquestionably out of tune with the party's Left-wing song-sheet, but that was the kind of thing the voters were prepared to listen to. Instead, the party drew up its full-blooded socialist statement, *Peace, Jobs and Freedom*, which contained 'most, though not all' of the policies that Benn had been campaigning for throughout the 1970s. It was endorsed at a special one-day conference at Wembley on 30 May 1980 by 5,000,000 votes to 6000.

By July 1980, Betty was being billed in *The Times* as one of 'Five women who could change the shape of Labour's future'. A feature article by one of the paper's intellectual leader writers, Geoffrey Smith, suggested that the trade unions were about to slacken their allegiance to the traditional horsetrading of you-vote-for-mine-and-I'll-vote-for-yours that had long dominated the election of the five women members of the national executive. Faced with the relentless onslaught of the Left, it was argued, moderate union leaders of the engineering workers, the GMWU general workers, the electricians, the shopworkers, the postmen, the railwaymen and the steel workers had joined forces to change the political balance of the NEC. Smith acknowledged that there had been only too many similar false dawns in recent years to have any great confidence this time.[3]

His reticence was amply justified. Standing as usual in the women's section in the elections at the October conference in Blackpool, Betty was runner-up but still a long way behind. On the policy front, the Left had a virtual clean sweep. The conference voted by 5,000,000 to 2,000,000 to withdraw from the Common Market. Mandatory re-selection was approved. Unilateral nuclear disarmament was carried overwhelmingly. By a narrow majority, the current system of drawing up the manifesto was endorsed, but delegates voted in principle to change the system of choosing Labour's leader and deputy leader.

This was a major new departure in British politics. Hitherto, the

choice of leader of the party had been the sole prerogative of Labour
MPs. Unrelenting pressure from the Left had now shifted this privilege
out to the unions and the party activists. There would be an 'electoral
college' in which MPs would share the right to determine who might
be a future Labour prime minister. The party was in chaos. Jim Callaghan threatened to stage his own leadership contest, with only MPs
voting, and warned Tony Benn, 'the Parliamentary Party will never
accept a Leader foisted on them'.

Once the principle of the electoral college had been agreed, the
fight over its composition began. Moderates seeking to salvage something from the wreckage of Blackpool wanted to give Labour MPs
half the votes, with the rest divided equally between the unions and
the constituency parties. The Left wanted as big a role as possible for
the unions and the CLPs, which were their power base. The argument
raged for another three months as arrangements were made for a
special conference, again at Wembley, to determine the outcome of
the power struggle.

Meanwhile, the social democrats within the party who had been
watching events with mounting horror and disbelief, began to gather
round the standard of Roy Jenkins. Labour's former Chancellor had
been plotting since the summer of 1980 to set up a Social Democratic
Party, on continental lines, shorn of the hard-Left and Labour's
umbilical links with the trade unions. In fact, the initiative went back
to the late 1970s, when the plotters' aim had been to install Jenkins
as leader of the Labour Party. Their convivial chats, Lord (David)
Owen has revealed, 'continued from time to time . . . usually at Harry
Walston's flat in Albany'.[4] There is no record of Betty ever attending
such gatherings at the home of her former employer, where she worked
until 1973.

The new year brought quite different news. On 10 January 1981, it
was announced that Betty had been appointed to the board of Thorn
Lighting as a non-executive director for three years. For some time
she had been a co-sponsor of the all-party parliamentary Lighting
Group associated with the Lighting Industry Federation, the industry's
trade body. The story only made a paragraph. Three weeks later she
would be on the front page of *The Times*.

In the interim, on 24 January 1981, Labour's special Wembley conference, after a day of classic Labour movement confusion, approved a formula for the composition of Labour's leadership electoral college. The Left had won hands down. The unions were to have the lion's share of the votes – forty per cent. The rest were to be divided equally between constituency parties and the parliamentary parties – thirty per cent each. In common with other Labour MPs, Betty's role in the leadership contest had been devalued overnight. Tony Benn confided to his diary: 'It will never be reversed, and nothing will be the same again.'[5] He was wrong on the first count, right on the second.

Appalled and self-satisfied in approximately equal measure, the Social Democrats moved quickly. The next day, the 'Gang of Four' – Jenkins, David Owen, Shirley Williams and Bill Rodgers – announced in the 'Limehouse Declaration' their formation of a Council for Social Democracy. Thirteen MPs immediately rallied to their cause, followed immediately by Lord George Brown, who had so often made a nuisance of himself at Betty's parliamentary elections.

On 2 February, Mrs Williams said she was going to quit Labour's national executive. In its splash story, *The Times* pointed out the next day that she would be succeeded by Betty, who had been runner-up in the women's section poll the previous October. A week later, Shirley Williams quit, agonizing in a letter to party general secretary Ron Hayward, 'I believe the party I loved and worked for over so many years no longer exists.'[6] Betty had no such qualms. She took the seat. She was fifty-one, and it was success at the fifth go, as it had been in her battle to enter parliament.

The question must be asked: why did Betty not follow where so many of her mentors had gone? Harry Walston had been one of the original Jenkins plotters, and he did not hesitate before joining the Council for Social Democracy, which was shortly to become the SDP. Bill Rodgers, Chairman of the Campaign for Labour Victory, which supported Betty's NEC bid the previous year, was one of the breakaway Gang of Four. The Social Democrats were pro-Europe, believers in a mixed economy, upholders of the consumer society and individualism, and pro-NATO. It would have been difficult put a credit card between their views and Betty's.

Yet she held aloof, loyal to Dewsbury rather than Albany. Oliver Walston, who joined the party his father helped to create says, 'He was instrumental in this, and Betty was not. There was no hint of any personal animosity at all. At no point did Betty feel she had been betrayed, still less did my father feel that she should have followed his example. She was on the right of the Labour Party, there was precious little between them but Betty's roots were in the Labour Party – and that is where she stayed. I am unaware that she was ever tempted.'[7] Much later, when the SDP was in its death throes, Betty and Oliver clashed over the issue. Oliver Walston argued that if she and like-minded Right-wingers had joined the Social Democrats, the Labour Party would have been reformed 'that much quicker'. With character-istic vigour, Betty replied, 'Hell, no! If you had stayed in the Labour Party, it would have been reformed that much quicker.'

Staying put brought its own political price. Betty did not have to wait long for the hard-Left's reformists to come looking for her. She must have been expecting them. As far back as October 1979 there had been reports of a Labour extremists' black-list naming a 'doomed dozen' moderate Labour MPs regarded as ripe for ousting from their seats. The *Sunday Express* revealed that she was 'said to be included' on the list.[8] Fanciful reports apart, Betty was a natural target for the Left. In April 1981, with the ink on the reforms barely dry, she had to stand for re-selection in her West Bromwich West constituency party. She received twelve nominations, while John Edwards, a Sandwell borough councillor, received eight nominations. Edwards, a fireman, was chairman of the area Tribune Group of socialists. He was a popular, young Left-winger cast very much in the mould of the reformers. In other words, he spelled danger.

The party's constituency executive decided to invite both candidates to a re-selection meeting. After frantic overnight moves, a meeting of the larger, more 'organized' general management committee was called for the next day. By twenty-three votes to twenty-one, the GMC decided to overturn the executive's recommendation and have a short-list of only one: Betty. 'That was the test,' said Edwards later. 'The same general management committee would have carried through the re-selection. If they had voted for a short-list of two, it would have meant there was a majority for me . . . She was fighting for her life. She knew how important it was. It didn't half frighten her. OK, she won and she kept her job. But the fact is, a couple of votes the other way and she could have lost it. And in all fairness, losing your seat if you are an MP, it's your whole life gone west.'[9] Unprompted, he added: 'She is a very pessimistic candidate. She always expects the worst. She's very jittery. She's an appalling woman to have around in elections. Not a good candidate, always expecting the worst. It may be that she has experienced the worst.' Others, including her most recent constituency agent Paul Jackson, say similar things. Jackson agreed, 'Betty is always convinced she is going to lose.'[10]

The incident rankled in West Bromwich. Betty's constituency agent, Bob Steventon, resigned in protest. 'If you have only one candidate, the re-selection is more or less a formality,' he complained. 'I have resigned as agent of the party, but not in protest against Miss Boothroyd, because I have no argument with her. If she had been selected in a fair contest, I would have been happy to fight for her.'[11]. He said further, 'You hear a lot about the narrow-mindedness of the Left posing a threat to democracy, but last night showed the narrow-mindedness of the Right and people who do not normally attend meetings and it was a defeat for democracy. When the Labour Party decided to democratize itself, it did not really want to see shortlists of one.'[12]

Betty regretted the loss of an 'incredibly efficient agent', but safely nominated, added, 'There has been an element in the Labour Party which has been shouting for mandatory re-selection for years, but when the process goes against what they want, they protest.' She spoke a little too soon. A week later, the national executive's organization sub-committee refused to confirm her re-selection. The 'OrgCom' said local party members should have more time to protest about selections if they wanted to. Despite objections from the new Labour leader, Michael Foot, and his deputy Denis Healey, the issue was deferred . At the end of April, Betty's re-selection was approved by the full NEC by twenty-nine votes to seven, a comfortable majority.

There was pressure to reopen the debate on shortlists of one, which rapidly became adopted by some moderate local parties as a neat way round mandatory re-selection. But Betty stayed put, and has never been challenged since, though she did make secret moves with her local opponent before the 1992 election, to ensure a free run in the poll critical to her ambitions to become Speaker. By now, she was in some demand by the tabloids for rent-a-quote appearances, and occasionally she was happy to oblige. Responding to reports that the Communist Party might press for a closer relationship with Labour, Betty told the *Daily Star*, 'Even to think of allowing the Communists in is a sure way of digging our grave.'

On the NEC, Betty was very much in a political minority . In July 1981, she was one of only three who opposed unilateral dismantling of all nuclear bases – British and American – on home soil and in territorial waters. Michael Foot pleaded with the NEC not to tie his hands, disclosing that he was about to visit Moscow to talk about disarmament with the Soviet government. It was an echo of his hero Nye Bevan's plea not to send him naked into the conference chamber, but it cut little ice with the Left. Betty was isolated with Denis Healey and John Golding, Right-wing leader of the post-office engineers, who was later forced to resign after 'kiss and tell' revelations by a prostitute.

Thankfully, there were other issues nearer her political heart to get steamed up about. In late July, Betty intervened in the shocking case of an eleven-year-old girl who was brought to trial in the Old Bailey, charged with stealing an iced cake and a doughnut. She was so small that her head could barely be seen over the wooden walls of the dock at the Central Criminal Court. A furious Betty thundered, 'It is shameful that a child of this age should have to go through a traumatic experience like this.'[13] She demanded that the Lord Chancellor, Lord Hailsham, should ensure that it did not happen again. The child, charged with her mother, was freed when the shop offered no evidence. In August, she was busy with an old bee in her bonnet – rising prices, this time petrol – in a complaint to Trade Secretary John Biffen. He did nothing.

With the autumn came the usual season of political dogfights for the executive, plus the added, frightening (for her) prospect of Tony Benn becoming deputy leader of the party. He did not get Betty's vote, but he did come within a whisker of realizing his ambition, taking 49.5 per cent of the electoral college vote to Healey's 50.5 per cent.

In September, *The Times* reported that moderate union leaders had drawn up a new 'hit-list' aimed at breaking the power of the Left on the national executive. They claimed a substantial success – five extra seats, by their reckoning. Betty was one of their favoured candidates.[14] This time, aided by the moderate union coalition, she made it in her own right, winning one of the five women's seats with a vote of 3,793,000 and coming second in her section. Her success earned her a place on the Organization Committee, a dubious honour since this was the body (chaired by Eric Heffer) that would have to begin the fight to rid the party of its incubus, the Militant Tendency. In November 1981, the OrgCom shied away from investigating Militant. Betty voted for the investigation, in a minority of two with John Golding. But she had put a marker down for the ensuing battle. It began in earnest the following month, when Foot's demand for an inquiry into Militant and the scale of its operations within Labour was approved by the full national executive by nineteen votes to ten – the most potent sign yet that the moderates were beginning to reverse the political tide.

Less than a year after succeeding Shirley Williams, Betty's voting pattern was now firmly entrenched. In Parliament, she was a member of the Right-wing Manifesto Group that was struggling to hang on to some kind of credibility with Labour's traditional supporters. On the national executive, she was part of the Right-wing loyalist core that sometimes fell as low as two or three votes – but could always be relied upon by the leadership. As crisis followed crisis in Labour's ruling circles, she set her face against the hard-Left. She supported moves to prevent the Militant-backed Pat Wall from becoming MP for Bradford North, and lost. She voted for the exclusion of Left-wing gay-rights activist Peter Tatchell, inglorious loser at the Bermondsey by-election, and won. When the hard-Left published voting figures on key political issues in 1980–82, she was one of only five members with straight 'A's (against). She began moving up the hierarchy, winning seats on the Home Policy, Organization, International, Press and Publicity Committee, Youth and Women's Committees.

In the new year of 1982, a truce of sorts was called between the warring factions. The Left agreed to go into the next election with the Foot–Healey leadership and the policies of the 1981 conference. David Basnett, General Secretary of the GMWU (Betty's sponsoring union) announced that 'peace has broken out' in the party. His choice of military words was apt, but premature. On 2 April 1982, General Galtieri's troops invaded the Falkland Islands. The invasion re-ignited hostilities within the Labour Party. Mrs Thatcher sent to the south

Atlantic a Task Force which, after much fighting, reoccupied the islands at a cost of more than a thousand British and Argentinian lives.

Once again, Labour was divided. Michael Foot, realizing that public opinion was overwhelmingly on the side of Mrs Thatcher's military solution, wanted to steer a cautious line somewhere between pacifism and the jingoism that was sweeping the country. The Left, arguing that this was a war to save Thatcher's face and restore her opinion-poll ratings, wanted a cease-fire and withdrawal of the Task Force. When the NEC's International Committee met at Walworth Road on 11 May, the cruiser *Belgrano* had just been sunk with huge loss of life. Judith Hart MP moved that Labour call for a truce with Argentina. Foot, supported by Denis Healey, wanted a more woolly formula seeking a settlement through the United Nations.

The meeting deteriorated into a shambles, with Eric Heffer, the Left-wing MP from Liverpool, becoming angry and shouting. Finally, Joan Lestor MP, in the chair, announced that she was going to make a ruling that she would accept a motion by Betty Boothroyd, seconded by Gwyneth Dunwoody. Betty moved 'the previous question'. This is a procedural device to bring debate to a halt. It was carried by eight votes to four, and effectively gave Michael Foot a free hand to do as he liked. Benn noted sadly in his diary, 'That is the first time in twenty-three years on the NEC that I have ever known a chairman accept a motion to prevent a vote.'[15]

With such a volume of party work and the onerous duty of chairing parliamentary committees, Betty might have eased up on her Commons appearances. But she was still there, fighting the same old causes. In February 1982, she introduced another ten-minute-rule Bill, this time giving the Trade Secretary powers to control the prices of essential goods and services. These were powers he most emphatically did not want. The Bill was given a formal first reading, but got no further. The debate did, however, allow Betty to point out that under the Tories, gas bills had gone up by 100 per cent and electricity by 70 per cent. National Insurance charges had also virtually doubled to £13.50 a week. Asking the government to safeguard prices, she roared, was like putting the train robbers in charge of silver vaults. She also called for legislation to prevent children getting hold of solvent-based glues

By midsummer of 1982, the national executive had settled into a new voting routine. The Right-wing camp could usually count on the support of a 'soft-Left' group, whose chief figure was Neil Kinnock, MP for Bedwellty and a Foot loyalist. The soft-Left/moderate coalition could normally muster a working majority in support of Foot. The prospect of an early 'khaki' general election, with Mrs Thatcher going to the country as the Falklands victor, was concentrating MPs' minds wonderfully.

In late June, at a seven-hour meeting, Foot tackled the issue of Militant head on. It was a secret conspiracy, he argued, and an appalling distraction from Labour's main task of attacking the government. The party's inquiry proposed the setting up of a register of politically acceptable groups, with the clear understanding that Militant would be unacceptable. This was approved by sixteen votes to ten, and afterwards Betty described the result as 'a boost for party morale'.[16]

On the eve of the party conference in Blackpool in late September 1982, Betty spoke at a fringe meeting organized by the Labour Solidarity Campaign, successor to the discredited Campaign for Labour Victory whose leading lights had left for the SDP. Sharing a platform with James Callaghan, Roy Hattersley and Peter Shore, she warned that the party would ignore at its peril the conclusions of the national executive's investigation into Militant. The Tendency was an unrepresentative minority shrouding Labour's real intent. Delegates evidently agreed with her, voting in the new register by a five-to-one majority. Expulsion of 'the Mils' was bound to follow.

Foot loyalists made more gains in the NEC elections that year, and Betty was edged into third place in the women's section, though her vote went up marginally to 3,794,000. The new Right/soft-Left majority coalition lost no time in making clear they were the masters now. Three weeks after the party conference, Betty was part of a coup against the Left that shocked even the most experienced political hands. In the 'Walworth Road massacre' of 27 October, Betty's old comrade in arms John Golding took on the role of chief purger. First, he ousted Tony Benn and Dame Judith Hart from the TUC–Labour Party Liaison Committee and substituted himself and Betty. Then, reported the *Daily Telegraph*, 'The purge rolled on, committee by committee.'[17] There was no quarter given. The Left lost every position

it held in the national executive committee structure. The power it
had sedulously built up over a decade vanished overnight.

Betty did not flinch from getting her hands dirty in this political
struggle. Indeed, she went further. She tabled a resolution to the
national executive demanding the curtailment of party study groups
because the emphasis should now be on gearing up for the impending
general election. The hard-Left *Labour Herald* described Betty's
move as 'sinister'. 'I suspect that first on her list would be the
women's rights study group,' wrote Janet Pickering. 'It was hoping
to tackle the problems of personal politics, an important area to
which Labour has so far regrettably given scant attention.'[18] Labour's
hard-line feminists plainly felt they had nothing to gain from Betty's
ascendancy.

All attention was now focused on the general election, which Mrs
Thatcher was expected to call when it best suited her and which Labour
was entering with a double handicap: a leader who 'simply did not
look like a potential Prime Minister'[19] and a manifesto designed to
appease virtually all sections of the party but alienate large sections of
the electorate, memorably described by Gerald Kaufman as 'the
longest suicide note in history'.

With inflation at a fifteen-year low, and a giveaway Budget under
their belts, the Tories were, not surprisingly, way ahead in the opinion
polls. Mrs Thatcher went to the country on 9 June. If 1979 was a
disaster, then 1983 was a political holocaust for Labour. Betty retained
her seat, with her majority slashed by more than 3000 votes to 6639.
The swing to the Tories in West Bromwich West was 7.7 per cent.
But nationally, the Labour vote fell by 3,000,000. Its share of the
popular vote – 27.6 per cent – was little more than two per cent higher
than the Liberal/SDP Alliance. The Tories now had a majority of 144,
the largest since Labour's post-war landslide in 1945.

Though she had still managed to win just over fifty per cent of the
popular vote in West Bromwich, Betty could see the political writing
on the wall. Soon after the election, she said out loud what many MPs
(and not a few union leaders) had been saying long before polling day:
that Michael Foot had been a 'disaster' as party leader, that Labour
must rid itself of the Militant incubus, and that the party must totally
recast its policies if it was ever able to become re-electable again. Her

comments made the front page of the *Daily Telegraph*, with a headline on the 'disaster' quote.[20]

As it quickly became clear on 12 June that Foot would step down, and there would be a two-horse race between Neil Kinnock and Roy Hattersley to succeed him, Betty said, 'What is needed is a solemn commitment from anybody in the leadership stakes that they will get rid of the headbangers in the party, and by that I mean the extremists and the Militants. There must also be a total reappraisal of party policy.'

Her characteristically forthright assessment went down well at Westminster, where Labour MPs were still reeling with shock. But there was a hostile reaction from the Tribune group in her constituency. Her old political sparring partner Councillor John Edwards called her comments 'deplorable'. It was unfortunate, he said, that she should choose to make a public attack on fellow party members, giving fuel to a hostile press. He assumed that the 'headbangers and extremists' were readers of *Militant* newspaper, yet only a few days previously these very same people were on the streets working to get her elected. 'There was no talk then of them leaving the party, and they were not told to go away and stop working for her.'[21] A fair point, perhaps, but not one that would weigh strongly in Betty's forthcoming jihad against Militant.

More to the point, Edwards said her calls for policy change did tremendous damage to the party because she had fought the election in support of its policy. 'If Miss Boothroyd cannot say anything constructive, she would really do better to say nothing,' he argued. This was wishful thinking. Betty may have fought on the manifesto, because she was obliged to. But she manifestly did not believe in it.

As a committed member of the leader-loyalist group on the National Executive Committee, she was dedicated to breaking the power of the Left, and had consistently opposed most of the hard-line commitments in the manifesto: unilateralism, hostility to the European Community and all the rest of the ideological baggage with which the Left had lumbered the party. John Golding, then Labour MP for Newcastle-under-Lyme, her political ally, was the unofficial (but nonetheless effective) whip for the leader-loyalist group. He said later, 'We put everything that the party conference decided into the manifesto. We knew we were going to be beaten. We may as well be beaten on this rubbish, and we were beaten on the rubbish.'[22] As leader, Foot was 'out of this world', he added. 'He had no idea how to fight a campaign at all.'

Betty returned to the fray two weeks later. In a speech to her local party in Wednesbury, she said Labour had to 'listen to the people' if it was to win back support. 'If the Labour Party is to make itself acceptable again to majority opinion, there is a need for a major rethink of the party's programme and its approach to the electorate.' Reminding party activists that Labour now had the smallest number of seats in the Commons since 1935, she warned, 'Nationally, we obtained the lowest popular vote in sixty years – millions of supporters deserted us. To recapture their confidence requires a serious study of the party's decline in its appeal to the electorate. In the process of winning back support we have to show a greater readiness to listen to what people have to say. The party of the people cannot turn a deaf ear to them.'[23]

She did not have long to wait. On 11 July, Labour's Home Policy Committee met at Westminster, and Geoff Bish, the party's head of research, presented a paper on 'policy development' proposing a radical streamlining of policy-making procedures in the wake of the election disaster. Bish, according to Golding, had been 'taken aback that the rubbish was put to the people and rejected', and was in a penitent frame of mind. His paper, in Tony Benn's assessment[24] conceded the view of Betty and her colleagues on the Labour Right, that 'we don't listen to the people, and that our policy is too inward looking'. Benn himself criticized the document, but it found a ready echo with Betty, and its themes were approved at a special meeting of the NEC on 12 September, shortly before the party conference in Brighton.

There, she was re-elected to the national executive with an increased majority; in fact, she topped the poll in the women's section with 4,834,000 votes, almost 100,000 clear of her nearest rival Mrs Ann Clwyd. In the other (rather more important) poll at conference, Neil Kinnock won the leadership with a huge majority on the first ballot, while Roy Hattersley, fellow tyke, political soul-mate and another West Midlands MP, was an easy winner for the deputy leadership after the Transport Workers' delegation defied an executive council instruction and voted for him. The election was run under the rules of the electoral college, but the Left's faith in this instrument as a means of political advancement proved misplaced.

1984 was dominated by one major social and political confrontation: the miners' strike. However, though Betty was of working-class stock, and hailed from a town that in her childhood teemed with colliers, she seems to have had virtually nothing to do with the dispute. It is a fair assumption that she disliked Arthur Scargill, the miners' leader and a close political associate of Tony Benn (who she 'hated', according to John Golding). There is no record of her speaking out against pit closures, though she did take up the cudgels on behalf of the civil servants at GCHQ, the Government's spy station, who had been sacked for refusing to tear up their union membership cards.

The pit strike dominated the early part of Labour's conference week at Blackpool in October and, after a lull, surfaced obliquely yet again on the final Friday morning when Betty was charged with replying to a debate on civil liberties on behalf of the national executive. There were three motions: one on GCHQ; one demanding a legal right of reply for all victims of distortion by the press and media and strengthening the Press Council (which Betty said had 'all the authority of a vegetarian in a slaughterhouse'); and a third, Composite 17, moved by the Society of Labour Lawyers.

This last motion strongly condemned 'the increasing use of the legal system for political ends' and recognized the 'serious deterioration of civil liberties in Britain today'.[25] It singled out 'the abuse of police powers in the miners' dispute', including well-publicized restrictions on the movements of miners, the 'clearly undemocratic use' of a centrally directed police force, the denial of bail, the 'persistent issue' of firearms and interception of telephones and mail.

In her response to the debate on all three motions, Betty virtually ignored the miners, though their plight had provoked most comment. 'In relation to Composite 17, which deals with the increasing power of the state and the need to see that power diminished, there *is* the power to stop motorists in Kent on suspicion that they are pickets on their way to Nottinghamshire. There *is* the power to detain a suspect for four days without recourse to a solicitor.'[26] And that was it. Less than one paragraph out of fourteen in her response. No word of condemnation for the police tactics or the attacks on miners' civil liberties. No word of sympathy for their plight, even though 100,000 men and their families were now beginning to see defeat and humiliation stare them in the face.

By contrast, Betty waxed lyrical over the sacrifice of the dozen or so GCHQ workers dismissed for defending union rights. 'There has been one erosion of civil liberties during the past year that was more shocking than anything else, and that was the persecution of the trade unionists at Cheltenham. We welcome them warmly today – we are delighted you have taken the trouble to be with us here in Blackpool. [Applause]

'Those people from GCHQ and our comrade we heard from today are the only substantial group of civilians in Britain today who are forbidden to promote a trade union, to found a trade union, to belong to a trade union. For them to do any of those things means a loss of job, it means having to move a home they have lived in for many years and were probably born in, it means uprooting their families. "Go somewhere else," says Big Sister, "we don't trust you. We don't want you. You can't stay here."

'One hundred and fifty years later, it is Tolpuddle all over again, and we won't have it! [Applause] Let's face it, comrades, governments – even Labour governments – rarely confer liberties; they are more inclined to take them away. I think, I hope, I believe that the next Labour government will be different.

'We badly need a Department of Justice – not one that rides roughshod over human dignity – but one that will nurture and develop human rights. Not one that will say the people *must* do that, but that says the law to be obeyed has to be a just law which protects civil liberties as it serves the interests of our people.' She sat down to prolonged applause, but by what she had not said as much as by what she had said, Betty had clearly indicated where her sympathies lay.

There were other battles to fight. In May 1984, Betty was one of twenty signatories to a Commons motion condemning plans to introduce harp music to the Harcourt room, a candle-lit dining suite at the Houses of Parliament where MPs could have a quiet conversation over dinner. The idea had been put forward by Charles Irving, Conservative MP for Cheltenham and Chairman of the Commons Catering

Committee. He wanted a harpist playing there in the evenings. Betty did not, and she was in some strange company, including Enoch Powell. Her fellow West Bromwich MP, Peter Snape, thought better of the idea, but suggested a jazz trio or quartet. Nothing more was heard of the harpist.

Betty featured in a lurid *Sunday Times* report that summer, headlined '2 5 LABOUR MPS FACE TAKEOVER BY LEFT-WING'.[27] Reporter Martin Kettle said Neil Kinnock had been warned of 'hard-Left moves' in the constituencies to dismiss twenty-five sitting MPs before the general election. The warning came from the Right-wing Labour Solidarity group, of which Betty was subsequently said to be a member.

Her own name figured in the 'hit list', along with some curious inclusions such as Norman Atkinson, the Left-wing MP for Tottenham, and (more understandably) Geoffrey Lofthouse, MP for Pontefract and Castleford, who was to become Betty's Deputy Speaker. The *Sunday Times* did not appear to grasp that Betty had already been re-selected by her local party, in March, by a margin of thirty-six votes to one.

At the time, Kinnock was under pressure to introduce 'one member, one vote' balloting for the re-selection of sitting MPs, and the *Sunday Times* story was clearly part of that campaign. It was almost a decade before 'OMOV' was finally agreed, under John Smith, but Betty survived nonetheless. Indeed, she flourished, despite attempts by groups such as the Campaign for Labour Party Democracy to oust her from the national executive.

CLPD published the voting record of the entire executive on seven key issues in 1983/84. Betty was one of only six NEC members (including Neil Kinnock and Roy Hattersley) who scored straight 'A's – Against the Left – on all seven issues, some of which were so arcane as to beggar description (like the appointment of a regional organizer in Wales) but all of which were regarded as politically barometric. She also appeared on another Left-wing hit list prepared by the Campaign group of Labour MPs. CLPD called on its supporters to oust Betty, but she was re-elected with a healthy vote of 4,607,000, third in the women's section behind her old friend Mrs Gwyneth Dunwoody. Betty immediately showed her mettle by voting for Neville Hough, an official of her sponsor union the GMB, against Dennis Skinner, the hard-Left

NUM sponsored MP, in the contest for vice-chairman of the party. On this occasion, the moderates failed. Skinner got the job, and went on to have his year of glory as chairman of the party, and performed very well.

In Parliament, 1985 was a largely uneventful year. In March, Betty told the Commons that for every year Mrs Thatcher had been office, 1000 jobs had been lost in her constituency. The total was now more than 7000, 'and they and their neighbours are sick and tired of being told that Britain is in the fourth year of economic recovery. The Black Country has yet to experience this recovery.'[28]

The issue of 'Smith Houses' – properties that look like conventional houses but are built of concrete blocks – brought Betty to her feet for a late-night intervention on 18 June 1985. She represented 189 families in her constituency who had bought Smith houses from the council, and now found the wall units were cracking and they were unsaleable. In the country as a whole, there were 4500 such homes, some owner-occupied, some tenanted and the government could not abnegate responsibility for the defects. She demanded 'natural justice, and no less'. The Housing Minister responsible, Sir George Young, an agreeable Tory 'wet', was wisely sympathetic and promised help.[29]

It came five months later, only a week after she was reconfirmed as a member of the Chairmen's Panel (still one of only two women). In November, Betty was told in a written answer from Environment Minister John Patten that the government would very shortly announce that owners of defective Smith houses would be given a statutory right to sell them back to the councils from which they had bought them. The *Guardian* hailed this as 'a victory for MPs led by Miss Betty Boothroyd'.[30]

But 1985 was memorable more for what took place outside Parliament than what happened on the floor of the House. In the wake of the election, and Betty's comments about 'extremists and Militants', pressure was building up for the leadership to strike hard at the Militant Tendency. At the party conference in Bournemouth in October, Kinnock made his famous speech denouncing Liverpool City Council, Militant's stronghold, excoriating them for 'playing politics with people's jobs'.

Kinnock stormed, 'Implausible promises don't win victories. You end up in the grotesque chaos of a Labour council hiring taxis to scuttle around a city handing out redundancy notices to its own workers.' Eric Heffer walked off the platform, Tony Benn, seeking to comfort a crying woman delegate, found himself in tears. The Left sensed what was coming: a political purge. The Right, led by Betty's political ally on the NEC, Ken Cure of the engineering workers' union, now urged an investigation leading to action. Betty concurred, 'We have a duty to the party to examine any individual who appears on a Militant platform. The NEC has a duty to investigate.'[31]

In November 1985, the national executive duly set up an investigation, comprising eight NEC members – including Betty, and Larry Whitty, general secretary of the Labour Party. The chairman was Charlie Turnock, a leading official in the National Union of Railwaymen, and reckoned (with justice) to be a tough operator in this field. The inquiry team travelled to Liverpool to begin its work on 8 December, and was immediately given a 100-page 'dossier' on alleged Militant malpractice within the district Labour party. It was claimed that day-to-day business of Liverpool City Council – a stronghold of the Militant Tendency – was discussed at district party meetings, including pay levels depending on which union council workers joined and employment practices favouring people 'with particular political outlooks'.[32]

The inquiry team spent two hours behind closed doors in the city's AUEW offices interviewing leading activists in the district Labour party, including Tony Mulhearn, district president, John Hamilton, district treasurer and leader of the Labour group on the city council, his deputy Derek Hatton, Terry Harrison and Eddie Loyden, MP for Garston – both vice-presidents of the district party – and Ms Felicity Dowling, its secretary. Hatton told the inquiry they had been carrying out their election promises to the people of Liverpool, while Mulhearn denied that there had been intimidation or irregularities.

This was just the beginning. In all, the NEC inquiry team visited Liverpool six times, and took oral or written evidence from all six constituency parties in the city, from nine party wards and one women's section, thirteen affiliated organizations, five groups of party members and seventy-one individual members. More than 120 members gave evidence, and no one from outside the party.

Betty's role was important. She had pushed for the investigation ever since Labour's failure at the polls, believing it to be a vital element in restoring the party's credibility with the electorate. But she was no Vyshinsky. The 'accused' Militant supporters can scarcely remember her being there. Tony Mulhearn insisted, 'I can't recall her particularly, really. Betty wasn't among the big names.'[33] Nor did she make much impact on Ms Frances Curran, then the Young Socialist member of Labour's NEC and a decade later a senior figure on *Militant* newspaper, who recalled that Betty was 'more personable than the others. If you were getting the tea, she wouldn't ignore you like Hattersley and others who wouldn't speak to you.'[34]

Affable she may have been, but the steel was there. The inquiry sat in secret, and made its report to the national executive in February 1986. In fact, there were two reports, a majority report signed by Betty and a minority report signed by the other two women on the team – Mrs Margaret Beckett MP for Derby South and later to become deputy party leader to John Smith, and Mrs Audrey Wise. Both were on the Left, to a varying degree. They took a less firm line than the majority, whose report was swiftly adopted by the NEC.

The majority report found 'systematic organizational irregularities' in the district Labour party and 'worrying features' in the activity of the party in the city. It recommended suspension and reconstitution of the district party under redrafted rules. It also named sixteen individual party members who should be investigated as possible members of the Militant Tendency. After further inquiries, general secretary Larry Whitty proposed taking a case against twelve of the sixteen, and despite legal moves to prevent the cases being proceeded with, hearings took place over five days in May, June and July 1986. Eight of the twelve – including Mulhearn and Hatton – were found guilty of membership of Militant Tendency and were expelled from the party. None of the eight exercised their right to appeal to the private session of the annual conference in Blackpool on 29 September. The expulsions were confirmed by 6,146,000 votes to 325,000. Betty and her allies had been vindicated.

Happily, life was not one long tribunal. In June 1986, Central Television, Betty's regional station (with whom she had a very good working relationship) filmed her 'reliving her Tiller Girl past'. The political magazine 'Central Lobby' shot a sequence of Betty getting into the swing of things at a youngster's tap-dance class in her constituency. The company's PR people told *The Times* diarist: 'Despite thirteen years in the more sedate surroundings of the Commons, she has not lost her touch.'[35] What they did not disclose is that they ransacked every film still and movie library they knew to find footage or photographs of Betty's Tiller days – and failed.

Grateful constituents in West Bromwich presented her with a gold pen in appreciation of her efforts over the Smith houses. That victory appears to have sharpened her constituents' appetite for housing problems. Hundreds of residents of Wednesbury asked her to take up the case of homes sinking into the ground because of subsidence in abandoned limestone workings. She led a deputation to see the Environment Ministry.

Otherwise, it was the daily round and common task of chairing Parliamentary committees, on which the Conservatives had such a preponderant majority that there was little scope for controversy – even had she wished it. It was not until the party conference in Blackpool in 1986 that Betty was in the limelight again, and she must have wished herself somewhere else. Chosen to reply for the platform on a tedious Monday afternoon debate on education, she found herself ambushed by the Left.

A composite motion, that device so beloved of delegates which brings together a hotchpotch coalition of demands, insisted that the next Labour government introduce an Education Act to abolish public schools. This would be done by withdrawing charitable status and then moving to 'the planned public ownership of the private school system'.[36] The national executive, anxious not to put off middle-class voters in the run-up to a general election, asked conference to 'remit' the motion – simply to hand it on without a vote, when it would promptly be forgotten.

Frances Morrell, Tony Benn's political ally and chairman of the Inner London Education Authority, demanded that Hattersley's first Budget as Labour Chancellor should withdraw every penny of taxpayers' money from public schools. 'The NEC is absolutely wrong to be timid about education. People want a bold, radical programme.

Let's give them one.' Labour conferences used to exhibit an alarming talent for running out of control. Scenting victory, delegates piled on the agony, accusing the platform of being mealy-mouthed and pussyfooting. Matthew Leigh, an eighteen-year-old student from Beaconsfield about to go up to Oxford, appealed to conference to reject the dithering of 'the weak-kneed people on the platform'.[37]

It was a rash boy who called Betty weak-kneed. But he caught the mood, and try as she might Betty could not swing the delegates back round. She delivered her prepared text competently enough, but they were not inclined to hear talk of 'further examination of the sub-paragraph' and 'remittance so that we can look at this and report back to you'. They didn't want to give their leaders 'more time to examine how to integrate public schools into the state sector'. They had swallowed defeat for the Left over Militant in the morning. Now it was time to have their own way over something.

The delegates applauded her politely, and carried the motion on a show of hands. It made no difference, of course. Shadow Education Secretary Giles Radice, plummy-voiced MP for Durham North and himself a product of Winchester College and Magdalen College, Oxford, simply reiterated the party's voluntarist policy, arguing that compulsory abolition might bring Labour into conflict with the European Court of Human Rights. The motion would not form part of Labour's manifesto, he promised.

Little did she know at the time, but Betty would never again be called on to defend the party line from the rostrum of conference. Less than a year later, she would be resigning from the NEC, and from the party itself – of which she had been a member since her teenage years – within six years. For now, she could savour the feeling of being re-elected to the national executive committee with an increased vote – up nearly a quarter of a million to 4,496,000 – while Eric Heffer, often accused of being an apologist for Militant, lost his seat.

Fortunately for Betty, Labour was also in the course of ditching its hard-line policy on renationalizing the state industries and services – like British Telecom – that had been privatized by Mrs Thatcher. This body-swerve towards 'social ownership', a minority holding with stronger regulatory mechanisms, effectively let off the hook those

Labour figures who had bought shares in privatized concerns. Such speculation was certainly against the spirit, if not the letter, of party policy.

It still came as a surprise in late March 1987, when the trade-union-funded magazine *Labour Research* disclosed that Betty was one of three Labour MPs whose names appeared on the register of British Telecom shareholders. She was in interesting company. George Foulkes MP and Ted Leadbitter MP appeared alongside her, together with the Princess of Wales, Prince Edward and Prince Andrew. Betty was named as holding 800 BT shares – the maximum for an individual. She denied buying the shares, and told *The Times* she had given her god-daughter some money. 'I know she bought some shares in BT.'[38] She must have given her god-daughter quite a lot of money: at least £1040. The shares were worth 130p at the time of purchase, and had almost doubled in value.

Politicians had rather more to think about than blushes over shares. Mrs Thatcher was edging towards calling a general election at the time best suited for her to win an unprecedented (in modern times, at any rate) third successive term of office. She moved on the afternoon of 11 May, announcing a snap poll on 11 June. Labour had by now learned many of the lessons of the calamity of 1983, and was projecting Neil Kinnock as a 'presidential' figure 'with an irresistible moral thrust'. Unhappily, the electorate seemed only too able to resist his thrusting.

Mrs Thatcher recovered from a bout of the political collywobbles on 'black Thursday' and took personal charge of a campaign that played on memories of the 'Winter of Discontent'. The economy was improving, even if it was to prove a disastrous boom, and people voted with their wallets. Mrs Thatcher stayed in Downing Street, with a reduced majority of 102, and Betty's own majority in West Bromwich West fell further to 5253 over the Tories, though she just retained an overall majority of votes cast – 50.5 per cent.

The first two Thatcher governments, which saw a progressive onslaught on the trade unions that were Betty's power base, and an economic recession that devastated the traditional metal-bashing industries of her adopted Black Country in the early 1980s, were a deeply distressing political and social experience for her. Factory after factory closed in West Bromwich, and while Betty is properly classified as on the Right of the Labour Party, the new brutalism of 80s Conservatism repelled Betty.

Speaking in 1991, she said of the Thatcher decade, 'This country hasn't really made any progress over the last ten years. When I see the areas that I love and represent that have made such little progress, the hard lives of the people there, the unemployment, the poverty, the low wages, that affects me tremendously. I see what changes could be brought about and I see people who want change and who have faith and confidence in that, and yet it has not been possible. It is very heart-breaking, very discouraging.'[39] Unlike some of her male colleagues, Betty did not exhibit a sneaking regard for 'the Iron Lady'. Nor did she see Mrs Thatcher as being on the same side in terms of improving the lot of women. 'I never think of Margaret Thatcher being a good role model for women, because she never advanced any women at all.'

Mrs Thatcher gave way to John Major as Prime Minister and party leader in the Conservative coup of late November 1990. But while Betty had not been a fan of 'the Iron Lady', she could not have any expectation of support from the new occupant of Number 10 in her quiet campaign for the Speakership. In this she was not to be disappointed.

CHAPTER VIII

CHOOSE ME FOR WHAT I AM

I T ALL BEGAN to slot into place 'very, very quickly' after John Major secured his unexpected re-election on 9 April 1992. Scarcely had the votes been counted and the result declared, when the telephone rang at Tanat House, John Biffen's country seat at Llanyblodwel in the Welsh Marches of Shropshire North, his parliamentary constituency.

It was Betty, asking if she could still count on his backing for the Speakership. Biffen's support was critical. As a former Leader of the House in Mrs Thatcher's second administration, and now a respected – revered, virtually – Tory backbencher, he was in an unrivalled position to deliver the critical mass of Conservative MPs that she would require to beat off the government's nominee. As an archetypal 'House of Commons man', he also represented the powerful strand of opinion, which goes right across the political spectrum, that argues that the occupant of the Speaker's Chair should be the choice of Parliament – not the executive.

Biffen was already on side. He had come to the conclusion long before polling day that, whatever the result, her competence as Deputy Speaker ought to be rewarded with the top job. As a Tory, he had no time for the time-honoured trade-union tradition of 'Buggins' Turn', the iron law of the labour movement which lays down that a long-serving number two must assume the number one position. But he was even less enamoured of the Conservative habit of giving the job to a Cabinet minister who was being put out to grass. Biffen had been mooted for the job himself and, though he must have been tempted, it says much for his loyalty to Betty that he stayed out of the contest.

Long before the election, MPs knew that Jack Weatherill was going to the Lords. Biffen took the initiative himself, contacting Betty directly to say that he hoped she would stand for Speaker. He would be very happy to support her. That was 'some months' – at least four, according to sources close to the Shropshire North MP – before John Major dissolved Parliament. Even though the election went in his government's favour, Biffen did not hesitate. He promised to propose her.

It was the most effective support she could have, and it triggered a telephone assault on MPs by her backers, which proved to be a conclusive pre-emptive strike. The votes were virtually sewn up before Parliament assembled, much to the fury of the government Whips, who were unable to get up to their usual arm-twisting and cajolery in the Westminster lobbies. 'It must have been very frustrating for the establishment,' said one senior Tory backbencher.[1] 'They normally like this place to be functioning so they can get hold of everybody and take them to one side, and give them a nice comforting chat or a kick in the pants. If they are all over the country and not required to come to London, they can't. MPs don't come before almost the evening ahead of the calling of Parliament. There is no great desire to be in London. After all, we spend most of our time here regretting we are not in our constituencies. One of the difficulties for the fragmented Tory vote was the Whips – they really didn't know their arse from their elbow, or who they should lean on.'

If the Tories were divided and disorganized, Betty was simply moving her election machine into fifth gear. She had been waiting for this moment for a long time, certainly longer than any of her rivals and much longer than most MPs would credit even today. One veteran Betty-watcher, who knew her in the USA thirty years previously, said, 'I think it is quite possible that she decided very early on that she wanted to be Speaker. She did pursue very long-term objectives.'[2]

It is true that she stuck at it for nearly two decades simply to get into parliament, but her ambition to be Speaker almost certainly gelled not long after she was appointed to the Chairmen's Panel in the wake of the 1979 election. That kind of appointment, in the words of Sir Marcus Fox, Chairman of the Tory 1922 Backbenchers' Committee, 'is usually given to people who have shown a sort of inclination for it. It is not normal for somebody who is going to achieve ministerial office to get it. It does, in a sense, map you out.'[3] When that appointment is coupled with her service on the House of Commons Commission for four years from 1983, in retrospect, Betty's career direction becomes clear.

There could not have been much doubt after the 1987 election, when she was voted by acclamation a deputy speaker – to be precise, Second Deputy Chairman of Ways and Means, which is number four in the hierarchy, below Speaker, Deputy Speaker and Chairman of Ways and Means, and First Deputy Chairman of Ways and Means.

Betty was thrilled. As she later told Rebecca Abrams, 'Never, never in a million years did I imagine [I'd become Deputy Speaker]. But things happen here, oh, it's a whirlwind here sometimes when things happen. My name was put to all the parties with perhaps two or three others, and it was finally agreed that I was a non-contentious personality and in June 1987 I was appointed. That was a great moment. That was one moment when I was really more sad than at most other times that my mother wasn't alive.'

It was no sinecure. She came in at 9.30 every morning, briefed herself on what was in the news and then attended the noon conference with Mr Speaker. In the afternoon, evening, and even early morning, she was chairing debates in the chamber, often for five hours a day. The media had little doubt about where Betty was heading. Less than six months after the 1987 election, when Speaker Weatherill was under fire from his own Tory Party for the impartiality that was to prove his hallmark, it was reported that Betty was being spoken of at Westminster as a prospective successor. She refused to be drawn, insisting, 'There is no vacancy.'

But that did not prevent the press from speculating. And Betty was not above helping the speculation along with interviews. In February 1988, she was profiled in the *Yorkshire Post* as 'Lady in Waiting'. Journalist Graham Brough, who is related to Betty, talked to her on the train to London from her Black Country constituency and found her ready to take on anything. 'I will do any job I am asked to do to the best of my abilities,' she insisted.[4]

Betty was honest about the pride she felt at being the MPs' choice. 'I enjoy it, and I was pleased to be asked because it is a position that is given by the entire House and has to have the approval of all the parties. There are ten parties in the House and to have them all agree is an accolade and a source of pleasure for me.' After chairing some difficult sessions – notably dealing with tricky Points of Order on a Government injunction banning a Radio 4 programme, 'My Country Right or Wrong' – she felt she was now getting the hang of the job.

'I try to avoid being schoolmarmish in the old-fashioned sense. You have to defuse the tension with a smile and a witty comment. It's a question of having jocularity in the right place with a smile on one's face when the temperature is rising. It is a feel you have to get about how a debate is going. I don't know if I have achieved it yet, but I'm certainly trying. It is a job you grow in, and I am just starting to grow.'

The following week, she confessed to Ewen MacAskill, political correspondent of the *Scotsman*, 'I have an inclination to be school-marmish in the old-fashioned sense of telling people to sit down, and I have to curb it.'[5] In July 1988, Frances Edmonds in the *Mail on Sunday*, writing a year after Betty's promotion, described her as 'the one woman with the power to silence Mrs Thatcher' whose popularity was such that 'even the congenitally superior Environment Secretary Nicholas Ridley is rumoured not to dislike her'.[6] Mrs Edmonds also discovered that Betty 'resolutely refuses to discuss' the prospect of becoming Speaker. But she cheerfully talked about the punishing schedule, the night sittings (of which she seemed 'to get more than her fair share'), and her innate showbiz sense of the theatrical that can defuse potentially difficult parliamentary situations. Above all, every story and profile recalled her response when asked by a genuinely bemused Peter Pike MP how MPs were supposed to address her. Betty replied: 'Call me Madam!'

No other member of the Speaker's team had ever had such a wide and sympathetic coverage in the press, usually complete with a smiling portrait, sometimes quite glamorous, sometimes almost matronly. It was brilliant public relations. While formally and publicly disavowing any ambition to become the first woman Speaker, which was wise and decorous in a Parliament jealous of its privileges and protocol, Betty was able to allow the image to grow of her natural accession to West-minster's throne. Of course, she could not have done it if she was not a popular and able deputy, and she cannot be held responsible for the natural curiosity of the newspapers. But she was canny enough not to discourage them.

That was the public face of a campaign that was also being waged in private. Neil Kinnock, the party leader, had already made up his mind that Betty should be Speaker. Immediately after he lost the 1987 election, Betty had to make the choice of staying on Labour's national executive, where she had played a key role in the 'leader loyalist' centre-Right group, or becoming a deputy speaker. She consulted with Kinnock in the Leader's Office. He had long been impressed with her crispness and firmness in the chair, and delighted equally in her capability of a wry word or a guffaw.

For Kinnock, there was no question about it. According to sources close to the then leader, it was important to ensure that Betty became the first woman Speaker. At that time, evidently, she already wanted the job, 'but only one-quarter believed she could get it and three-quarters disbelieved it because she was a woman and there were some doughty opponents.'[7] The first thing was to get her into 'the Speaker Stakes'.

Talks through the usual channels established that there was a vacancy created by the departure of Ernie Armstrong, Labour MP for north-west Durham and a leading member of the Chairmen's Panel. With the intervention of senior Labour figures, it emerged that a consensus existed in the House for Betty to get the job. 'There was certainly an easy consensus about her moving into that position,' said the sources. 'There would have been a less easy consensus about her becoming Speaker. What is thought to be a little bit distasteful is to have a long-ranging ambition in that situation.' It would not have looked right for Labour to have made her the heir-apparent to Speaker Weatherill, and to be fair 'she didn't make any assumptions about the possibility'.

Once installed as Third Deputy Speaker, Betty impressed Labour's front bench and the other side of the House with her clarity, and her personality. The word was quietly put about. 'Long preparation was the essence, and spreading the idea very gradually that she was *the* person,' said a Kinnock aide. Much was made of the views of Speaker Weatherill who 'thought a lot of her', because she did not shrink from responsibility and making decisions.

But Kinnock did not have a totally free hand. He may have had a master plan to create the first woman Speaker, but he could not simply bulldoze her through the Parliamentary Labour Party, much less the Commons as a whole. There were two very large constraints on his freedom of action. One was the substantial body of opinion on the Conservative side that wanted to break with the growing assumption – to many MPs, a parliamentary convention – that the Speakership should alternate between the parties.

This notion dates only from the 1960s, the so-called ABAB pattern, which saw Labour's Horace King in the chair from 1965 to 1971, then the Tory Selwyn Lloyd, the former Chancellor of the Exchequer, from 1971 to 1976, giving way to Labour's George Thomas (now Lord Tonypandy) from 1976 to 1983. After Jack Weatherill, a Tory, was in post from 1983, said the Labour Whips, it must be our turn. Their Tory counterparts hotly disputed the existence of any such convention. Kinnock's advisers warned him that the turn-and-turn-about rule was 'like most conventions, not worth the paper it was not written on – unless you can get MPs to respect it'. And that was by no means certain. It was not an idle question, because of the Tory dissatisfaction with Speaker Weatherill, who was felt to be less than friendly to the government: that is to say, he had been doing his job only too well. There had been rumours of putting up against him, the names of Sir Giles Shaw and Cranley Onslow being in the frame. Many Conservatives argued that being the majority party, the Speakership was within their gift.

The other great obstacle to a Betty shoo-in was the diminutive figure of Harold (now Sir Harold) Walker, who as the existing Deputy Speaker and Chairman of Ways and Means since 1983, was unquestionably more senior. Not only that, he also wanted the top job. Moreover, his political credentials were impeccable. He had been Under-Secretary and then Minister of State at the Department of Employment throughout the Wilson–Callaghan administration, an assistant Whip before that and a front-bench spokesman on employment affairs subsequently. A former engineering toolmaker from Manchester, he sat for the mining constituency of Doncaster Central, had been very active among trade-union-sponsored MPs and had a substantial following on the back-benches. Andrew Roth described him as 'combative and shrewd' in his Parliamentary Profiles, but also conceded that he was volatile and short-fused. Michael Foot had once called him 'difficult'.

Kinnock had to admit that Walker, short, balding and tough-talking, was very well thought of and had a real lobby – on both sides of the House. He was also a long-standing Deputy Speaker, and he had friends in the serious press. Edward Pearce wrote in the *Guardian* that Walker was 'on merit in *any* parliament, the very best choice . . . [he] just happens to know everything there is to know about procedure and its laws. He is a twinkling disciplinarian who will take no nonsense from anyone. He reveres the Chair and the House and would put them before anything.'[8]

The Labour leader proceeded with a twin-track approach. He had to win over sufficient Tory backbenchers to acceptance of his nominee, and persuade his own side that Betty was 'the man to beat'. He appreciated that whatever he did by way of advancing Betty's cause would mean offending Harold. His advisers argued that despite the pro-Walker lobby on the Conservative benches, 'there was a feeling that he could not be guaranteed to win'. Walker was sparky enough, very individual, and certainly blunt, but he 'was not universally supported in the chair, partly indeed because of his bluntness'. Some Labour MPs regarded him as 'pompous', others claimed that he favoured fellow Yorkshire MPs when it came to choosing who was allowed to speak. He was said to have upset the Chief Whip, Michael Cocks. It was even bruited that he never bought a round of drinks, a slur that his friends vigorously reject and certainly not true in the author's experience.

Such charges are brought against most MPs at one time or another, and Deputy Speakers are not exempt. But the Westminster back-chat helped to destabilize Walker's position, allowing Betty's virtues to come to the fore. Kinnock laid his contingency plans in 1991, certainly by the spring of that year. If Labour won the election, Betty would definitely be Speaker. If not, she would be Labour's nomination, and the Opposition would use such pressure at its disposal to secure the operation of the 'convention'. He spoke to her privately on a regular basis. The meetings were so secret they did not appear in his daily diary. He was convinced that she was not only his choice, but that of Speaker Weatherill also. There was no real dissent in the

Shadow Cabinet, though Buggins' Law was mentioned. Kinnock retorted, 'Buggins is not going to be nominated!'

Kinnock's political adviser, Charles Clarke, vast, bearded son of a Whitehall mandarin Sir Otto Clarke, took on much of the behind the scenes lobbying to win over Labour doubters to the Betty camp. Contacts were maintained with sympathetic Tories in the event of Labour losing the general election. Well before the election, Kinnock arranged that Walker's hurt pride would be soothed with a peerage. In any case, it was a long-standing tradition that a retiring Chairman of Ways and Means went to the Lords – not least because the holder of the office is supposed to sever all party links. As events played out, Walker had to be content with a knighthood, though that left him free to return to the back-benches and resume normal political activity, which he did with a characteristic vigour. 'He dealt with it very well, actually,' said a source. 'He didn't become bitter and twisted. At least, not publicly.' Privately, however, he was a deeply disappointed man, and not without reason. In the summer of 1994, he announced that he would not stand at the next election.

For their part, the Conservatives were in a fix. Rather to the surprise of a good many of them, they won the election with a hugely reduced majority. Labour's campaign for Betty was just maturing. The Tories had to find a successor to Jack Weatherill virtually overnight. There was no shortage of candidates. In fact, there was a large embarrassment, but it was not of riches. No fewer than five Tory MPs allowed their names to be considered.

The best known was Peter Brooke, MP for the City of London, aged fifty-eight, who until the election had been Secretary of State for Northern Ireland. An amiable man with an abiding passion for cricket, he had earned the sobriquet 'Babbling' Brooke for an easy garrulity that culminated disastrously when he sang 'Darling Clementine' on Dublin TV the day after an IRA terrorist outrage in Ulster. He came from a blue-chip Tory family, his father Lord Henry Brooke having been a notoriously hard-line Home Secretary in the Macmillan government. The *Financial Times* said he was 'admired for his wit, patience and courtesy, but some Tories have said they would not support him because they think the office of Speaker should not go to someone so fresh out of the Cabinet.'[9]

The other Tory hopefuls were Paul Channon, MP for Southend West, aged fifty-six, scion of the famous business family and son of the MP-diarist 'Chips' Channon; Terence Higgins, sixty-four, MP for Worthing, Chairman of the All-Party Treasury Select Committee and of the Liaison Committee of Commons committee chairmen, who was thought independent but dull; and Sir Giles Shaw, MP for Pudsey, a popular ex-minister, a member of the 1922 Executive, and former chairman of committees considering legislation. He had strong backing from the dwindling band of Conservative 'knights of the shires', and was regarded as a safe pair of hands, 'pragmatic and a consensus-seeker'.[10] The only Conservative woman in the frame, Dame Janet Fookes, who was a more junior member of the Chairmen's Panel. But the *Guardian* reported that she was 'not popular', and also her Plymouth Drake constituency was marginal. None of the Tory hopefuls had a machine to match Betty's and the government's Whips were just as divided as the backbenchers.

Channon, a former Cabinet minister who had been Trade Secretary and Transport Secretary, had been an MP for thirty years. And despite his underwhelming performance at the Despatch Box – particularly against John Prescott, his pit-bull Shadow at Transport – he had actually been promised the Speakership during the contest to succeed Mrs Thatcher. But by the wrong man – Michael Heseltine, the loser, not John Major, the winner. Alan Clark, the wayward Defence Minister, recounts in his *Diaries*, 'Michael himself is quite shameless in offering all and sundry what they have always wanted. For example, he would probably have got Paul's [Channon] support anyway, but he "sealed it" with an assurance that Paul would be Speaker in the next House.'[11]

Earlier in the parliament, there had been suggestions that Labour should adopt a high-profile candidate – a man, of course – who could stand comparison with these political heavyweights. The name of Peter Shore, who like Betty had worked at Transport House in the 1950s and who had gone on to senior office in Harold Wilson's Cabinet, was canvassed. 'They were looking for an elder statesman,' admitted one MP who was on Betty's side. 'Shore's name was mentioned, so was Bryan Gould.' Gould, an unpredictable but charismatic politician, was then MP for Dagenham, and a senior figure in the Shadow Cabinet. He became disillusioned with Westminster, and gave up his seat to take up an academic post in his native New Zealand in 1994. 'Names were coming up and falling away very quickly, and by that time a lot of people were saying they would like her. A lot of meetings were going on behind the scenes, and the longer it went on, basically because the government was stalling over the general election, the better it became for Betty, because the clearer it became that Harold would not get the Labour votes.'[12]

This well-placed MP remembers that these 'behind the scenes meetings' took place at a flat in a block off Marsham Street, Westminster. It was, he recalls, the Tufton Street home of Lady Helen de Freitas, widow of Betty's much-loved employer. The MP was 'very quietly asked' to go along and meet a few like-minded people. There, he found Labour members from every strand of party thinking 'and even a few Tories'. These gatherings, he insisted, were organized not by Betty, but by friends. 'One thing that Betty did not do was declare that she was in the running. She just got people talking all the time about her running for it. This is Betty's style – to be there and let other people do the talking. She is a different character now than she was when she was deputy. She was more of a listener. She knew the rules inside out. She knew that given more time, her time would come, and she could not lose because Harold was dead and buried.'

Another Labour MP – who also voted for Betty – recalls these parties well. 'It began in the summer of 1991, or it could have been late spring. A series of parties began to happen. "At Homes", they were called. At that time no one knew that Jack Weatherill was standing down. Officially, certainly, as far as we were concerned, Harold Walker was in the running if Weatherill ever went because by convention it would have been our turn. So when the invitations went out – and they were always personally delivered – you never knew who was going to be there. On the face of it, nothing was going on. It was just Betty Boothroyd being nice to people, and the parties took place. The one I went to was in the evening.

'It was extremely pleasant. And that was the first time I heard a hint that there might be a new Speaker in the next Parliament. To be fair, it was all passively done. I never got the impression that there was any canvassing. On the contrary, it just seemed a nice party, as if they were saying thank you to people.

'I remember going away from the party with a friend of mine and saying, "That was a lovely evening," and he said, "There was a purpose behind all this." By the time the election was called, it was widely known that Jack Weatherill was standing down, but I cannot remember being approached by anybody with a view to garnering support for the next Speaker.

'Then, at 11 o'clock on the Saturday morning after the election, I was in my constituency, taking a surgery, when I got a telephone call from somebody in the Leader's Office saying did I know that the preferred candidate was Betty? What did I think about having the first woman Speaker? I remember saying, "Surely, it must be Harold?" I was then told, "No, we think the precedent of a male Speaker must be broken." And in the days that followed, several people telephoned me and said virtually the same thing. By the time I returned to London on the Sunday night, I had heard nothing from Harold, and it seemed to me it was a *fait accompli*. Once the House began to gather in the days before the first formal meeting, there seemed to be a consensus of opinion. It became imperative that we had a single candidate because the Tories were split several ways. Her election was inevitable because the PLP acted as a single block vote.

'I was to learn subsequently that in the quiet group that sometimes meets, particularly in the mornings before 10 a.m. in the Commons Tea Room, the idea of Betty Boothroyd had been canvassed for a very long time. But the ordinary member of the PLP is not to be found in the tea room at that hour.'[13]

Apart from the Leader's Office, there was much activity by the Labour Whips. Don Dixon, the Deputy Chief Whip and (like Betty) sponsored by the GMB union, 'went around saying she's the woman', according to inside sources. 'Don cleaned up the votes. At the end, it was clear what the vote would be.'

There was one other potential problem. Most pundits believed that Labour would perform well at the general election, whenever it came. John Major's shilly-shallying did not noticeably improve his government's standing in the opinion polls, which pointed to either a narrow Labour victory or a hung parliament with Neil Kinnock in a

position to form a minority administration, with or without Paddy
Ashdown's Liberal Democrats. But Betty, the eternal electoral pessi-
mist, still worried about what might happen back at West Bromwich.
Suppose she might still be challenged by her old rival, John Edwards,
the Tribunite activist in her local party?

By this time, the West Bromwich West party had been purged.
There had been an influx of new members, and loyalist delegates from
the TGWU were installed on the general management committee.
'They were lobby fodder,' insists Edwards. 'Their mission was to see
that Betty never again came that so to defeat, and she never did.'[14]
The events of 1981, when Betty came within two votes of a lethal
challenge to her position could not be allowed to happen again.

And yet, and yet. There was a nagging fear. Edwards, now chairman
of the constituency party, tells a remarkable story of how he was dis-
suaded from mounting any fresh bid to unseat Betty. 'Before the last
election, it must have been in 1990, when I was chair of Finance on
Sandwell Borough Council, I got invited to the palace [of Westminster]
to talk to four MPs about Sandwell's finances. They were getting
questions about the Poll Tax, and they wanted me to brief them on
the financial situation. It was Betty who organized it.'

The meeting was over in about ten minutes. Edwards had gone
armed with reams of information. Essentially, Betty and her colleagues
wanted to know why the Poll Tax couldn't be set any lower. High
Poll Taxes were a political problem in some marginal seats, even
though John Major had promised to abolish the hated tax.

Then something unexpected happened. 'Betty took me into the
Members' Dining Room and bought me a cup of tea and crumpets.
She had never done that before. I had never been to the Commons at
Betty's request before. I was excluded – the old wounds are still there.

'She bought me the crumpets and asked me if I intended to attempt
to run against her in 1992, for another re-selection. She was certain
[to win] beyond question. By this time, we had gone over to the electoral college system, and the trade-union vote would deliver it for her.
But from what she said to me, she was going to run in 1992 and she
would almost certainly be the Speaker and she didn't want the indignity
of a selection contest in the constituency.

'She knew I couldn't win, because the trade-union block vote would deliver it for her, but I would almost certainly pick up the same branch nominations as before. She knew that three party branches out of six in West Bromwich would almost certainly nominate me, and she didn't want to be seen to be winning by the use of the block vote – when three of her own branches were not even prepared to nominate her.'

According to Edwards, Betty was evidently anxious. 'She said, "Are you going to run?" I said I might consider it. I wasn't particularly intending to. I didn't want a humiliation. I said, "It depends on your future plans. What are your plans for the future? Will you stand in 1996 and the end of the century?" She said, "I just want one more term. Neil wants me to be Speaker. Clearly, I would like to be Speaker. It would be a boost for women's issues generally. I want one more term, but that would almost certainly be the end of it." She wanted to do it as Speaker, but after that she was almost certainly not going to run again because it was a very lonely life and people didn't under-stand the hours and the fact that you have no social life and no family life and no time for anything other than parliament.'

Edwards was taken aback, both at her unaccustomed frankness and the faint whiff of a possible deal in the air. 'We didn't come to an agreement, but I said, if you are going to do one more term, I would not want to contest you if this is your last term. I said to Betty, I gave her an assurance I would not seek nominations from branches to run against her, and we left it in that state. There was no formal under-standing, but she made it clear to me that she wanted one more term, as Speaker, which she was fairly certain she would get. She would do that term, and then bow out gracefully. That seemed reasonable to me. It would leave a vacancy in the mid 1990s, which I would be interested in contesting.'

Since this was a private conversation, there is no way it can be corroborated except through Betty herself. But it has the ring of verac-ity. Her electoral nervousness is well established, attested to even by her loyal agent Paul Jackson. Her ambition to become the first woman Speaker is equally well documented. It would have been quite agreeable to see off any local opposition by such a charm offensive. Edwards was not to know that her parliamentary position would be rendered iron-clad by a subsequent Labour Party change of rule that permits

no Labour challenge to her position as candidate in West Bromwich
– even though she is no longer a member of the party.

So, well before the election, Betty's position was about as powerful
as it could be. As her mother would no doubt have put it, she had
'set her stall out'. She had the PLP discreetly in her grip, an unknown
but influential number of Tory MPs backing her, and the main
group of Conservatives loyal to whatever the government told them
was at sixes and sevens. Her side was united, and the other side was
in disarray.

The General Election result of April 1992, the return of a Conservative government for the fourth time in succession, albeit with a reduced
majority of twenty-one seats, was a personal triumph for John Major.
By the same token, and despite a three-per-cent swing across the
country from Tory to Labour, it was a terminal political disaster for
Neil Kinnock, Betty's parliamentary patron. Major was delighted that
he and his much-derided soapbox had triumphed over Labour's glitzy
media-orientated campaign. He now had to take on a rather more
doughty opponent: the lass from Marriott Street, safely returned by
the voters of West Bromwich West with her majority increased by
more than a third from 5253 to 7830.

Major's problems were compounded by the fact that nobody
seemed to be in charge of the Conservative campaign to retain the
Speakership. Very soon after the election, the Downing Street news
machine had pumped out the story that the Prime Minister was to
stay aloof from the parliamentary fray. None of the candidates
would get his blessing, though in the event most of his Cabinet voted
for Peter Brooke. The Conservative Whips were actively canvassing
support, but they were hampered by the long list of possibles on
their side, and by the hostility being aroused to the prospect of an
ex-Cabinet minister of such recent vintage being punted as chief
contender for the job.

Then the 1922 Committee Chairman Cranley Onslow got in on
the act, canvassing the prospects for his vice-chairman, Sir Giles Shaw.
Frantically seeking to pick up Major's electoral theme, friends of Sir
Giles insisted that he would be 'the classless society candidate'. It was
all too little, too late. 'We were all over the place,' one Tory MP
conceded sadly. On the eve of the contest, Brooke's backers claimed

their man was in the lead. A head count of the 336 Conservative MPs gave him sixty per cent of the government side.

It was nowhere near enough to mount a successful challenge to Betty, as Brooke later conceded. Nor did the Tories get a good press on the issue. If the outcome had been left to the media, there would have been no contest. Newspapers vaguely of the Left (the *Guardian*), of the self-styled 'hard centre' (the *Independent*), and of the Tory-supporting Right (the *Mail on Sunday*) vied with each in pushing Betty's candidature.

Peter Dobbie, political editor of the *Mail on Sunday* came closest to the truth with his prediction that Betty would be dragged with seeming reluctance to the chair. 'But she will have no compunction. It is the realization of a long-nursed ambition she has worked cleverly and, some would say, ruthlessly to secure.' He added, generously, 'But it is a job that she richly deserves, bringing a vivacity and glamour to the role.' Describing Betty as 'a natural performer' who delighted in ceremony, Dobbie said she would enjoy the Speaker's robes and props of office, the huge salary and the sumptuous official apartments. The *Mail on Sunday* even commissioned a cartoonist to draw a caricature of what Betty would look like in a wig, though she was never to wear one. Dobbie remarked, 'For Miss Boothroyd, this is something she has dreamed about, a fantasy fulfilled . . .'

The *Independent*, under a headline BETTY BOOTHROYD IT SHOULD BE, argued in a lead editorial that there was an overwhelming case for giving her the job. Generosity to the Opposition while embarking on their fourth term of office would do the Tories credit, and above all the choice of a woman would help to redress the hopeless imbalance of the sexes in the Commons where even after an influx of new faces only nine per cent of MPs were women. Having shown her impartiality and ability to control the chamber, not to mention a sense of humour, she was the best candidate. 'The democratic life of the nation will be the loser if she does not get the job,' pronounced the voice of City Road.

The *Guardian* was a little more guarded. Under the politically correct headline, MS SPEAKER BOOTHROYD, the paper lamented that Betty's chief sponsor, John Biffen, former Leader of the House, was not himself a candidate. The paper conceded loftily that Harold

Walker 'might also do the job well', before suggesting 'even at the risk of tokenism, we would like to see the job go to a woman. The choice of a woman would symbolize another blow at the grotesque male domination of Parliament.' It was surely more than symbolism. The paper's sagacious political commentator, Ian Aitken, her friend of thirty years or more, observed that 'the election of the admirable Betty will unquestionably add to the gaiety of life'.

On the eve of the contest, Betty's hand was strengthened by a speech in his Southend constituency by Sir Teddy Taylor MP, in which he publicly backed her and urged his colleagues to do the same to avoid a challenge. Sir Teddy, a Right-wing populist Tory, bitterly opposed to European integration and therefore virtually everything she stood for politically, commands quite a body of support on the Conservative back-benches.

His intervention, plus the discreet leaking of John Biffen's name as Betty's chief sponsor, helped turn the trickle of Tory supporters into a stream. The Tory Whips put a three-line whip on their MPs to turn out – though they could not actually instruct them who to vote for. The papers were full of 'eleventh-hour Stop Betty' stories, but the tide was going the other way. Senior Tories conceded that 'ten to fifteen' independent-minded backbenchers on the government side might vote for Betty. A dozen would be enough to overturn the government's twenty-one-strong majority.

As the day dawned, early editions of the London *Evening Standard* reported Betty leading the field, gathering the kind of support among Conservatives that she would need to win. Peter Brooke was a clear front-runner among the five Tories who might stand, with 119 MPs committed to his cause. The Tories, who dislike defeat more than the next man, were getting crotchety. There were private complaints about the 'aggressive behaviour' of advocates of Sir Giles and Terence Higgins, while Paul Channon and Dame Janet Fookes were now counted out of the reckoning.

On the Labour side, Betty's position as sole Labour nominee was formalized. All 271 Labour MPs were called to a special meeting of the Parliamentary Labour Party at noon in Committee Room 14 at Westminster. Stanley Orme, veteran MP for Salford, was in the chair. 'There is only one item of business,' he told MPs – forty-four of them new to the House – 'and that is the Speakership. The Shadow Cabinet is recommending Betty Boothroyd.' Her nomination was agreed by acclamation, and the meeting was closed. 'It was a quick fix. People came out astonished,' said one long-standing MP. 'New members couldn't believe what was happening.'[15]

But still nobody actually *knew* how 'the most sophisticated electorate in the world' (as MPs often describe themselves) would vote. This was unfamiliar territory for all concerned. Normally, the question of the Speakership is settled in discreet exchanges between the two front benches in Parliament, representing the government and the Opposition. Their agreed choice is nominated by a senior MP, and he (hitherto, it had always been a he) is elected unopposed by the full House.

With potentially five Tories and certainly one Labour candidate in the running, this was bound to be the first Speakership election contested between the government and the Opposition since 1951, an event that few could remember. On that occasion, Clement Attlee's defeated Labour Party opposed the election of the Conservative W. S. 'Shakes' Morrison with its own candidate, Major Milner. The Opposition was soundly thrashed for its pains. There was another contest twenty years later, though this was caused by backbenchers, not by political contest between government and Opposition. When Selwyn Lloyd, a former Cabinet minister, was offered for election with the approval of both main party leaderships in January 1971, Robin Maxwell-Hyslop, a Tory back-bench expert on procedure, rebelled. He nominated Sir Geoffrey de Freitas – Betty's former employer – as Speaker.

John Biffen wrote later, 'De Freitas had no warning of this unsought accolade. His demeanour registered both bewilderment and horror. Here was a candidate who would again have to be dragged to the chair. Happily, he was spared.'[16] Selwyn Lloyd was elected by 294 votes to fifty-five. But the back-bench rebellion did trigger a review of the Speakership election by the Commons Select Committee on Procedures. The outcome of this review was a greater degree of consultation between front and back benches on whose name should go forward.

That reform was of little help two decades later. Not only was this the first election contest between government and Opposition for more than forty years, but the very first at which there was a multiplicity of candidates. There was no precedent for such a competition; one had to be found.

By parliamentary tradition, the Father of the House – the MP with the longest continuous of service in the legislature – takes the Chair for the Speakership election. Sir Edward Heath, the newly knighted former Conservative Prime Minister and MP for Old Bexley and Sidcup since 1951, had just taken over this honorary title. Accordingly, he took charge of proceedings on the day, 27 April 1992. He had been in discreet talks with the Clerk of the House, Sir Clifford Boulton KCB, for some days, on how to handle this tricky operation. They had to think of every eventuality, including the possibility that none of the candidates would be able to command a majority of MPs' votes (in which case the House would be adjourned to discover whether 'the usual channels' could agree on a common candidate) and the prospect of a tied vote (in which case, according to custom, Sir Edward would vote with the government). 'We didn't reach that situation, fortunately,' said sources close to the former premier.

Sir Edward outlined the procedure that he intended to pursue. First, he would call for a candidate to be proposed and seconded. A debate would then take place on 'that Question'. At the end of that debate, the MP who had been proposed could speak, and indicate 'his or her willingness' to accept the office. This was the first time the faintest hint of a woman Speaker had been recorded in the annals of Parliament.

At this point, MPs could propose an amendment, striking out the first name and inserting a new name. A debate on the amendment would follow, at the end of which the member would signify willingness to accept office. Sir Edward would then call on MPs to vote on the Question, as amended – that is, on the rival. If there was no amendment, MPs would vote on the first name. If the amendment was carried, no further names could be put. This ingenious system of exhaustive ballot would work strongly to Betty's advantage.

So much so that David Harris, Tory MP for the Cornish fishing and farming constituency of St Ives, and a former political correspondent with the *Daily Telegraph*, appeared to smell a rat. 'On a point of order,' he asked Sir Edward, 'could you explain in which order the candidates will be proposed to the house? Have you decided in which order the names will be chosen?'[17] The Father of the House sidestepped the question, simply announcing that Sir Michael Neubert, Tory MP for the Essex constituency of Romford, would propose the first candidate.

Sir Michael rose and moved Mr Peter Brooke 'do take the Chair of this House as Speaker'. After some pleasantries about democracy he indulged in a bit of flattery to the chair. 'This parliament – if you will approve the metaphor, Sir Edward – will not be plain sailing,' a reference to the former Prime Minister's great passion in life, after music. Then it was straight into business: 'Unusually, we have a choice of candidates. In particular, on the Conservative side, it seems that we have an embarrassment of riches.' *Hansard* recorded '*Laughter*'. It was an invidious start to the new session.

Sir Michael ploughed on. Since Mr Brooke's entry to the House in 1977, the Chamber had had 'an essential magnetism for him'. He had filled with distinction a number of ministerial posts, culminating in the Cabinet post of Northern Ireland Secretary. But throughout, there had been no doubt in his mind of 'the primacy of parliament'.

Sir Michael followed up this slightly specious attempt at giving Brooke a 'House of Commons man' credibility with a reminder that there had been Speakers since 1258, and since the Second World War, the Speaker had always come from the majority party in the House. This custom and practice had worked well. And there was no reason that his time as a minister would make Brooke any less forthright in defence of backbenchers' rights or less jealous of the Speaker's independence than his predecessors.

'My right honourable Friend is steeped in the traditions of this place,' he gushed. 'Both his parents were parliamentarians. Parliament is in his blood. He has a grasp of history which would guide him if he were to take his place in that long line of Speakers. He would bring dignity, erudition and wit to the exercise of the office and the stature to ensure firm handling of our often stormy debates.'

Finally, Brooke was agreeable and affable in his dealings with MPs of all parties. He would be an admirable ambassador outside, and he had the strength, stamina and family support needed for the task. In short, he had all those qualities that the House looked for in a Speaker. This short paean of praise – it took only six minutes – may have been pitched a little high, even for a cricket-loving minister with friends on both sides of the House. The little-noticed mention of 'family support' was certainly below the belt, it being well known that Betty had no family.

Seconding Brooke, Sir Tom Arnold, MP for the Cheshire seat of Hazel Grove, praised his impartiality, and predicted that he would protect the rights of backbenchers. On a personal note 'and without wishing to be impertinent' he commended Brooke's bushy eyebrows which made his friends wonder what he was thinking.

Sir Tom sat down at 3 p.m., a signal for the House parliamentary enthusiasts to get their oar in. Tam Dalyell, Labour MP for Linlithgow, seized the opportunity to ask whether the new Speaker would be more lenient towards back benchers' private-notice questions, and whether science would be given a better parliamentary hearing in future. James Wallace, the Scottish National MP for Orkney and Shetland, pointed out that the Speakership of the UK Parliament of Great Britain and Northern Ireland went back only to 1801, and the English would forget that at their peril. And Tony Benn, Left-wing Labour MP for Chesterfield, argued that the House needed a reforming Speaker, and signalled his support for Betty. 'If Parliament is to survive, it must be as a workshop, not a museum,' he thundered. Nicholas Winterton, the awkward-squad Tory MP for Macclesfield, Cheshire, echoed Benn's remarks.

Only then could Peter Brooke get his word in, at the request of Sir Edward. It was a good speech, replete with historical reference, jokes and personal modesty. He promised to avoid the example of the turn-of-the-century peer, whose memoirs were held up at the printers for three weeks because the printers had run out of the capital 'I'. He told MPs his first visit to the House was when he was a nine-year-old schoolboy 'lugubriously to report, on the day that the then Mr Speaker FitzRoy died, which I suppose constitutes a thread of continuity.' There were other threads, less lugubrious. His forebear, Sir Robert Brooke, was the first Speaker to represent the City of London. But that was in 1554, in Queen Mary's second parliament, and he did only last for five weeks, from 2 April to 5 May. He decided 'in the reign of Bloody Mary, and in an office which then often led to summary execution, that discretion was the better part of valour'.

Brooke prayed in aid his wife, who possessed 'a vivid and willing understanding of the role that falls to a Speaker's wife', and sought to defuse the row over his proximity to Cabinet office by insisting: 'I shall be my own man.' He counted it as an honour to have been considered 'at least worthy of nomination' and expressed his gratitude to those who encouraged him to stand, and sat down, after speaking for only six minutes.

It was not the speech of a man who expected to win, and probably could not have been. He must have been given a snapshot of the likely result by the Whips before MPs gathered in the Chamber, but he carried it off with some dignity. How dismaying must it have been for him to watch the next man to rise to his feet: John Biffen, Tory MP for Shropshire North, to move an amendment, deleting Peter Brooke, and inserting Miss Betty Boothroyd.

Biffen, whose role as a discreet champion of Betty's claims over many months, pleaded for 'total myopia about party affiliation' and about the various conventions as to power and precedence, arguing that the overriding consideration should be 'the test of merit'. He was 'most happy' to commend the honourable Member for West Bromwich, who had been an MP for twenty years.

Most of that time, he pointed out, was spent on the back benches, learning the endless frustrations of that kind of life. 'Those of us who are looking for fraternity in suffering will therefore well consider her merits,' he said. 'Also, and providentially, the honourable Lady's innocence was tempered by service in the Fagin's Den known as the Labour Whips' Office. As it now seems that service in the Whips' Office is almost a *sine qua non* of consideration for the Speakership, that tells us something about either the Whips' Office or the modern Speakership.'

Biffen commended Betty's performance as Deputy Speaker since 1987, a role she had exercised with authority and courtesy, often in difficult circumstances. It was 'an apprenticeship carried out with great skill'. He concluded, 'If I wanted to make the recommendation, I should say merely: look at the record, look at the experience.'

Betty's seconder, Gwyneth Dunwoody, MP for Crewe and Nantwich, had worked with her in Transport House where her father, Morgan Phillips, was general secretary of the Labour Party, and was characteristically robust. 'She was highly thought of, not least because my father was known to say that if they were any damned good they went, and if they were no damned good, one could not get rid of them,' recalled Mrs Dunwoody. 'The honourable Lady, of course, was one of those who moved on.'

She was also the first to play the gender card. 'It is time we had in the chair someone whom we shall vote for not just because she is a woman, but because she is a woman parliamentarian whose intelligence and ability have proved themselves time and again in the protection of all Members of Parliament of all parties.'

As if this were not enough, she harped shamelessly on Betty's origins. Warning of attempts at undue influence upon the Speaker by government and Opposition front benches alike, Mrs Dunwoody argued, 'It is therefore essential that we elect a woman who comes from one of the tribes of the United Kingdom that is well known for its ability to speak its mind plainly and with wit. I refer, of course, to the people of west Yorkshire.'

Her warmth and good opinion was supported by Sir Russell Johnston, veteran Liberal Democrat MP for Inverness, Nairn and Lochaber, who commended Betty's fairness, sense of humour and decisiveness. Had the outcome been in doubt hitherto, it must have been dispelled by the next two speeches from the Tory back benches: the first, from archetypal Tory 'wet' Robert Adley, the train-loving MP for Christchurch, and the second from Barry Porter, a tough-guy of the Tory Right, who sits for Wirral, South. Adley, tragically to die of a heart attack only a year later, appealed for a non-partisan, cross-party consensus in support of Betty, and Porter extolled her credibility and experience.

At precisely 3.42, two minutes under the hour since the debate began, Sir Edward invited Betty to make the speech of her life, 'to submit herself to the House if she so wishes'. She began by paying the customary tributes to the former Speaker Weatherill, which in her case was not simply obeying a custom because he was 'my teacher and my friend'. Then she recalled that Speaker Weatherill had once been asked his guiding rule when he was in the chair. He had quoted St Bernard of Clairvaux: 'Notice everything. Correct a little. Cherish the Brethren.'

This, she thought, was not a bad rule for a Speaker, and one that she would wish to follow. 'Although I shall certainly cherish the brethren when I am in the chair, I can be relied upon to cherish the sisters as well,' she added. This brought her to 'another factor', Betty went on. 'Much has been written recently about the possibility of having a woman Speaker for the first time. Some right honourable Members might consider it desirable, others conceivably not, but this House must know that, although having a competent woman Speaker may be a good thing, having a bad woman Speaker would be disastrous. It would be a tragedy for this House, it would be bad for the country, and it would be bad for the cause of women everywhere.'

Conceding that the House could on such occasions become sentimental, Betty argued that when it came down to basic, MPs were essentially hard-headed. Therefore, she did not have to tell them to make their decision solely on the grounds of her conduct in the chair and her time as an MP. Then, in that memorable line, she appealed: 'I say to you, elect me for what I am, and not for what I was born. That is crucial.'

Recalling her twenty-year membership of the House, Betty admitted, 'For me, the Commons has never been just a career: it is my life. I have known it in all its moods – sometimes very dull, although even at its drowsiest it is always capable of erupting at the most unexpected moment.' She had also, unfortunately, known it at its most docile before the Executive, and when it was mutinous. 'I have witnessed moments that are the very stuff that our history is made of.'

Now, millions outside shared those experiences through the introduction of television into the Chamber, which showed events not only to British viewers but to living rooms thousands of miles away. And though she understood the very strong and robust feelings (a phrase she has often used since) so often revealed, people at home and abroad expected the highest possible standards of conduct from MPs.

Though she had been a Deputy Speaker, 'always at heart I have been a backbencher'. She had never sought, and never expected, to occupy one of the great offices of government. Administrations had grown enormously in size over those two decades, but 'I have always been aware that it is the back benches which provide the overwhelming majority of the House when all is said and done.' Betty thanked her proposers and supporters, and promised to endeavour to justify the faith placed in her, concluding, 'I now have to offer myself as the voice of the House – sensitive to the concerns of every member, aware of the supreme duty of the Speaker to safeguard the rights of this House, abandoning all my previous commitments to party and content to serve the House for as long as it may require.'

It was a show-stopper. Betty had pressed all the right buttons. It was the speech – as the late John Smith put it about himself – of someone seeking the right to serve. At 3.53, Sir Edward put the Question 'That the amendment be made', and the House divided. Robert Adley and Giles Radice, Labour MP for Durham North, were tellers for the Ayes; Peter Bottomley, Tory MP for Eltham, and Sir Anthony Grant, fellow Conservative MP for Cambridgeshire South-West, were tellers for the Noes. The result was even more dramatic than her campaigners had hoped for: MPs voted 372 to 238 to elect her, a decisive majority of 134 votes over Peter Brooke. Apart from the overwhelming support of the PLP, Betty picked up the backing of all the smaller Opposition parties, ranging from the Liberal Democrats to the Reverend Ian Paisley's firebrand Democratic Ulster Unionists, picking up the Scottish and Welsh Nationalists on the way, and the moderate SDLP and the official Ulster Unionists. The most interesting name missing from the Ayes was Harold Walker

Most critical, however, was the support of seventy-two Conservative MPs who broke with the candidate of their party and put their faith in Betty. Nor were they all of a political piece. There were Tory women, of course: Emma Nicholson, Mrs Edwina Currie, and Mrs Elizabeth Peacock, the miners' champion. Some, like Jerry Hayes, the gaudy, gabby MP for Harlow, Jim Lester (Broxtowe), the sturdy supporter of Britain's aid programme, and John Bowis, the chubby MP for Battersea soon to become junior Health Minister, were regarded as on the 'wet' side of the party. But there were also hard-line Right-wingers – the exotic Bill Walker (Tayside North), together with Sir Rhodes Boyson (Brent North) and Sir George Gardiner (Reigate), both luminaries of the 1922 Executive. Betty won the vote of the man sometimes (and wrongly) cast as the House misogynist, Sir Nicholas Fairbairn. And she even won the support of five senior Conservative ministers, the hard-line Thatcherite, John Redwood, Local Government Minister who later went into the Cabinet; Anthony Nelson, Economic Secretary to the Treasury; Robert Jackson, Minister for the Civil Service; Michael Forsyth, Minister of State for Employment; and Peter Lloyd, Minister of State at the Home Office. Five junior ministers backed her, and three members of the Cabinet (including John Major) abstained – though sixteen Cabinet ministers supported their quondam colleague Peter Brooke. All five Tory hopefuls for the Speakership voted against her. All in all, it was a remarkable coalition of support for Betty, stretching from the old-fashioned Conservative knights of the shires to the inner-city hard-Leftists of the Labour Party.

The Main Question, as amended, was put and agreed to, and *Hansard* notes it was resolved: 'That Miss Betty Boothroyd do take the Chair of this House as Speaker. Whereupon Sir Edward Heath left the chair and Miss Betty Boothroyd was conducted to the Chair by Mr John Biffen and Mrs Gwyneth Dunwoody.' Standing on the upper step in front of the chair, Betty, now Speaker-elect (her election having to be confirmed in the Lords the following day), thanked the House for the 'very great honour' it had bestowed on her. 'I pray that I shall justify its confidence, and I pledge that I shall do all in my power to preserve and cherish its traditions.'

Offering his warmest congratulations, John Major showed his agreeable side. The fact that her election was contested 'only adds to your success and in no sense detracts from it', he insisted. 'It will enhance your authority in the House and it reflects also the richness of experience available to us in choosing our Speaker.' He concluded, 'I have no doubt that your Speakership will be long and distinguished, underpinned by adherence to the principle so eloquently proclaimed by Mr Speaker Onslow, who stated: "I have loved independence and pursued it. I have kept firm to my original principles and upon conscience have never deviated from them to serve."'

Neil Kinnock could not resist celebrating Betty's election 'also because of the fact that you are a woman'. After six centuries and 154 previous Speakers, her elevation could hardly be described as an overnight success for women's rights. He heeded her 'elect me for what I am' admonition, but welcomed her election as 'a step forward for the majority of the people of the United Kingdom who, after all, share your gender'. He topped this show of political correctness with a quip to make the House squirm: 'I say with the greatest warmth and sincerity, may all your points of order be little ones.'

After tributes from the defeated Peter Brooke and the minor Opposition parties, Tony Banks, House stand-up comic (Labour, Newham North-West) rose on a point of order. Madam Speaker-elect made her first observation from the chair: 'Today would not be complete without a point of order.' Banks said two MPs had not voted for her – Betty herself, and himself, because he was late. 'I had intended to vote for you. I hope that, when you read *Hansard* [where votes are listed by name] you will not hold that against me,' Betty retorted, 'That is the most bogus point of order I have heard this session.' There would be many, many more. She was on her way.

CHAPTER IX

ORDER! ORDER!

HUNDREDS OF FAN-MAIL letters poured in every week after Betty took up her post. 'It is all terribly flattering, and she is trying to reply to every single letter personally,' said an aide. She was an overnight success on television too, fast becoming a cult figure on American cable TV. Letters also appeared in the newspapers. She had caught the public mood perfectly. Diana Mead, an estate agent's valuer in Penarth, south Glamorgan, wrote to the *Daily Express* to say her election had been 'a terrific thing'. She added, 'No one should feel discarded and pensioned off at sixty – life is there for the taking. Betty Boothroyd is a wonderful example to us all.'

The Queen's Speech a week after Betty's election brought a foreboding of what was to come. Among the measures enunciated from the throne was implementation of the Treaty of Maastricht, which would later cause near anarchy in parliament. Betty was in danger that day of upstaging the monarch. In the *Daily Mail*, veteran Westminster-watcher Colin Welch wrote, 'One thing we all must have noticed – the resplendent, smiling and life-enhancing deportment of Madam Speaker Boothroyd. People often say she was once a beauty. No need to – she still is.'[1]

Betty was appointed to the Privy Council, the Queen's body of private counsellors, a month later. She settled into the Commons chair very quickly. But it was not long before Speaker Boothroyd faced the first test of her authority in the House, and from the most predictable quarter, a small area of constant turbulence below the gangway on the Labour side: the traditional seat of Dennis Skinner, MP for Bolsover. Skinner, for so long her hard-Left opponent on Labour's national executive, was not called 'the beast of Bolsover' for nothing. On 2 July

1992, he described John Gummer, the garrulous and bespectacled Agriculture minister as 'a little squirt' and 'a wart'. Betty called on him to withdraw his remarks, on the grounds that they constituted unparliamentary language.

He refused, saying, 'I am not prepared to do so, that is how I picture him.' Madam Speaker ordered him to leave the chamber. He then took refuge in the Members' Tea Room, arguing that he had been told only to leave the chamber, not the precincts of the Palace. Several Tory MPs volunteered to effect a citizen's arrest, but Skinner eventually left after words with Labour's Chief Whip. It was the ninth time he had been expelled since 1979, but the press reported the incident as Betty's first 'blooding'. Only the week before, she had vouchsafed, 'I have a very broad back, and I am developing a rather thick skin.'

On the whole, however, her chairmanship brought forth murmurs of approval from both sides of the House. Her first historic occasion in the chair, for the opening of the debate on the Maastricht Bill on 20 May, was the occasion for dissident Scots Labour MPs to carry out their threat to disrupt parliament. One cried, 'I spy Strangers,' a parliamentary device to clear the public gallery and bring proceedings to a halt. Betty allowed the storm to blow itself out and normal business was resumed, prompting the *Guardian*'s witty sketch writer Andrew Rawnsley to point out that, as Speaker, Betty was proving to be 'a velvet fist in an iron glove – exactly the combination that MPs, particularly the men, were looking for when they chose to make her their Madam'.

It was a remarkable tribute to Betty that little more than six months after she ascended to the chair, she was voted Parliamentarian of the Year by the *Spectator*, the weekly periodical known for its stylish writing and reactionary views. At an awards lunch in London in late November, the judges praised her as 'the first new Speaker of the House of Commons in modern times to show immediately that she is the right man for the job'. Dominic Lawson, editor of the *Spectator* (and son of the previous Conservative Chancellor), disclosed, 'She was our unanimous choice. She has already achieved the mastery of the House.' It was the first time a Speaker had been honoured in this way, and commentators put it down to the firm but good-humoured way she slapped down naughty backbenchers. 'The House must come to order, instead of bawling and shouting like this,' she would rap out crisply.

She had also begun to show off her own style, ending each Prime Minister's Question Time with an admonitory 'Time's Up!' at 3.30 p.m. precisely. This was to become her parliamentary catch-phrase, rather like a comedian's gag line. Reminiscent of a barmaid's cry at closing time in the pub, it had most men in the Chamber in her thrall. Some Tories, however, thought it rather common. None of them dare say so in public. Nor, though they affected to be shocked, did they protest when Betty put her hand over her mouth and mimed an ostentatious yawn to curb one particularly long-winded government minister.

Betty had also stamped her personality in other ways. She ruled that the menus for her official dinners should be written in English instead of French, the traditional language of banquets. 'It's not chauvinism, or anything of that kind,' she insisted. 'But the language of our Parliament is English, and it seems only right that any hospitality I give here should be in English too.'[2] She even gave English wine – an award-winning Chiddingstone 1989 – to the Speakers of Saxony, Brandenburg and Thuringia (the new democratic regions of eastern Germany) to eat with their avocado and lime salad, together with House of Commons claret and breast of chicken Westminster. There were other things not to her liking, where being a woman did not help. Betty banned Labour front-bencher Mrs Ann Clwyd from parking her Ford Granada in Speaker's Court, the gloomy but convenient quadrangle reserved for the Speaker and ministers' chauffeur-driven limos, threatening to have her clamped if she did not obey instructions to use the underground car park for ordinary MPs.

Inside the chamber, many Scottish members were restive. After a general election in which the people of Scotland had voted overwhelmingly for a Labour government, but had once again got a Conservative administration committed to 'the union' with England and deeply hostile to devolution of power, Scots Labour MPs had been threatening to disrupt parliament. They lived up to their word on 17 December 1992, just before MPs went off for the Christmas recess.

Outraged by a 'hole in the corner' written government announcement by Scottish Secretary Ian Lang of the first eight hospital trusts

– self-governing commercials units within the National Health Service
– north of the border, they first brought business to a virtual standstill
by bogus points of order. When this tactic failed to secure a ministerial
statement, angry MPs led by Ernie Ross (Dundee West) and George
Galloway (Glasgow Hillhead) of the Scotland United faction left their
seats and stood protesting in the centre of the Chamber, facing the
mace, symbol of the Crown's authority.

Betty's deputy, Michael Morris, appealed for seasonal goodwill, and
when his pleas fell on deaf ears he ordered a five-minute suspension.
When that was over, Betty took the chair, but she was no more able
to persuade the fiery Scots to abide by the rules of the House. She
suspended the sitting for nearly three hours, losing six short debates
in the process. When she returned, Madam Speaker announced the
Royal Assent for several Bills, and swiftly adjourned the House until
the new year.

It was an unhappy end to the year that had brought Betty her greatest
happiness. But she was undeterred, telling her local paper after
returning from a Commonwealth Speakers' Conference in Namibia,
'The year of 1992 was really magnificent for me – but it looks as if I
am going to be as busy as ever in 1993.'[3]

Though the Speaker is not allowed to engage in parliamentary or
partisan politics, early in the new year Betty signalled her support to
the founding of a political fund-raising organization, Emily's List UK,
to help women fight for seats at Westminster. On the seventy-fifth
anniversary of the granting of votes to women in Britain, she told the
BBC that sixty women out of 651 MPs at Westminster was 'nowhere
near enough'.

The main reason, she thought, that there were not more women in
the House was because they thought their place was in the home.
'They are the only sex that can give birth, and many of them want to
be at home with their children to bring them up. Secondly, it is awfully
difficult for women to fight their way through the selection committees
of the major parties. These committees are male-dominated and they
tend to look to a man. They ask women how they would cope with
children, yet the question is never put to a man.'

There were times when the men must have thought she was getting
her own back, for Betty proved to be an absolute stickler for procedure.

Early in 1993, she ticked off the new Conservative member for
Kincardine and Deeside, George Kynoch. His crime was to allow a
parliamentary clerk at the Scottish Office to send in a question to the
Commons table office on a blank form that Kynoch had already signed.
This allowed a back-bench Tory MP to offer a 'dolly' catch to a
minister, in this case Ian Lang, the Scottish Secretary. Such tactics
were an abuse of procedure, boomed Betty, and there must be
no recurrence. Kynoch and Lang grovelled and apologized. On
another occasion, a Tory MP cut short his lunch and ran back to the
Commons for environment questions. 'I wanted to ask a question,
but Betty is so strict she won't call you unless you've been there
from the start of the session,' he explained breathlessly. And another
Conservative backbencher, Barry Porter, complained that a Labour
member had used the word 'pillock' four times. Was this not unparliamentary language? Did she know what it meant? Betty, whose textile-
town origins must have brought her into frequent contact with this
item of male slang, affected not to know what it meant. 'Funny, that,'
observed *The Times* political sketch writer. 'She's in charge of 650 of
them.'

Maastricht proved to be the issue that challenged her skills as
Speaker to the limit. As the Bill giving effect to the Maastricht Treaty
moved towards the end of its Commons committee stage in mid April
1993, Betty's deputy Michael Morris MP, handed down a controversial
decision ruling out a vote on the Social Chapter. His rejection of a
vote on this key issue prompted Labour to move adjournment of the
night's debate – effectively a censure of the chair.

The Social Chapter, confirming and extending the social rights of
people at work, had been specifically excluded from the British version
of the Treaty of Maastricht by the 'opt-out' negotiated by John Major.
Labour and the Liberal Democrats wanted the chapter reinserted, and
John Smith in particular was willing to use every parliamentary device
to compel the government to accept Europe's social dimension.

However, the Opposition refused to listen to the siren voices of
hard-line anti-Maastricht Tory rebels, who were hoping to derail the
treaty's legislative progress by proposing a motion of no confidence
in the Deputy Speaker. Labour decided to wait until the Bill came
back for its final Report Stage, when Betty would be in the chair. As

the days dragged by, and tension increased, she talked behind the
scenes to key players in the political drama and promised a verdict on
4 May.

Westminster watchers calculated that with support from the Liberal
Democrats, the Scottish Nationalists, two Northern Ireland minority
parties, the DUP and SDLP, and as many as nineteen rebel Tory
'Euro-sceptics', Labour's Amendment 2 reinstating the Social Chapter
would command a majority. If this proved to be the case, it would
humiliate John Major and force a vote of confidence in his administration. He would almost certainly win the vote, but his would thereafter be a lame-duck government.

So Cabinet ministers spent an anxious weekend, privately hoping
that Madam Speaker would come to their aid by supporting her deputy.
Publicly, they played down the risk that she would not, by arguing
that defeat on the Labour amendment would not alter the government's resolve. They would simply press ahead. For its part, the Opposition stepped up the pressure on a Speaker it had installed in office.
George Robertson MP, Labour's razor-like European spokesman, said
there would be 'widespread anger and dismay' if Betty refused a vote.

Loyalist Tories, who had voted against her getting the Speakership,
warned that she would undermine the authority of her own deputy if
she overturned his ruling, which was based on the confidential advice
of the Commons clerks. However, her old friend the columnist Alan
Watkins urged her not to be bullied. 'Miss Boothroyd may be concerned not to appear to contradict her deputy or to favour her former
party. Nevertheless, justice requires a division [vote].'[4]

This crisis of personal confidence in the job, and how to cope with
warring political interests, comes to every Speaker sooner or later.
Betty's Labour predecessor George Thomas has related how the major
parties try to look after their interests. 'Key people from the Opposition and the government would come to sound out what my rulings
were likely to be on certain issues and it was not unusual for me to be
told that a poor view would be taken if I decided to rule in a particular
way. I soon became convinced that both sides were engaged in an
effort to gain the ascendancy over me. Polite but barely hidden
menaces would be forthcoming in the privacy of a chat in my room.'[5]
Thomas finally threatened to walk out and resign, telling parliament

Picking up the baton from Shirley Williams in 1981, Betty was known as a 'Hammer of the Left' during her years on the National Executive Committee.

BETTY Boothroyd
She speaks for the people **92**

'Speaking for the people' was Betty's address in the 1992 General Election. She was already hot favourite to become Speaker.

Above: Madam Speaker, accompanied by Black Rod, leads the Members of the House of Commons to the House of Lords to hear the Queen's speech at the State Opening of Parliament.

Left: Madam Speaker meets her deputies, the Clerks and the Serjeant at Arms to discuss the day's business. Her Deputy Speakers are Michael Morris *(on Betty's right)*, Geoffrey Lofthouse *(opposite Betty, in the centre)* and Dame Janet Fookes *(on Geoffrey's left)*.

Right: Order, order!

Below: A packed House of Commons at the start of the day's business.

Red carpet treatment: the entrance to the Speaker's House in the Palace of Westminster.

The Great Bed of State: 'Of course I've bounced on it,' says Madam Speaker, 'and it's far too hard to sleep in. I prefer my comfy one upstairs.'

The first woman Speaker's coat of arms. Betty composed her own motto, 'I Speak to Serve.' The red background of the crest represents her career as a Labour MP, the mace her Speakership and the white rose her Yorkshire origins.

why he had done so. The front-benchers backed down, protesting that they simply wished him to know their party viewpoint.

Under similar pressure, a year and a week after she had been elected Speaker, Betty took the hardest decision of her career in public life. She first met Sir Clifford Boulton, Clerk to the House, and then her three deputies. Having taken advice, the decision whether to allow a debate and vote was her own. She threw out ministerial objections and ruled that the Commons could, after all, have a direct vote on the Social Chapter. MPs were in turmoil. Downing Street put on a brave face, saying that even if Labour's initiative was approved, it would not affect ratification of the Treaty. The Liberal Democrats promised John Smith their backing, and with the die-hard Tories already on side, defeat was staring John Major in the face.

This was a full-blown political crisis. In the aftermath of Britain's humiliating withdrawal from the European Exchange Rate Mechanism, the government's popularity was already in steep decline only a year after being returned to power. The Conservatives faced defeat in a key by-election in Newbury, Berkshire, and in the county council elections, only two days later. By allowing the vote demanded by Labour, Betty could expect to be accused of political partiality, or worse. But outside Westminster, opinion across the spectrum supported her. The Tory-supporting London *Evening Standard* immediately responded, 'The only aspect of the current dispute over the Maastricht Treaty that anyone can fully grasp is that the Speaker, Betty Boothroyd, has come well out of it . . . Mrs (sic) Boothroyd is agreed to have shown admirable decisiveness. Which is more than one can say for any of the other players in this drama.'[6]

The Left-of-centre *Guardian* agreed, 'By deciding that MPs could vote on this key issue, Betty Boothroyd did a service both to earthy common sense and to the loftier theories of representative democracy. If she had not done so, Parliament would have been an ass.'[7] In the *Observer*, Alan Watkins was ecstatic, proposing that readers raise a glass to the toast 'Betty', adding *sotto voce*, 'God bless her!' Certainly, he argued, no one should underestimate the courage it took for her to take that decision . . . 'and yet she did the right thing.'[8]

Happily for Madam Speaker, she is not allowed to give reasons for her rulings. Newbury duly fell by a landslide to the Liberal Democrats, and the Tories suffered their worst drubbing for decades in the county council elections. But nobody blamed the Speaker. She had, after all, only been doing her job, guided by her own convictions. They had proved more reliable and responsive to the mood of the country. MPs waited anxiously for the vote to be taken.

Betty's second honeymoon proved short-lived. Lurking round the corner was another messy affair, this time reflecting on the integrity of an individual MP rather than the viability of a government. Michael Mates, Conservative MP for Hampshire East and a Minister of State in the Northern Ireland Office responsible for security in Ulster, came under pressure to resign at the end of May over his links with the financier Asil Nadir who had jumped £3.5 million bail on fraud charges and fled to his native northern Cyprus.

As his involvement with the fugitive tycoon emerged, including leaked letters to the Attorney-General and the gift of a watch inscribed 'don't let the b—s get you down', Mates bowed to pressure and reluctantly resigned his ministerial office. But he had one last shot in his locker. By tradition, outgoing ministers are allowed to make an uninterrupted statement to the Commons, explaining the circumstances of their resignation. Mates informed Madam Speaker of his intention to take advantage of this privilege.

Proceedings against Nadir on thirteen charges of fraud and false accounting involving £30 million were still very much alive in the courts. And since 1963, MPs have been bound by a self-denying ordinance not to raise in debates, motions or questions any matters awaiting decision in the criminal courts. The Speaker decides what is and what is not covered by this sub judice rule. Betty privately asked Mates if he was going to say anything that might prejudice Nadir's impending trial. After speaking to him on the telephone, she thought she had full assurances on this score.

The day of the drama, 29 June 1993, began well. As she made her way through to the chamber, the Central Lobby was packed with mainly working-class pensioners lobbying their MPs about the imposition of value added tax on fuel. They recognized her, and burst into very unparliamentary, but spontaneous, applause. A Commons policeman shook his head, saying, 'I've been here sixteen years and I've never seen that before.'

Just for once, the television cameras were not broadcasting. Both BBC channels were screening live tennis from Wimbledon. They missed some great parliamentary theatre. On his feet immediately after Prime Minister's Questions, as is the custom on such occasions, Mates threw caution to the wind in his blistering resignation speech. He told a crowded House he had been foolish, but had done nothing improper. He excoriated the Serious Fraud Office, responsible for bringing the prosecution, accusing it of improper pressure, including claims of conspiracy involving Nadir's defence lawyer Anthony Scrivener QC and the trial judge, Mr Justice Tucker.

Betty, given whispered advice by her clerks (though her most senior Clerk, Sir Clifford Boulton, was missing from the Commons, in Stoke-on-Trent to accept an honorary law degree from Keele University), grew visibly restive in the chair. Mates, a heavily built former Army officer, lumbered on with one astonishing and contentious allegation after another, insisting that Nadir had been denied his rights under the law. Mates's girlfriend, Christine Robinson-Moltke, watched from the gallery. She urged him on so vigorously that a gallery attendant asked her to desist.

Betty reminded the Hampshire East MP that Nadir was still facing charges on which he might stand trial. Mates protested about the seizures of documents from Nadir's bankrupt company Polly Peck International. Madam Speaker intervened again, cautioning him about the sub-judice rules and promising, 'I will see they are carried out.'

Mates replied, 'I hear what you say. Please trust me.' There were further exchanges with the chair, and Mates appeared on the point of surrendering. Nine times she intervened, and nine times he kept going. At one point, after repeated clashes, Betty bellowed, 'I am now requiring you to resume your seat.' Then, extraordinarily, a group of Labour MPs, some on the Left, rallied to him. Clare Short, one of Labour's most prominent women, sought vainly to make a point of order in his defence. Betty would not let her speak, pointing out that personal statements could not be interrupted. 'You've interrupted it,' retorted Ms Short.

Mates sensed that the House was on his side, not Betty's. Invoking the language of Speaker Lenthall, he said to Labour cheers, 'If one cannot speak in this place, not about innocence or guilt, not about trials, not about sub judice, but what is wrong with the system, then what is the point of being here?' He finished his thirty-minute statement and sat down, the chamber abuzz. Betty had been worsted. She had told him to sit down, and he had not done so. She had warned him not to rehearse matters that might come before the courts, and he had ignored her. His bravado had faced down her authority. She had not 'named' him, as she could have done. Had he persisted after her doing so, she could have ordered the Sergeant at Arms, Sir Alan Urwick, to escort him from the chamber, difficult though that would have been.

Unquestionably, the burly ex-Major had got away with defying the Speaker. The import of what had happened was not lost on the parliamentary press lobby. 'DEFEAT IN THE WAR OF WORDS IS THE FIRST SET-BACK FOR SPEAKER' headlined the *Daily Telegraph* report, which spoke of Betty suffering the first real blow to her authority as Speaker. It was, the paper thought, probably her most difficult time since being elected. Many MPs thought she relied too much on the advice of her clerks. They backed Mates's view that since much of the information was already in the public domain, it was the duty of the Speaker to protect the right of MPs to raise issues of importance in Parliament. 'There is also some concern that by repeatedly trying without success to prevent Mr Mates making his allegations, her own authority has been weakened. It could be more difficult on a subsequent occasion to prevent an MP raising issues which she rules are before the courts.'9

Lawyers outside the House also took a more lenient view than Madam Speaker. Some said that even if Mates had repeated his remarks outside the House, it was doubtful if contempt of court proceedings would have ensued. David Kirk, head of the fraud unit at City solicitors Stephenson Hardwood, admitted that the Polly Peck issue was still technically sub judice, but Betty had taken the ruling too far. For there to be a contempt, a 'substantial risk of serious prejudice' to a fair trial had to be established. It was arguable that there was no realistic prospect of a trial taking place that could be prejudiced by Mates's impassioned attack on the SFO's handling of the Nadir case. If the case did come to court, it was unlikely to be for two years and 'the courts have always taken the view that time is a great healer as far as prejudice is concerned. Betty's arguments, taken to their logical conclusion, would mean that if the trial never took place, then no one would ever be able to comment on the case again.'[10]

According to a well-informed parliamentary source, John Major consoled Betty over a drink. 'He was very sympathetic, and very fed up with Mates,' said the source. That is as maybe. But it did not stop the Prime Minister from putting her in a similarly difficult position a year later. Nor did it prevent the media from speculating that there was 'concern among ministers' about her handling of the affair. Andrew Marr, columnist for the *Independent*, sprang to her defence, disclosing that Mates had promised to Betty on the telephone only forty-five minutes before he spoke that he would not say anything that would prejudice a fair trial for Nadir. He read her a short extract, beginning, 'I do not know whether Mr Asil Nadir is innocent or guilty . . . that is a matter for the courts.' Betty thought she had a deal 'and was gob smacked when Mr Mates ambushed her'.[11]

Marr also mentioned newspaper stories alleging that Betty was taking a holiday to open a hotel in Cyprus, on an expenses-paid junket. Betty was 'very hurt' about this. Senior MPs said she was paying for the trip herself, and had agreed to open the hotel for a friend before she became Speaker. Pretty trivial matters, thought the *Independent*'s man, not normally worth discussing. 'But a whispering campaign against the Speaker is another matter. And that, say Mrs (*sic*) Boothroyd's friends, is what she has been facing.' He recalled a previous whispering campaign against Speaker Weatherill, which he had 'weatherilled'. Marr opined, 'My guess is that Speaker Boothroyd is even more popular than he, and that these whispers against her will blow away with no harm done . . she has more friends here than any minister does. So don't mess with Betty.'

This seems to have been something of an over-reaction to a brief item in the *Evening Standard*'s Londoner's Diary, which claimed that ministers had met to discuss the Mates affair. No evidence of such a meeting was ever produced. The *Standard* item also quoted the manager of the five-star Coral Beach hotel in Paphos, in the south of the island – a long way from Nadir's hideaway in the Turkish-controlled northern sector. Her presence would allow people 'to see we have guests of high calibre'.

Not very much to object to here, even if the *Standard* did add bitchily

that 'the Speaker is indeed a guest of high calibre. Far too high for
hotel-opening junkets.' Betty was – and is – a family friend of the
hotel's owner Michael Leptos, a wealthy property developer. She has
been a regular visitor to the island for twenty years. It rivals Sri Lanka
in her affections.

But her involvement with the Leptos development did upset
environmental campaigners in Cyprus. They claimed that the 670-bed
Coral Beach hotel had been allowed to encroach on an unspoilt beach
in violation of planning regulations. By performing the opening ceremony, Betty had given a stamp of approval to the island's 'over-
development', they said. The inauguration went ahead on 18
September. It was a grand affair, featuring laser and firework displays,
and attended by President Glafkos Clerides of Cyprus and a minor
galaxy of ministers, bishops, business leaders and diplomats. Betty's
'Order! Order!' speech certainly did pull in the crowds, who appreciated her tribute to the warmth of the Cypriot people.

Scarcely much to make a whispering campaign of here, admittedly.
But with the vital Maastricht vote virtually upon them, ministers were
understandably nervous and disposed to look around for someone to
blame for their predicament. Affairs took an even more bizarre course
when a group of Conservative Euro-sceptics headed by the columnist-
peer Lord Rees-Mogg went to the High Court for a judicial review
of the whole Maastricht business. MPs were alarmed. Tony Benn MP,
for so long her political opponent on Labour's national executive,
wrote to Betty arguing that the case could constitute a breach of privilege of the House. He suggested that the process of judicial review
was going too far, with the High Court being invited to rule whether
parliament, as well as government, had exceeded its powers. He asked
for the matter to be referred to the Committee of Privileges, one of
the most august bodies of the House, which as its name implies guards
the privileges of members.

Instead of writing back privately, as is the custom, Betty preferred
to say what she had to say before the whole House. In a historic
statement greeted by cheers from MPs, she asserted her role as protec-
tor of Parliament's power and underlined its supremacy over the
courts. The Euro-sceptics were arguing before the courts that the
Maastricht Treaty ratification process was legally and constitutionally

flawed. The Speaker is duty bound to be on the look-out for any attempt to infringe the freedom of MPs, and Betty clearly saw one here.

Citing the 1689 Bill of Rights, which asserts the sovereignty of parliament, she said she treated 'with great seriousness' any potential questioning in the courts of proceedings in the Commons. Article 9 of the 304-year-old Act lays down that 'the freedom of speech and debates or proceedings in Parliament ought not to be impeached or questioned in any court or place out of parliament.' She went on: 'I am sure that this House is entitled to expect, when the case referred to by Mr Benn begins to be heard on Monday, that the Bill of Rights will be required to be fully respected by all those appearing before the court.'

It was a timely reminder, rather than a threat, and it did not impress all the lawyers. Professor Trevor Hartley of the London School of Economics argued, 'There have been cases when the courts have clashed with Parliament. But Lord Rees-Mogg's action is challenging the government, rather than Parliament.'[12] However, it was enough for Tony Benn to claim victory. He told Madam Speaker, 'I hope the judges will now drop the case brought by Lord Rees-Mogg. To proceed, after what you have said, could constitute a breach of privilege.'

His Lordship demurred, but in the paper he had edited for so long, The Times, came a further riposte the next day from Tony Benn, and praise for Betty. Citing a recent House of Lords case (Pepper v Hart) which ruled that the courts could assess the significance of words spoken in the Commons to help in the interpretation of statutes, Benn warned that this 'incursion' was a major shift of political power from an elected chamber to unelected judges.

'The issue here is not dissimilar,' he argued. 'If the Commons were to capitulate to a claim of jurisdiction by the British courts, a similar transfer of power would be taking place.' It would be open to anyone who disliked legislation to ask the courts to intervene, and that would cancel out the authority of any future government.

'That is why Speaker Boothroyd's statement yesterday can be compared to that made by Speaker Lenthall, when he told Charles I he had no business to interfere with the House of Commons,' Benn wrote triumphantly.'[13] Betty may well have blushed to find her remarks compared with the most famous affirmation of Parliament's democratic sovereignty, but it must have been a quietly satisfying moment.

She had little time to savour it. The Commons returned that day, 22 July 1993, for the critical Maastricht vote. For weeks, John Major, his ministers and the Whips had been cajoling and bludgeoning wayward backbenchers to get them back in the fold. Some of the most difficult, including John Carlisle, the swashbuckling Right-wing car salesman from Luton North, had been persuaded to drop their opposition to the Bill. But a hard core of Euro-sceptics was determined to vote for Labour's wrecking amendment restoring the Social Chapter to the Treaty of Maastricht.

After an emotionally charged debate, the tense House divided. Astonishingly, MPs recorded a tied vote. This impasse required Betty to use her casting vote, a rare procedure, and the only time the Speaker does vote. It had last been used three years previously, when Sir Paul Dean, Betty's immediate superior as First Deputy Chairman of Ways and Means, used his casting vote to prevent a last-minute change to the Human Fertilization and Embryology Bill, which would have curtailed the rights of women to get late abortions.

Speaker Boothroyd observed parliamentary procedure punctiliously. This requires that if government and Opposition record the same number of votes, and further discussion is out of the question, the Speaker's casting vote on an amendment must leave the Bill in its existing form. When the result of the division was announced, Betty rose and read a prepared statement to a hushed Commons. She said, 'The numbers being equal, it is my duty to cast my vote. It is not the function of the chair to create a majority on a policy issue where no majority exists among the rest of the House. In accordance with precedent, I therefore cast my vote with the Noes. The noes have it.'

So Betty broke the deadlock in favour of the government. Ironically, of course, it had been her decision two months previously to overturn the ruling of her deputy Michael Morris that allowed the vote to take place at all. She had decided, after much self-doubt ('I tossed and turned. I put the light on and read,' she told Sue Lawley) to allow MPs a vote on the Social Chapter. It may be idle to speculate, but her political record would suggest that she was privately in favour of the

Social Chapter. Yet parliamentary custom compelled her to vote against it.

There was understandable dismay on the Labour benches, and huge relief on the Tory side. Indeed, some of the whisperers against her now began to say she had redeemed her Speakership. Back in West Bromwich, there was some confusion among the party faithful. Her agent at the time, Paul Jackson relates, 'There was unease. A lot of people found it very difficult to come to terms with Betty, perceived as a "Labour Speaker", voting with the Tories to keep them in power. That didn't go down particularly well. I got some telephone calls from electors – they didn't understand the difficult position she was in.'[14]

As that momentous parliamentary session drew to a close, seasoned parliamentary observers were inclined to draw up a balance sheet on Betty. Her admirer Alan Watkins, handed out end-of-year prizes in the *Observer*, giving pride of place to the imperturbable Foreign Secretary Douglas Hurd, but finding room for a special commendation for Betty. He praised her courageous decision to allow a vote on the Social Chapter, adding: 'Though she has made mistakes – her failure to control resignation speeches in general and Michael Mates's in particular, her clumsy intervention in the Rees-Mogg case – there is a special prize too for Miss Betty Boothroyd.'[15] Watkins, for long the doyen of his trade, is about the only writer who regularly describes her as 'Miss Boothroyd', presumably out of an old-fashioned insistence on accuracy.

But there were deeper tones to the discussion. Some commentators thought that, *pace* the Mates case, Betty's bark was worse than her bite. If she had not upheld the strictest interpretation of her duty in the Maastricht vote, it was pointed out, John Major would be packing his bags for a rather longer stay in Huntingdon than the parliamentary recess.

An anonymous profile writer in *Scotland on Sunday* suggested that Betty had acquired an altogether different kind of glamour in office than that of her Tiller days. 'But showbiz is still undoubtedly in her blood. Capable of being both seductive and authoritarian, she has an ability to probe hidden psychological depths of the mostly male members in her charge.'

Though mostly using her larynx – with the familiar 'Time's Up!' 'Awwwdaaargh, awwwdaaaaargh!' and 'I am on my feeeeet!' – she could while making considered comments from the chair use the plummy tones of the nouveau-establishment, and when it came to keeping order she resorted to 'full-fishwife'. To many Tories 'she evokes the childhood nanny, the public-school matron, a She-Who-Must-Be-Obeyed to replace that great lost matriarch, Lady Thatcher. There is something in Betty's female fierceness that makes the inner man squeal and turn to water. To the other side, especially the many Scottish MPs on the Labour benches, it is the primary-school mistress in Betty Boothroyd that compels obedience. Though sometimes, as in primary school, that obedience is less than total.'[16] Few profilists can avoid reaching for the schoolmarm image, though it is also flatteringly used by her oldest friends. There is something about her that makes you want to stay behind after class, even while dodging the well-aimed chalk.

One of the tests by which Speakers are traditionally judged is the readiness to grant emergency debates, which put governments on the spot on an important issue of the day and allow the Opposition to score much-needed points. Betty has proved sparing in her disbursement of these golden parliamentary opportunities. But she did relent in June 1993, granting Labour an emergency debate on the decision of Defence Secretary Malcolm Rifkind to award a £5 billion refit contract for Britain's Trident nuclear submarine fleet to the West Country dockyard of Devonport, rather than Rosyth, on the Fife coast. It was a controversial step by the government, and it infuriated Scottish Labour MPs. They had shown how their wrath could take a distinctly unparliamentary form, but on this occasion the storm blew over. The government survived with an unusually large majority of seventy-two on a technical motion to adjourn the House.

Betty's growing stature in the chair was confirmed in late September when the *Guardian Political Almanac* chose her as one of The Year's Politicians. In his citation, Simon Hoggart, the paper's parliamentary sketch writer, said Madam Speaker's darkest hour had been when she failed to halt Michael Mates's resignation speech. 'But such is the respect Betty commands her position was undiminished.'

She was soon to need all her powers of control. When the House returned for the 'spillover' – the brief period of unfinished business from the last session, before the Queen's Speech – it was clear that

Labour was in a mood for guerrilla warfare, particularly over the Bill privatizing British Railways.

The 'dirty tricks' campaign culminated in the first week of November 1993, when the Opposition, encouraged by a rebellion against rail privatization in the Lords, engaged in what it regarded as legitimate time-wasting ploys in the Commons. These included shenanigans in the voting lobby: switching tellers, forcing extra votes, stuffing bound copies of *Hansard* against a door handle to prevent the Sergeant at Arms investigating delays in a division, and even locking lavatories in the 'engaged' position to confuse Commons staff.

John Major complained that the behaviour of Labour MPs had been 'a disgrace to Parliament', and his Chief Whip Richard Ryder formally lodged objections to the chair. Betty was not amused. 'I happen to think that there was disgraceful behaviour on the part of many members in an attempt to disrupt our procedures. I can assure you the matter will not be left there. I will make my own inquiries.' The Lords, however, dropped their objections to the privatization Bill once they realized they could be prejudicing their own existence as a second chamber, and the measure passed.

Nothing more was heard of Madam Speaker's inquisition . . . except in the gossip columns. The *Observer* disclosed, 'The Tory whips are sucking their teeth at remarks made by the Speaker, the estimable Betty Boothroyd, at the eve-of-session knees-up at Number Ten. In a short and funny speech, the Speaker commented on the chaos with which the summer session ended. Some Whips apparently took this as a rebuke . . .'[17] She made another appearance in the *Evening Standard* diary about this time, confirming what the paper called 'her burgeoning political disinterest'. The *Standard* reported that Rotherham Labour Party had asked her to address them. She declined, on the grounds that she was 'no longer a member'. Her public affairs spokesman, Terry Lancaster, said her response was exactly as it should be. 'She wouldn't even take part in a coffee morning,' he said. This was the first public mention of her quitting the Labour Party. Leaving the political organization that had claimed her parents' allegiance and shaped her own social development was unquestionably a wrench. But her loyalty now lay to parliament.

As if to underline the change, Betty did not take too kindly to having her dignity mocked on 18 November 1993, the day of the Queen's Speech. While she was in the Lords listening to Her Majesty reading out the government's programme of legislation, the Commons was the scene of some extraordinary agitprop theatre. A number of Left-wing Labour MPs who scorned the day's pomp and ceremony were sky-larking in the chamber. Dennis Skinner, long a thorn in Betty's side, took it on himself to sit in the Speaker's chair. He proposed a motion abolishing the House of Lords and the monarchy. Laughter echoed round the virtually empty chamber.

When MPs returned for business, Skinner told Madam Speaker that whilst most people – including her – had been to witness the pomp and circumstance of the Queen's Speech 'some of us did see the irony of having a little exercise in which we took part in "abolishing" the House of Lords and the monarchy – which was, unfortunately, a split vote.' She would be 'pleased to know' that there were not enough MPs in the chamber to carry a motion.

Pleased, she was not. Betty told the Commons she regarded the Left-wingers' jape as 'a travesty of the proceedings of this House' which she viewed with distaste 'and even contempt'. She added, 'I take the most serious view of this kind of horseplay. It is not for Mr Skinner to decide to take the chair, even in a piece of temporary buffoonery. And it is not for other Members of his persuasion to become his accomplices by supporting him in this way.' This regal rebuke did not faze the impossible Skinner. He pointed out that MPs of all parties often sat in the chair during the mornings, while showing visitors round. 'I don't know what all the fuss was about. There was nothing to it,' he complained.

That he did not know what the fuss was about, while she did, was a measure of their relative notions of parliamentary high seriousness. Betty is tirelessly vigilant in this respect. In December that year, she ticked off three MPs who accepted a wager from the makers of a game called 'Balderdash'. The first to get one of three obscure words into *Hansard* won £1000-worth of toys to give as Christmas gifts to a charity of his choice. Betty got to know, and chided them for 'game playing and tomfoolery'. The words? Reverist, a person inclined to dream a lot; victrix, a conquering woman; and embolalia, the use of virtually meaningless words.

Similarly, a few months later, she publicly upbraided Edwina Currie MP for not getting permission before using the parliamentary portcullis logo on the cover of her 'bodice ripper' novel, *A Parliamentary Affair*. The crowned portcullis motif figured prominently on a woman's stocking, and Betty told MPs she took a dim view of anyone bringing the symbol into disrepute. She hauled Mrs Currie in for a private ear bashing, according to *The Times*. 'Not that anything involving Mrs Currie can be kept private for more than a nano-second. She reeled out of the wigging, and exclaimed indignantly, "Betty has joined the establishment!"'[18] Politics apart, the two women were never close. That may have had something to do with a cheeky little leak by Mrs Currie within forty-eight hours of her becoming Speaker. Debates under Betty would be shorter and sharper, because 'Madam Speaker cannot go for long without a cigarette'.[19]

These episodes reveal how deep runs Betty's respect – reverence, even – for the traditions of parliament. But they are a sideshow compared to the actual job of maintaining order and ensuring the free-running business of democracy. Betty has never argued that the Commons should be a model debating chamber – far from it. 'Ours is an adversarial and robust House,' she argues. 'People come here to change the flow of the Thames, to make change in our society, and therefore one has to expect robust behaviour, which I enjoy. What I do not want is for us to lose our traditional common courtesies here. By all means let us have robust argument, but good temper costs nothing.'[20]

Accordingly, she is tough on the House bullies. As the new session of 1993/4 got into its stride, she had to cope with the ranting, baleful figure of the Reverend Ian Paisley, leader of Ulster's Democratic Unionist Party. The House was listening agog to the government's admission, prompted by press disclosures, of secret contacts with the IRA going back many years, despite regular official denials. John Major had decided the best way to handle the crisis was to come clean, admit the contacts, publish the exchanges – and try to salvage something from the wreckage by way of pushing forward efforts to find peace in Northern Ireland.

Sir Patrick Mayhew, the Northern Ireland Secretary, was put up to defend the government's position. Immediately after his emergency statement, Paisley, MP for Antrim North, stood up and accused him of 'issuing falsehoods'. Betty pointed out that this meant 'lying', which is strictly unparliamentary language, and repeatedly called on him to withdraw or leave the House for the rest of the day. Instead, Paisley stood up again and thundered, 'I stand by what I said. It was a false-hood. It was worse – it was a lie.' Madam Speaker had no alternative. She 'named' him, and when he refused to leave his seat, ordered a vote which recorded a 272-to-25 majority in favour of suspending the fiery Protestant preacher from the Commons for five days.

Looking more satisfied than chagrined, Paisley left the House saying defiantly, 'I would rather be outside as a true man than inside the House with Paddy Mayhew the liar.' Naturally, his suspension made the evening television news, as it was meant to. The Speaker often has to weigh the merits of disciplining a wayward MP who may only be looking for publicity for himself or his cause. Though Dr Paisley was genuinely outraged (indeed, he gives a very fair impression of being in a semi-permanent state of outrage) his expulsion from Parliament probably did him no harm among his hard-line followers in Ulster. And it was not his first offence. He had been 'named' twelve years previously for calling a previous Northern Ireland Secretary a liar. A few days later, Labour MP Andrew Faulds, an actor with a powerful voice who can usually make himself heard, got off rather more lightly than Dr Paisley. He lost his temper with chattering Tory backbenchers and shouted, 'Listen, you berks!' but his apology was accepted by the chair.

The year ended with another first for Betty. Traditionally, the choice of the House of Commons Christmas card is made by the Works of Art Committee, an obscure body chaired by Patrick Cormack, rotund, engaging Tory MP for Staffordshire South. His taste ran to old-fashioned religious or mediaeval scenes. Without waiting for his choice, Betty decided that cards should have a picture of Speaker's Tree, adorned with fairy lights, in New Palace Yard. She got her way.

But a rather nasty Christmas present was in store, courtesy of the *Sunday Times*. On 19 December, the paper's senior political correspon-dent, Andrew Grice, reported that Betty was 'the victim of what her friends are calling a "dirty tricks" campaign, emanating from parliament's most exclusive male bastion: the Tory Whips' Office.' Prominent Tories denied the charge of foul play – chiefly gossip stories in the press – but then made wild allegations that she was giving Labour preferential treatment in her handling of Commons business.

The gossip 'revelations' were easily dealt with. Betty had been accused in the Peterborough column of the *Daily Telegraph* (a much-used and entertaining notice board for the Tory parliamentary party) of being keener on entertaining foreign delegations than MPs. Yet that same day, the paper's court and social page reported that Madam Speaker had entertained three Tory and three Labour MPs the previous evening, when the main dinner guest was the chairman of the Czech national council.

Speaker's House records offered no evidence that she had been 'niggardly in rolling out the welcome mat': since being elected, she had fed nearly 290 out of 651 MPs at Speaker's House – though some of these were buffet meals. Her alleged preference for foreigners at table was also a misapprehension. Distinguished overseas guests are mostly wished on her by the Foreign Office, and visiting Speakers naturally expect to be entertained at the mother of parliaments. The Christmas card 'row' was also recalled.

As if the anonymous criticism of the Tory whips was not enough, the Tory Sunday tabloids were also claiming that Betty was the subject of 'a bitter carping campaign' by Labour front-benchers who felt she had turned her back on the brothers and sisters since being elected Speaker. She was spoken of as 'a Queen mother figure' who stood aloof from the parliamentary cut and thrust. Speaker's House was being dubbed 'Balmoral'. Again, there was no supporting evidence. One Shadow Cabinet member insisted, 'She's even handed. Her job is to protect the rights of backbenchers in all parties and she does that very well. She is not a branch of the government.'

There are two separate questions here. Gossip writers have to fill their columns every day, and politicians are not only self-important busybodies but inveterate gossips to boot. Hence their regular appearances in the diary pages. Add to that the bottles of champagne or good claret that political correspondents get from their papers for good gossip tip-offs, and you have the making of a non-stop word cabaret. However, Betty is in an almost royal position: she cannot gossip about

MPs, while they are free to prattle about her. She can only answer back through her public-relations man, or 'friends'. To that extent, she will always be in a no-win competition with the press.

The second, political question is more serious. At the turn of 1993, parliament was still in the grip of guerrilla warfare being waged by the Opposition in its rage over government 'arrogance' in whipping through measures that ought to have been debated. The system of 'pairing' MPs that allows MPs from rival parties to be absent from the House at the same time by agreement was in abeyance. Labour was refusing to do deals through 'the usual channels'. Every night could herald a parliamentary ambush on John Major's depleted parliamentary majority. The Tory whips were on a tight rein – and a short fuse. They were angry that Madam Speaker failed to discipline Labour's 'awkward squad' for their disruption of the latter stages of the rail privatization Bill.

In fact, Betty rebuked the Labour whips, and demanded assurances that the behaviour would not be repeated. But this discreet assertion of her powers was not enough for rattled Conservative business managers. One senior Tory was quoted by the *Sunday Times* as saying, 'She just swept it under the carpet.' Not that their nerve extended to going public. 'Don't print my name or the Speaker will never call me [to speak] again!' said one senior backbencher. This useful sheltering alibi allows MPs to carp and criticize at will, safe in the knowledge that Betty cannot directly answer *them* back, either.

John Smith, the Labour leader, kept the cold war against the government going right through to Easter 1994, ensuring that tension was always just below the surface. But as parliament returned in the new year, there were jokes, even if they were in poor taste. Tony Banks, Labour MP for Newham and the House jester, called for a condom machine to be installed in the Commons. This was the heyday of John Major's much-trumpeted 'back to basics' political campaign, which had been mangled into a moral revival by the tabloid press – exposing the sexual peccadilloes of a number of Tory ministers and backbenchers. 'I realize that the installation would come rather too late for some Tory MPs,' smirked Banks. 'The more circumspect amongst us would welcome it. Alternatively, of course, perhaps we could seek some advice from Lorena Bobbitt' – a reference to a current court case in the United States where Mrs Bobbitt was accused of cutting off her husband's penis with a kitchen knife. This was too much for Madam Speaker. She halted him with the intervention that his remarks were in 'extremely bad taste'.

Parliament had been back only three weeks when one of Betty's closest friends, Jo Richardson, MP for Barking, died at the age of seventy after a long illness. They had been close friends, if not always politically compatible, for more than four decades. As Speaker, Betty had to make the announcement of an MP's death. She was close to tears as she told the House, and her spokesman Terry Lancaster told reporters, 'It was genuine emotion. She was terribly upset. They had known each other for forty years when they were both Labour candidates.'

But grief did not deflect Betty from her duty. On 24 February, she gave MPs what one seasoned observer called 'the biggest shock of the parliament' – by announcing that Question Time must be limited to questions and answers. This was a demand almost as radical as a requirement that politicians tell the truth. It provoked due conster-nation at Westminster, though MPs should have seen it coming. For weeks, if not months, she had been getting increasingly restless at the behaviour of MPs at Question Time – particularly the weekly Prime Minister's Questions – and at the undue formalization of the exchanges, which means that very few questions are properly answered. Question Time may be good theatre, attracting a large television audi-ence, but it was becoming less and less satisfactory as a parliamentary occasion. On 17 February, for instance Madam Speaker intervened repeatedly as the Prime Minister tried to struggle through interrup-tions. She called for order, saying, 'This is enormously time-consuming, I urge the House to be quiet,' and 'Order! I am prepared to name people today. The Prime Minister is giving a serious answer and I want us to hear the end of it in silence.'

A week later, MPs were astonished to hear Betty say that the new rules limiting Question Time to questions and answers would in future be implemented – and that they had already unanimously agreed to the reform. So they had, in a sparsely attended debate on procedure, with only enthusiasts for the rule book present, that approved the measure without a vote. 'There is a growing tendency to regard

Question Time as an opportunity for debate rather than question and answer,' said Betty firmly. Too few MPs who put down questions actually got answers. Most questions on the order paper were not being reached before she called 'Time's up!' She was determined to change this. She wanted short, snappy, questions and brisk replies. Members would in future ask only one question, and ministers would have to give a proper reply instead of giving lectures.

Few commentators thought that Betty's strictures would alter the behaviour of MPs, and looked forward to the next session of the bear-garden. They were wrong. Betty beamed, 'I have to say, I am agreeably surprised.' The sketch writers could scarcely contain themselves: 'At the first test of obedience to Betty's new regime, MPs have come through with flying colours,' vapoured Matthew Parris in *The Times*.[21]

Madam Speaker hustled MPs and ministers alike, through a series of questions on issues as complex and contentious as the Child Support Agency and Britain's arms-and-aid deal with Malaysia. Chiding the government benches with remarks like 'The minister will know that I've asked for brisk answers', she had them panting through texts prepared by civil servants who plainly had not grasped that she meant what she said. No such doubts existed in the Chamber. Parris spotted bouffant-haired Tory MP Michael Fabricant in such a lather to be brief that he condensed a question on our sixth place in the world overseas aid league to: 'Britain is equal to six in the world.' Betty congratulated her charges, promising, 'Tomorrow, I want us to do even better.'

Within days, however, it was back to the trenches. On 3 March, a gradual walk-out of members over a variety of issues left a lone Ulster MP to face the government benches. Dale Campbell-Savours, MP for Labour Workington and a one-man anti-corruption unit, opened hostilities with a charge that a Tory MP, Right-winger Alan Duncan, who was at the centre of the Tories 'right to buy' policy for council house tenants, had himself 'ripped off' the ratepayers of Westminster by buying a desirable property in the environs of the House. He refused Betty's entreaties to withdraw his unparliamentary language, and Betty banned him from proceedings for the rest of the day. Soon afterwards, Labour and Liberal Democrat MPs walked out over a Tory MP's accusations of 'sleaze, gerrymandering and corruption' by Welsh councils.

Try how she might, Betty could not persuade MPs to moderate their language. And sometimes even Madam Speaker allowed unexpected laxity. When John Prescott, the Shadow Employment Secretary, accused the government of sending to the G7 heads of government conference in Detroit a document on jobs and training that was 'no more than a tissue of lies', she did not intervene.

Perhaps she did not hear. Ann Widdecombe MP, Under-Secretary of State at Employment, did. She stepped in to upbraid the Hull East MP, and was rapped on the knuckles by Betty for her impertinence. Miss Widdecombe complained that Prescott, who in private discourse is as robust as most former seafarers, had used 'decidedly unparliamentary language'. Betty shot back, 'Order! Had that been the case, I would have asked the honourable Gentleman to withdraw.'[22] Nobody decides what is unparliamentary language but the Speaker, and, with Betty in the chair, nobody is allowed to forget it.

Two disputes of potentially greater significance than the niceties of parliamentary language blew up in mid March. Both involved Left-wing Labour MPs with constituencies in Wales, and both went to the heart of the rights of members and the powers of the Speaker. On 14 March, Llew Smith, MP for Blaenau Gwent, who entered the House in the 1992 election, protested that his Commons questions to ministers about the arms-to-Iraq investigation had been blocked unfairly.

He tried to raise the issue on a point of order, and Madam Speaker stopped him in his tracks as he began, 'I am being treated differently from other members . . .' with a reminder that she had been in correspondence with the MP and a declaration that he could not raise the matter as a point of order. 'I've taken weeks to try to help you with the procedures of this House,' she admonished. 'You are still unfamiliar with them.' This put-down did not halt Smith, a former MEP not entirely ignorant of parliamentary ways, who continued to protest. He said later that the Commons Table Office, under Betty's jurisdiction, had disallowed sixty-five questions from him over a period of twenty months, while other MPs' questions were allowed.

Almost simultaneously, Peter Hain, Tribunite Labour MP for Neath, and a one-time turk in the Young Liberals known for his strong

anti-apartheid views and his disruption of visiting South African sports
events, stirred a hornet's nest by raising Conservative MPs' losses at
Lloyds of London, the insurers. He tabled an Early Day Motion – a
device to gain publicity rather than a debate – naming twelve Tories
who had made potential losses estimated at £6 million. They had all
refused to disclose in the Commons Register of Interests to which of
the Lloyds loss-making syndicates they belonged.

Hain's allegation was based on calculations made by a former Lloyds
underwriter with access to official figures, but it was still only an
estimate. Hain's motive was clear: to flush out the actual losses, in the
expectation that some of the MPs might have to declare bankruptcy
and thus under the rules of the House resign their seats. A string of
by-elections under these conditions and at this time – the government
having just lost two 'safe' seats at Christchurch, Dorset, and Newbury,
Berkshire – could bring down John Major's administration.

But Betty refused to allow Hain to publish under parliamentary
privilege a breakdown of the individual losses, even though these esti-
mates had been in the original version of the Early Day Motion
approved by the Commons Table Office. She did not give a reason
for this step, as she is not obliged to. It may be that she did not trust
the arithmetic of Hain's informant, or that publication was a potential
infringement of privilege.

Whatever the reason, her ruling was only partially successful. A copy
of the original version of the motion came into the possession of the
Independent on Sunday, which promptly published the list of estimated
losses, which ranged from £100,000 to £1.5 million.[23] It was an
impressive roll-call, including a clutch of ministers and the former
Prime Minister, Sir Edward Heath, as well as well-known backbenchers. Sir Edward was volcanic. He denounced Hain's move as
'sleazy desire' to imply that the Conservatives could lose office, adding,
'As far as I am concerned the figures are not only entirely untrue, but
they bear no relation whatever to the proper provision made for loss
by myself and no doubt other members of Lloyd's.' Hain retorted that
if the MPs disputed the figures, they should declare what their actual
losses were. And there the matter rested, for the time being.

It was not all such hard going. That month Betty headed a list of
contenders for the imaginary post of President of Great Britain

published in the *Guardian*. Her name was up there with Lord Jenkins of Hillhead, the entrepreneurs Richard Branson and Jimmy Goldsmith, David Jenkins, the Bishop of Durham, Gulf War hero Sir Peter de la Billière, and Princess Anne. The item compared her with Ireland's president Mary Robinson, and enthused, 'Just think of the impact on the campaign posters . . . Betty's popularity would stem not from her personality but from her perceived fairness and love of Order.' This was only a half-serious feature, but joking aside the idea that the Speaker could figure in the presidential stakes would have been unthinkable hitherto. It was a measure of Betty's achievement that she was now firmly fixed in the public mind as a national figure known for her fairness and order. Indeed, a 'presidential' opinion poll for the BBC Radio programme 'The Radical Option' shortly afterwards put her in third place after Princess Anne, with fourteen per cent of the votes.

Madam Speaker also now acquired her own coat of arms, emblazoned on the oak-panelled wall of her office. The diamond-shaped coat of arms has a red background representing her career as a Labour MP, the upright Mace her Speakership and the White Rose her Yorkshire roots. There are also slices of the arms of Kirklees (as Dewsbury's local authority is now called), the owl; and of Sandwell, where her West Bromwich constituency lies, the millrinds. Atop the whole is a green knot. Betty explained this unusual device, 'As an unmarried lady, I have to indicate that by means of the "forget-me-not bow", and that is in, painted in the green of Commons.'

She composed her own motto, I Speak To Serve, and insisted that it was not in Latin. 'I only speak English. I had the menus changed in here from French. This is an English-speaking country. It seemed sensible.' The newspapers all commented on the absence of any reference to her 'Tiller girl days'. Betty explained she had a diamond-shaped lozenge instead of a shield because it was said in heraldry that women did not go to war. Her public-relations man raised his eyebrows, 'They obviously didn't know women MPs.'

Some dark days followed. During Prime Minister's Questions on 14 April 1994, Madam Speaker had cause to rebuke John Major. This is virtually unprecedented. It is not supposed to happen. Prime Ministers should not give cause for reproof from the chair, and the Speaker is

placed in an impossible position if the premier refuses to accede to
her wishes fully. But it did happen on this occasion, and it left a nasty
taste in the mouth of parliamentarians.

At the outset, Betty was in determined mood. She cut into a long,
tendentious question by Iain Duncan-Smith, Right-wing successor to
Norman Tebbit as MP for Chingford, with an intervention: 'Order!
I am determined that this should be Question Time, not speech time.'
Margaret Beckett, Deputy Leader of the Labour Party standing in for
John Smith, got in with a supplementary question about elderly people
being denied the right to hospital treatment on the grounds of their
age. Was this not proof that the NHS was now a two-tier service?
Stung by the accusation, an ill-tempered John Major retorted, 'Despite
the fact that the right honourable Lady has peddled an untruth and
continues to do so, there is no policy . . .' *Hansard* records:

> HON MEMBERS: Withdraw
> MADAM SPEAKER: Order. I am sure that the Prime Minister will
> reflect and I hope that he will withdraw that last remark.
> THE PRIME MINISTER: Despite the fact – (Interruption)
> MADAM SPEAKER: Order. I will have order in this House.
> THE PRIME MINISTER: Despite the fact that what the right
> hon. Lady says is inaccurate and she has just been told so again –
> (Interruption)
> MADAM SPEAKER: Order. I do wish the House would listen to
> the comments that are being made and not make such a row. I have
> asked the Prime Minister politely to reflect and I hope that he will
> withdraw what he said. (Interruption) Order. I am sure that if the
> House were to listen, it would hear him do that.[24]

The House heard no such thing. Major ploughed on with his refu-
tation of Labour's charges, arguing that Mrs Beckett had 'misled the
House'. He did not withdraw the 'peddling of untruths' allegation.
Only six questions were reached that day. The Chamber was agog. An
MP had refused a polite instruction from the Speaker. But that MP
was the Prime Minister. What could Betty do in the circumstances?
She could hardly throw the premier out of the Commons. She kept
her counsel, and did nothing.

But just over half an hour later, Nick Brown, Labour MP for Newcastle East, rose with a point of order, pointing out that Major had rephrased his point. 'However, I think that the record will show that the Prime Minister did not withdraw his unparliamentary remark and did not apologize for it.' He asked Betty to check the record, and ask the Prime Minister to withdraw and apologize. David Shaw, the egregious Tory MP for Dover, tried to muddy the waters by alleging 'lies about the National Health Service', but Betty cut him and others short with a statement.

'I have captured the spirit of the House on this matter . . . of course I heard clearly the Prime Minister's remarks which, I have to say, I felt were unparliamentary. However, it is for me to decide whether the rephrasing that he offered was acceptable, and I deemed that it was acceptable.

'In any event, I should like to remind the entire House – this relates to Back Benchers as well as Front Benchers – of the very wise words of Erskine May: "Good temper and moderation are the characteristics of parliamentary language."' MPs should remember those fine words, said Betty. 'Let us conduct ourselves in that spirit in future.'[25]

That was not the end of it. On the following Sunday, the *Observer*'s political editor Anthony Bevins drew together various strands of dissatisfaction in the Opposition to discover a strong Labour front-bench attack on Madam Speaker for 'alleged bias towards the government'. Betty, he reported, had been made aware of disquiet about her perceived favouritism. 'Critics believe she is a prisoner of the establishment. It is said she has applied the iron fist to her former colleagues while treating rowdy Conservatives with kid gloves.'[26]

Bevins, one of the most brilliantly mischievous members of the parliamentary press lobby, compared a rebuke to Hilary Armstrong, John Smith's aide, before Easter with the treatment given to John Major three days previously. Madam Speaker had 'backed down when he ignored her', said Bevins, and cited this as evidence of Labour critics' accusation of 'pro-Tory tilt', with Betty being over-protective to an already powerful government. For good measure he threw in the Llew Smith arms-to-Iraq and Peter Hain Lloyd's List affairs as supporting material.

The *Observer* quoted a highly placed Labour source saying that the

Speaker had created a problem for herself because MPs would now use *Hansard* to show that 'peddling untruths' was an acceptable parliamentary device for calling an opponent a liar. Bevins's prediction matured only two days later, when Mrs Ann Clwyd, MP for Cynon Valley and a Labour spokesperson on employment, accused British Coal and the President of the Board of Trade of lying through their teeth over pit closures. Betty ruled that unacceptable, and asked her to withdraw it. Mrs Clwyd did so, inserting 'blatant untruths' instead. Betty was in good humour. 'Order!' she cried. 'The English language is very rich. I am sure that the honourable Lady can do even better and I ask her to try.' Mrs Clwyd did so, using the expression 'peddling untruths'.

The debate moved on, and it was a little time before Madam Speaker realized what had been said. She said the phrase had been unacceptable to her the previous week, and was still unacceptable to her now. She asked Mrs Clwyd to rephrase her remarks. The Opposition spokesperson struggled gamely on. 'I understand that the Prime Minister was not asked to withdraw that particular phrase.' Betty said he had been, and asked Mrs Clwyd to do the same. With a minimum of grace, she did so, using the acceptable term 'misled the House'.[27]

This saga is of more than philological interest, as the *Observer*'s skilful interest showed. Other commentators observed that this was thought to be the first time that a Prime Minister had gone over the top since the days of Harold Wilson. It was suggested that John Major was being deliberately combative at the Despatch Box because he was acting on his spin doctors' advice to look tougher. He certainly asserted himself over Madam Speaker, by ostentatiously going only part-way towards meeting her request for him to withdraw. There was a view in some quarters of the House, however, that the Prime Minister had been graceless and ungallant. He had compromised his reputation for decency, whereas she had emerged from the episode with enhanced standing.

But the discontent did not die down. On 9 May 1994, Madam Speaker was obliged to investigate the use of parliamentary counsel – that is, government lawyers – to help kill a back-bench Bill aimed at outlawing discrimination against the disabled. Dale Campbell-Savours MP complained to Betty that these lawyers had drafted scores of amendments which had then been tabled as their own by Tory MPs assisting Nicholas Scott, Minister for the Disabled. Their aim was to talk out the Civil Rights (Disabled Persons) Bill.

This unsavoury manoeuvre came to light when Scott first denied that his department had been involved in drafting the wrecking amendments, and then admitted that he had misled the House. Angry Labour MPs called on the deeply apologetic Scott, hitherto a popular Tory 'wet', to resign. He was later sacked in a summer government reshuffle, but not before his conduct focused attention on the issue of misleading parliament once again.

William Waldegrave, then Minister for the Civil Service, had earlier told a Commons Select Committee there were certain limited exceptions when it was permissible to mislead parliament. He was supported by John Major, who argued that ministers who knowingly fail to give accurate and truthful information should resign – save in quite exceptional circumstances, such as devaluation or in time of war, or where there is a danger to national security.

None of these categories fitted the Nicholas Scott affair. His shameful parliamentary behavior had simply been directed towards saving money. Ministers claimed the Disabled Bill would cost industry, commerce and the public services £17 billion to implement, a figure that expert sources rejected as grossly inflated. MPs expected Betty to be hard on Scott. They were disappointed. On 11 May, Madam Speaker announced to a hushed chamber that she would take no further action over accusations that Scott was guilty of contempt of the House.

'Shock waves of disappointment and anger swirled amongst Labour MPs,' reported the *Daily Telegraph*. 'They were so certain the government was on the run ... Now they felt let down by the chair, the traditional guardian of back-bench rights.' Campbell-Savours, who had initiated the contempt complaint, was livid and challenged the chair. With all the respect in the world (usually the precursor of a hefty dose of disrespect), he said, the Speaker's ruling was 'utterly astonishing'.

He protested, 'A precedent has now been set whereby any minister can come to the Commons and deliberately mislead the Commons in the knowledge that if they are subsequently found out, suffice that they come before the House and apologize and, in their view, provide the facts. If that were to happen, then contempt would no longer

be of relevance to the Commons. In fact, the last application for contempt may have been brought, insofar as you have opened the door
to ministers deliberately misleading in the event that they know they
can simply apologize.'[28]

Betty rode out a barrage of similar protests from the Labour side,
arguing that her powers were limited, and the decision had been 'mine
and mine alone'. For the future, she insisted that any similar incidents
would be determined on their merits. There were later reports that
she had made her displeasure at the government's actions known to the
Commons Procedures Committee, which had begun an examination of
wrecking amendments.

The hubbub over the Scott affair had not died down before tragedy
struck political life. The next day, 12 May 1994, John Smith, Leader
of the Labour Party and the man widely expected to become the next
occupant of 10 Downing Street, collapsed from a massive heart attack
in the bathroom of his Barbican flat. He was pronounced dead on
arrival at nearby Bart's Hospital. The nation was stunned. Many were
convulsed with grief. It fell to Betty to announce the news. The
chamber was packed but silent as the time approached for the opening
of business. Sketch writer Simon Hoggart caught the sense of occasion
best: 'Perhaps it was the formal announcement which was most affect-
ing. At exactly 2.33 p.m. the House was jammed, not with its usual
ragged sprawl, but as if MPs were already at the funeral, sitting stiffly
upright, the rowdy benches turned briefly into pews. Betty Boothroyd
said very simply: "I regret to have to report to the House the death
of the Right Honourable John Smith QC, member for Monklands
East." It seemed touch and go whether she would reach the end without breaking down.'[29]

Margaret Beckett, who immediately became Acting Leader, recalled
that, at a gala night dinner the day before, John Smith had said, 'The
opportunity to serve our country is all that we ask.' Mrs Beckett said,
'Let it stand as his epitaph.' There was an unconscious, but poignant,
throwback. Only six weeks previously, Betty had unveiled her heraldic
motto, I Speak To Serve. They believed in the same thing.

Normal politics were suspended for the next ten days until John
Smith was laid to rest on the Island of Iona where Scottish kings are
traditionally interred. Then it was business as usual. Betty reprimanded

MPs for encouraging disabled people to get out of their wheelchairs and crawl up the steps of Parliament's St Stephen's entrance for the benefit of the media. The disabled had been demonstrating over the 'murder by proxy' of the Bill that would have extended their rights.

Madam Speaker saw the media stunt as demeaning to the dignity of the disabled. And when Lady Olga Maitland, Tory MP for Sutton and Cheam, returned from a parliamentary mission to Malawi, she felt the rough edge of Betty's tongue for the misleading terms of her apology over the Scott affair. She had initially denied using government-drafted amendments, and persisted in a tortuously worded self-exculpation until Betty delivered a strong rebuke and compelled her to apologize to the House. 'Her statement did not so much mislead the House as exasperate it,' fumed Betty.

As the warmest summer for years closed over Westminster – never the best place on a hot day – the House got tetchy. Just before the recess, yet another scandal broke cover. Over the years there had been unsubstantiated rumours that certain MPs were prepared to sell parliamentary privilege, by taking money for 'placing' Commons Questions to ministers. Nobody had ever been able to prove it. Then, on 10 July, the Sunday Times disclosed that a member of its Insight investigation team had persuaded two Tory MPs to accept £1000 each to ask questions in the House that had been given to them by a reporter posing as a businessman. Both had later returned the cheque.

At Westminster, the balloon went up. Labour MPs demanded an immediate inquiry, and the banning of 'MPs for hire'. Tory MPs, embarrassed by the disclosures, tried to turn the fire back on the Sunday Times for its 'entrapment' of members and for secretly taping an MP within the confines of the House. On 12 July, Betty made a statement encompassing both issues. She reminded MPs of the first report of the Select Committee on Members' Interests, 1991/2, which laid down that Members must not bring the House into disrepute, and that a financial inducement to take a particular course of action in Parliament may constitute a bribe and thus be an offence against the law of Parliament.

She considered there was 'an urgent need to clarify the law of Parliament', and though not passing judgment on the present case she also thought that the conduct of the newspaper – in offering the payment and in making a clandestine recording – should also be considered under the general heading of breach of privilege. The Commons agreed without a vote to stage a formal inquiry composed of senior MPs. But Madam Speaker refused the plea of Joe Ashton MP, veteran Labour campaigner against sleaze, that the hearings should be held in public. Tory MPs found themselves inveighing against Rupert Murdoch, proprietor of the *Sunday Times*, when normally they would be praising his Wapping titles for all they were worth.

Simon Hughes, Liberal Democrat member for Bermondsey, probably judged feelings outside the House right with his remark that 'the public has the view that we are here to make a profit for ourselves, that we do very well and that our snouts are in the trough. If we are to enhance democracy the [inquiry] committee should take this issue as widely as possible, otherwise we will be regarded as open to the same corruption as other democracies around the world.'

It is easy to imagine Betty saying 'hear, hear' to that. It had been a long, nasty and sometimes brutish parliamentary session, culminating in the worst allegations of sleaze for decades. Betty had taken the House through trying times. Her 'reward' had been sniping from Labour Left-wingers, hurtful fire from some senior people – and heavy but anonymous salvoes from the Tory big guns cowering in the Whips' Office. It was time to get away from the place. She set off in late July for her home in rural Cambridgeshire, before embarking on a three-week tour of India, Bangladesh and Nepal.

Betty had always been an intrepid traveller. Holidaying in the High Atlas mountains of Morocco in April 1995, she and her companions were caught in a landslide. Betty was forced to trek miles through torrential streams and dodge falling rocks before finding help in a lonely hamlet. Even in this remote quarter of North Africa, Madam Speaker was recognized. 'The police knew exactly who I was, because they had all watched satellite television, she said later. Despite her ordeal, Betty was back in the chair days later, in time for the re-opening of Parliament on Easter Tuesday, which was more than many MPs managed. She admonished their 'very bad behaviour'.

CHAPTER X

TIME'S UP!

'HANC UBI DOMUS communis primam prolucutricem creauit, raro melius et sibi profuit et spes hominum expleuit, ad munus illus uia numquam brevis, feminisque ne ad domum quidem facile peruentum est...' So began the Orator of Cambridge University, when Britain's oldest seat of learning awarded Betty an honorary Doctorate of Laws on 9 June 1994.

She was in unusually distinguished company. In James Gibbs's classical 260-year-old Senate House that summer morning, her fellow honorands included Dr Richard von Weisacker, President of the Federal Republic of Germany, Dr Robert Eames, Anglican Primate of All Ireland, Claudio Abbado, principal conductor of the Berlin Philharmonic, and the actress Dame Maggie Smith. Conferring the degrees was no less than the Duke of Edinburgh.

Translated from the Latin, the Orator's traditional address of commendation opened: 'Seldom has the House of Commons better served itself and matched the hopes of the people than in electing our next guest as its first woman Speaker. The path to such office is never short. For women, the path even into the House is not easy. But the wise electors of West Bromwich have now supported her with their votes seven times, and the House has understood her devotion and her skill in serving it, and because she has been faithful over some things it has made her ruler over many.'

The Orator invited the university congregation to take their picture of her from the previous summer, the 2500th anniversary of the beginning of democracy, when Betty stood at the tiller of a reconstructed Greek trireme sailing up the Thames to Westminster. 'Who better than she to hold the tiller of such a ship, driven as it used to be by

citizen power on either side,' asked the Orator. 'Was ever a figure of
speech so refreshed?' Quoting Virgil's *Aeneid*, he continued, 'She went
her radiant, busy way between them,' and then 'throned herself on
high, giving her rulings to the men, and distributing tasks in fair shares
or putting them to a ballot'.

Concluding on the Speaker's traditional reluctance to take the office,
Orator said admiringly, 'Fear not: with her sense of fun and her wit
she wields the vote of Athena amid the confidence, the approval and
the delight of all.'[1] After Ave Marias and the national anthem, the
honoured graduands paraded from the Senate House in their robes,
to the music of a trumpet voluntary. A news release from the university
pointed out that she was no stranger to the city: 'Miss Boothroyd lives
locally and shops regularly in Cambridge: she recently opened the new
building of our much loved local departmental store, Eaden Lilley's.'[2]

This bump down from the sublime to the everyday detracts little
from the honour bestowed on Madam Speaker. It was a proud moment,
becoming an honorary graduate of the university where her much-
loved mentor Geoffrey de Freitas had been such a brilliant student.
However, her Cambridge LLD was only the latest in a long line of
similar honours. Betty had already been given honorary degrees by
Leeds Metropolitan University, the University of Birmingham,
London's South Bank University – and the University of Leicester,
the city in which she fought her first by-election. In 1993, she was
elected Chancellor of the Open University.

Barely six months after her election as Speaker, she became the first
woman to be given the Freedom of Kirklees, as the local authority of
her home town had become. Tears of joy ran down her face at the
ceremony in Dewsbury Town Hall, and she confessed to *Yorkshire
Life*, 'It would be hypocritical to deny that the proudest day of my life
was when I was elected Speaker. But being granted the Freedom of
Dewsbury came a very close second. I cried that day, but they were
tears of joy – and I don't cry very often.'

There is more, much more. Betty has her own coat of arms. Her
portrait has been painted in oils to hang in Speaker's House for as
long as there is a Parliament. She has a state carriage. She was honoured
as Parliamentarian of the Year. She travels the world, and has a cult
following on C-SPAN television in the United States. She was

applauded by the US Senate, and described in the *Washington Post* as 'the charismatic matriarch of British politics.'[3] She is spoken of as a prime candidate for the presidency of the United Kingdom, admittedly an eventuality less likely than forgetting to wear her crested-portcullis jewelled brooch – but indicative that she is as much a household name as Richard Branson and not much less so than the Princess Royal. The fact of her Speakership gets everywhere, even into a short story in the *Daily Telegraph*. The trappings and the honours come with the job, and they will increase. Even more satisfying is the knowledge that no previous Speaker has so captured the hearts and minds of the British people.

However, there is a down side to her success. Deeply, even passionately, attractive to men, she has never married or formed a strong enough relationship to bear children. Betty admits bluntly, 'If I had married, I doubt if I would have become Speaker.'[4] An American writer observed that Madam Speaker talked about her chamber with more affection than many politicians display for their spouses, and she admitted to him: 'I am wedded to our system . . . that is the most crucial thing in my life at the moment.'[5]

It was not always so. From her early days as a schoolgirl singer and dancer in the Swing Stars, she attracted admirers. Laurie Ward, trumpeter in the band, remembers, 'She was a smashing person. She was quite adult, really. Betty was a very pretty girl, there was no doubt about that and she went out with various lads. She was a normal girl, a fun-loving girl.'[6]

Molly Walton, who got to know Betty in 1950, describes her then: 'She was a very, very attractive woman, really beautiful. Her hair was naturally wavy and a beautiful rich chestnut brown. I often wonder why she never married. She certainly had the opportunities. The opposite sex certainly found her very attractive. Perhaps the right person never came her way.'[7] Another friend from her teenage years confides, 'She really is as you see her. I have never seen her glum. She was absolutely dedicated to her political career, but not to the exclusion of her friends. I never knew anyone who did not like her.'[8]

This *joie de vivre* survived her unhappy experience as a chorus girl. When she went to London to work at Transport House, she joined a high-spirited circle of young people loosely attached to the Hornsey constituency Labour Party in north London. There, her conviviality bloomed. She was greatly sought-after, but showed no great interest in forming any lasting attachments. Betty was particularly close friends with Jo Richardson, a lass from the north-east who was then secretary to Left-wing Labour MP Ian Mikardo and who was also later to become a member of parliament and indeed of Labour's Shadow Cabinet.

One of the 'Hornsey Group', a veteran observer of the political scene, recalls, 'Betty and Jo were like a couple of northern Likely Lads: lots and lots of one-night stands – and not very sentimental about it. They treated their love lives like men, which in those days was not frightfully befitting. Girls were meant to do it for love.'[9] Jo was the more bohemian of the two 'always rather scruffy', whereas Betty was always 'terribly well turned out'. She always said she inherited her good taste from her father, who encouraged her to pay 'just that bit extra' for better quality clothes. There wasn't much money over for expensive socializing.

The Hornsey group (sometimes known as the Second Eleven, mostly Bevanites) used to congregate in the Flask public house in Highgate. Betty's tipple since she could afford it has been gin and tonic. Then, 'she had halves of bitter like the rest of us'. Ted and Barbara Castle occasionally turned up, as did Terence Lancaster, then a young journalist who also harboured unfulfilled ambitions to become a Labour MP.

Betty still paid regular visits back home, though some friends thought that 'Dewsbury very quickly grew too small for her'. On one of her return visits home she confided to Vivien Meakin, her former dance teacher, that she did not restrict her favours to her own Party. 'And she's never married, you see, but she used to say to me, "But I have a good time, you know, and I go out with the Tories as well as the others." I used to kid Betty because I wasn't Labour, she knew I wasn't. I used to say, "Why don't you go on the other side?" And she said, "Oh, I go out with them." She is attractive. She wasn't a spinster type.'[10]

Her entry into Westminster as secretary to Geoffrey de Freitas, Labour MP for Lincoln, drew her into a more glamorous and ambitious social orbit. 'She adored Geoffrey, no doubt about that,' said a friend at the time.' And with good reason. He was a delightful man.' De Freitas was married to Helen Graham Bell, a graduate of Bryn Mawr who he had met on the liner *Berengaria* on his way back home from Yale in 1936. She was the daughter of a well-known Left-wing Democrat, on her way to Moscow to study children's plays in the Soviet Union. They married two years later, and had three sons and a daughter. De Freitas and Betty became particularly close. He supported her parliamentary ambitions, going on the stump with her when she stood in by-elections. In return, she remained close to him, even nursing him at her home in rural Cambridgeshire in the weeks before his untimely death in 1981.

But Betty also made friends in the London media scene. One journalist recalls first meeting her in the late 1950s in The Cogers, a pub in Salisbury Square just off Fleet Street, a favourite haunt of Beaverbrook Group newspapermen. She was with a *Sunday Express* man. 'She was brought in by Llew Gardner. It was quite clear that she was his girl-friend, although Llew Gardner was married at this stage. She was then secretary to Geoffrey de Freitas. She was a very attractive girl, and very ambitious, and made it clear to me that she was going to be a Labour MP.'[11] Llew Gardner had been a Communist journalist on the *Daily Worker*, but he quit the Communist Party over the crushing of the Hungarian revolution in 1956. A talented writer, he was taken up by Beaverbrook as so many other 'Lefties' had been, and he became a roving political reporter on the *Sunday Express*. In all probability they met when he was covering the Leicester South-East by-election in 1957. Equally, Betty could have met him in any of the bars of the House of Commons, which in those pre-IRA 'troubles' days were very open and sociable places, or in the north London political scene, which was a Bevanite playground.

Betty clearly liked the easy-going company of political journalists, most of whom were men, and was tough enough to stand her corner with them, propping up the bar with a cigarette in one hand and a gin and tonic in the other. She took up smoking at the age of twenty-one because she felt it was 'vogueish', and would regularly get through twenty Rothmans a day. It was her smoking habit, she later joked, that gave her such a resonant voice. This worldly self-confidence stood her in good stead later when she had to take on the unreconstructed male bastions of the trade union movement to get into parliament. It also, perhaps, scared off the more timid would-be suitors. Even so, as she confessed to Sue Lawley on 'Desert Island Discs', there was 'no lack of admirers'. She did not decide against marriage and a family. Simply, 'It didn't come at the right time.'

Betty's attractions were admired wherever she went. As noted earlier, her risqué negligee certainly caused a stir in the Swift household in Peterborough in the General Election of 1959. Her attraction also cut a swathe through Labour's ranks in the sleepy railway city. They had never seen anything quite like Betty. 'All the young lads asked for their leave at the same time,' recalls Charles Swift, chairman of the constituency party at the time. 'For the first time, they got a sleeper van. One young lad in particular drove here everywhere. They gave up their holidays, because some of them were really attracted to her, know what I mean?'[12] There was also a mysterious Army officer some-where in the frame, a friend of Betty's by the name of Ian Archibald Wandsworth-Bell, for whom Swift obtained a proxy vote.

But, disillusioned with the 'old men' of European politics, she moved on from the provincial flatlands of Cambridgeshire to the vast expanses – social, as well as geographical – of the United States. She toured the country with the John F. Kennedy campaign, and then settled in Washington. She was hugely popular around the dinner tables of the capital. She had her own basement flat, 'not at all squalid, a perfectly nice apartment', in the words of an admirer of the time. He was thrown out at five in the morning, because Betty was afraid of scandalizing the neighbours.

Another suitor remembers her apartment being in 'a very gloomy block of flats', but at least 'she had her bits and pieces about her'. According to him, he enjoyed a brief, whirlwind romance with Betty that included a passionate trip to the deep South. But it is suggested that she was most strongly attracted during the two years she spent in America to Bruce Rothwell, an Australian journalist who worked first for the liberal *News Chronicle* and then for the Tory *Daily Mail* when it took over the title. He later moved to the Murdoch empire, and was slated to become editor of the *Observer* if Murdoch's takeover bid had succeeded. He did later become editor of the *Australian*. At this period of his life, he was married to an imperious Czech woman, who belonged to the pre-Communist haute bourgeoisie, and had still had sufficient contacts to go back home to central Europe for long summer holidays.

Rothwell, a sharp-featured, dark-haired and immaculately clean-shaven man, was said to be deeply attracted to Betty. A confidant of the time says: 'It was very much on the cards that he would leave [his wife] ... it would be the great love affair. But it never happened.' Betty later told an interviewer that she loved the States, and 'perhaps if I'd met somebody who'd asked me to marry them, maybe I would have stayed'. Evidently nobody did and, just as she had abandoned the chorus line, she quit America and returned to Europe. Even back home, according to another informant based in Washington at the time, she was pursued to London by a CIA officer who was 'madly in love with her'.

This period was a critical watershed in Betty's life. She confessed later, 'I think sometimes, when I look back on it, maybe I have missed out in not marrying and creating a family of my own. I think there's a tide in the affairs of men – and women – as Shakespeare said, "which taken at the flood, leads on to fortune".

'It wasn't that I didn't have a lot of men friends, I did, but if you've spent your life going off to Vietnam, going off to America, going off to France, being very independent, there's no man going to wait until you come back. I mean, he wants to see you, he wants to take you out, he might want to propose to you. You can't say, "Can you hold on until I get back?" And then you get back, and you're packing, and you're off again! Nobody's going to wait around for you like that. It wasn't part of my planning. There was nothing planned about it. If it had come my way, wonderful, but it didn't.'[13]

Betty was taken on 'sight unseen' by Harry Walston as his personal secretary in 1962. Like de Freitas, Walston was a man of means, only very much bigger means. A friend at this period observes, 'She liked rich men. She always had a taste for the high life. She liked doing things in style.' Betty became virtually part of the Walston family, going down to the farm at Thriplow at weekends. Eventually, Walston provided her with a grace-and-favour cottage on his estate, which is still her home today. 'I think it is above and beyond the call of duty for an employer to build a dower house for his secretary, as Harry did,' commented an insider in this political circle. The implied suggestion is strenuously denied by someone who was in a position to know.

Walston, created one of Labour's first life peers by Harold Wilson, was extremely wealthy by his party's standards, a cereal baron in Cambridgeshire with discreetly luxurious rooms in The Albany. His first wife Catherine led him a merry dance with novelist Graham Greene, but she and Betty were very close. That, argues his son the writer and broadcaster Oliver Walston, is compelling evidence that the relationship between Betty and the socialist millionaire was a purely professional one.

'My father was an interesting chap, who had lots of girlfriends in many walks of life. Betty was not one of them. Betty is a normal heterosexual human being, no question about that. But in the case of my father, absolutely no – and I would have known,' he insists.[14] Catherine Walston 'couldn't abide' her husband's girlfriends, yet she was very friendly with Betty. That was the litmus test, a clear indication that there was nothing between Betty and her boss.

At the time she got into Parliament, Betty confessed that marriage had its attractions. 'Well, I would like to get married at some stage,' she told Laura Gillan. 'Now you're going to ask why I haven't. I think the answer's just that I had so many interests at the time when there were men around who wanted to ask me.

'I was always off on delegations and conferences, and if a man rings up to say he's got theatre tickets for tomorrow he's not going to wait around if you say, "Sorry, I'm not free till next week." But the companionship of marriage is an enormous possession. I'd love to have a husband waiting at home for me when I get back from the House, saying, "Here's a cup of tea for you, luv."'[15]

In recent years, Betty's consistent escort has been John Ginnery, formerly an executive with the Independent Broadcasting Authority. In the words of an MP, 'He is the perfect foil. He holds the coat, and she does the grand entrance.'

Betty approaches the issue of being a woman in a man's world in a characteristically no-nonsense fashion. 'I hate to spoil the fun, but I do get a bit fed up with all the books and articles written by, and about, women in politics,' she has written. 'Some of them reek of the "plucky little woman" attitude. Can you imagine men contributing to this ballyhoo and still hoping to be elected in large numbers?'[16]

All sorts of arguments are advanced for the failure of women to reach the Commons, she pointed out: cultural attitudes, the crazy working hours, the public-school tradition, and the 'mystical bonding' of male-dominated trade unions. Even Britain's long-suffering electoral systems gets the blame.

She conceded, 'I think a positive barrier to Westminster is the obvious biological factor: only females can give birth. So most women devote their prime years to bringing up and looking after the children, and all the et ceteras. In spite of their complaints, most women like it, they are good at it, and I reckon it's a satisfactory occupation not to be sniffed at. To obtain even partial relief to take another demanding job requires money for a nanny, or a gem of a granny. For me, there are no family complications to the arduous commitments of political life.'

Betty has made clear that this was how she wanted it. Not long after becoming Speaker, she was asked – by a woman interviewer – if women intent on achieving must be prepared to forfeit a close personal relationship. Looking back over her own lifetime, she replied, 'Well, women had to make a choice. I deliberately didn't have a family. Sometimes I regret this, but I don't complain. It is what I chose.'[17] Earlier, she had implied that the choice was less than deliberate. 'I guess there are times, I admit to you, when I feel sorry for myself that I haven't got [a family] of my own,' she told Rebecca Abrams. 'But I am not sure I could've done what I have done. You've got to make choices in life, and maybe unconsciously I made my choice.'[18]

Deliberate or unconscious, making that choice set her apart from the average woman, and she learned that it could just as easily arouse jealousy and put-down sentiments among 'the sisters' as admiration. As she has often observed, women selectors have traditionally judged women harder than they do men. In her long battle to enter parliament, Betty got 'tremendous encouragement' from men, but was never once nominated by a women's section. She was even accused at West Bromwich of not knowing what it was like to slave over a kitchen sink.

'I don't think it goes on quite like that now, but it is still hard for women because they are often accused of not having had a family, but if you do have one they want to know how you are going to look after them – the sort of question they never ask of a man. If I had married I doubt if I would have become Speaker.

'I hope the fact that I have broken through into this male stronghold will be an example to other women. I am very impressed by those who have come in here recently; the way they get up and challenge and ask questions and seek adjournments and never give up.'[19]

The House of Commons may sometimes be a place of romance, but it is suspicious of glamour. Betty has managed to steer a dignified course through this potential minefield, even prompting admiration from Sir Nicholas Fairbairn, the late Tory MP for Perth and Kinross. He expressed delight at the increased intake of women after the last election, but bewailed that they did not give him a feeling of femininity. 'Why has womankind given up the exaltation of herself – that attempt to attract, to adorn, to glint?' he asked in the *Spectator*. 'They all look as though they are from the 5th Kiev Stalinist machine-gun parade. Except for Betty Boothroyd. Now she's got style, fragrance.' The record shows that he voted for her in the Speakership election, too. And *Elle* magazine listed her among the House's 'party girls', reporting, 'Madam Speaker Betty Boothroyd as a young woman 'oozed sex' according to one of her admirers and, indeed, suitors.'[20]

For all the glitz and the ceremony, there is a homely side to Madam Speaker, which comes out best in her Cambridgeshire hideaway. She calls it 'my little fourteenth-century cottage near Royston'; it is actually in the village of Thriplow. Inside, the house has exposed beams and antique furniture with flowered tapestry coverings, giving the place a faintly chintzy feel. A portrait of her by John Bratby, commissioned by Betty before she became Speaker, hangs on the wall. She also has paintings of the old foundries in her constituency, again paid for by herself. When she 'pops her clogs', as she puts it, they will go to Wednesbury Art Gallery.

When not travelling to exotic parts she tries to spend a whole day at the cottage every week, usually travelling down by car. She has something of a set routine. 'I love lighting a fire when I arrive and going to bed early, and wild horses wouldn't drag me out on a Saturday night,' Betty has confessed.[21]

On Sunday mornings, she gets up and makes a cup of coffee and takes it back to bed and reads for an hour or so. In the days when she had to wash her own clothes – perhaps even now – this was when she did her weekly wash. Her mother would have frowned on her for washing on a Sunday, she fears, but excuses herself with a slice of homespun wisdom: 'the better the day, the better the deed'.

Betty is a Christian, though not a practising one. 'I love spending Sunday pottering round the house and fixing things.' She goes for afternoon walks in the undulating countryside, and relaxes by doing patchwork which she finds 'very soothing'. Her reading tastes are middlebrow rather than intellectual – Mary Wesley's novels are a favourite. Cast away on the BBC's 'Desert Island', however, she chose Vikram Seth's epic love story of post-independence India, *A Suitable Boy*.

'Music means a lot more to her,' says a close friend. 'It's more important than reading.' Her tastes in music are similar to those in books, but she has a remarkable showbiz repertoire. Put on a Glenn Miller record, and Betty can sing all the words, even now. Her choice of records for 'Desert Island Discs' gave the game away: the overture to Offenbach's 'Orpheus in the Underworld' which reminds her of the 'zip and glamour of Paris', where she worked with Geoffrey de Freitas; Flanagan and Allan's 'Underneath the Arches', the humour of the dispossessed; 'Rockaby Your Baby'; Ted Heath's Band playing 'Opus One', which reminds her of nights jitterbugging at Dewsbury Town Hall; Tchaikovsky's 'Sleeping Beauty'; Placido Domingo singing 'You Are My Heart's Delight' ('this melts my heart and brings me to order'); Fred Astaire's 'No strings, no connections, I'm fancy free . . .'; and Ethel Murman singing 'No Business Like Show Business'.

Sunday lunch is often taken at the Walstons, but if she has someone staying or friends coming in, Betty enjoys making traditional Sunday 'dinner', as he mother would have called it. 'I really enjoy cooking,' she told the *Sunday Times*. 'It's plain English cooking – casseroles, roasts, fresh veg.' She is 'not very good on afters' but neighbours offer to bring dessert. Although she is 'a loner', in the sense that she is on her own and her family is confined to one half-cousin and a god-daughter, Betty is a gregarious woman. 'I absolutely adore company. I've never been lonely,' she insists.

As her seemingly eternal tan shows, Betty also loves holidays. Ever since her lazy, hazy days in St Lucia, her passion has been islands. Her favourites are Cyprus and Sri Lanka. The media attention given to 'the Cyprus connection' has already been noted. Less is known about her links with the former Ceylon, the 'tear below India' as it became known during the bloody Tamil Tiger insurrection aimed at creating a separate Tamil state of Eelam in the north and east of the island. Her links with the island are an instructive lesson in Betty, leisure and politics.

On a visit to Sri Lanka in late 1993, Betty told a friend she has visited the island no less eighteen times. According to official sources, all the visits but two have been private, though she was an official of the British–Sri Lanka Parliamentary Group at least as far back as 1983. Most of the trips have been during December and January, when the House was in recess.

However, Betty took part in a ten-member British Parliamentary team of inspection which visited the island for a week in the early summer of 1984, presumably at the invitation of the Colombo government of President Junius Jayewardene. The group met ministers, travelled to the war-ravaged areas, and met leaders of opposition parties including the mainstream non-violent Tamil Reformists. At the end of this tour, three of the MPs, Betty, Michael Morris (who was Chairman of the British–Sri Lanka Parliamentary Group, and is now her Deputy Speaker) produced a report entitled 'Some Impressions of Sri Lanka'. In it, they said, 'Our conclusion is that we see no basis for the call for Eelam. The majority in the Eastern Region are totally against it, and in the North it represents a demand for realistic regional devolution.'

While this is predominantly the case, the verdict of the MPs would have come as music to the ears of President Jayewardene, who like most of the government, the army and the ranking civil servants, belongs to the majority Sinhalese community which was fighting to put down the Tamil revolt. The civil war was a no-quarter, merciless affair, which prompted international concern over the suppression of civil rights and random murders by the security forces, which could have hindered the flow of aid and materiel to Sri Lanka. The MPs' endorsement of its policies would have been a welcome boost to the Jayewardene administration.

However, Betty can scarcely be said to have capitalized upon it. A well-placed informant in Colombo says that while Madam Speaker has close friends in the government and in the public and private sectors, she has 'declined with thanks' Foreign Ministry offers to make her an official guest. However, says the source in Colombo, 'on several occasions the Foreign Ministry provided her a limousine with fuel and chauffeur for her travels within the country. Everyone describes her as a 'good friend of Sri Lanka'. She has a good knowledge of Sri Lankan affairs, particularly about the ethnic conflict. Whenever Labour MPs wanted some background about the situation in Sri Lanka they always went to Boothroyd and she provided them with an unbiased and objective account.

'During her visits, she used to stay at a five-star hotel in Colombo for a couple of days and then visit the island's historical and cultural centres such as Anuradhapura, Polonnaruwa, Kandy (where she saw a tooth relic of the Buddha), and Sigirya. She loves the sea and often spent hours swimming or lazing on the beaches of the south-west coast. Her favourite places were the beach resorts at Wadduwa, about thirty miles south of Colombo, and Unawatunna, near the southern capital of Galle, seventy-two miles south. A Sri Lankan who knows her well says she is a very friendly and informal person, despite being an MP and the Speaker. He described how she rang him one day from her hotel and said 'I say . . . I've run out whisky. Can you spare a bottle?' He obliged of course . . .'

Betty, said the informant, likes the island's spicy rice and curry, but not too much chilli. And when she goes home she always takes a kilo or two of fresh limes. 'What she used the lime for is not known.'[22] Most Asians, ignorant of the ways of Annie's Bar, would not know of her penchant for gin and tonic, which tastes so much better with fresh limes.

Quite apart from holidays, Betty's official globetrotting is something to be admired. She was on a Commonwealth Parliamentary Association delegation to Kenya in 1983, and the following year saw her on an expenses-paid official visit to Hong Kong, funded by the colony's government. 1984 also saw her in Moscow, in a four-member all-party group, the first parliamentary delegation to be given visas to meet Jewish 'refuseniks' in the former USSR.

In 1990, Speaker Weatherill sent her to a Speakers' Conference in

Harare, Zimbabwe, where she was chosen to respond to President Mugabe's speech. 'I enjoy what I do,' she said later. 'I do feel at the heart of things, and very privileged.' In late September 1993, she announced that a 'thrilling day' when she got a round of applause at the US Senate in Washington left her with 'tear stained eyes'. The *Washington Post* reported that she was flying on to Colombia 'to continue her parliamentary proselytizing'. Next stop after that, Brazil. Her winter to the sun that year took her to the South Seas, she confided to parliamentary journalists. This is the shape of things to come. 'When I retire, I shall travel as much as I can,' she has remarked.[23]

In late 1993, replying to the author's request for an interview, Betty wrote, 'I have only been Speaker for eighteen months. The office I hold is surely the most important fact in my life so far. To write my life story now is, I feel, a trifle premature.'[24]

By now, autumn 1995, however, she has been Speaker for just over three years. Not long enough, in all conscience, to come to a final verdict on her Speakership. Since the war, Speakers have served an average of seven years. Even Selwyn Lloyd, who served the shortest period, was in the chair for five years.

But after nearly forty years in Westminster, from secretary to MP, from junior member of the Wilson government to second highest Commoner in the land, surely sufficient time has elapsed allow one to strike something of a balance-sheet. How has her Speakership been received in the House? How long is she likely to remain in the post? Has the long haul from the back-to-backs of Marriott Street given Betty the kind of success she so clearly craved? And, on a personal note, has the sacrifice to politics of a normal woman's life – the attention of a husband, the joys of children, the enduring satisfaction of family life – been worth it?

Serving MPs are reluctant to make a public judgment on Madam Speaker. This is not too surprising, as they have no desire to create difficulties for themselves. But Neil Kinnock, the man who did more than most to win her the post, is in no doubt. 'She enjoys it and is thriving on it. She doesn't have that sense of loneliness that often afflicts Speakers. If the Tories melt down with by-elections, and we find ourselves in a hung parliament, Betty will be a tower of strength because she has bags of guts.'[25]

Her deputy, Geoffrey Lofthouse, Labour MP for Pontefract, agrees: 'She really enjoys the job, and is always on top of it. I think she enjoys what goes with the job – being a public figure. She is a household name. People say 'Oh! Isn't she marvellous!' Sometimes, I wonder where she gets the energy from. She is very good at calming the House down, and she is always very sharp with her decisions. She doesn't shirk them. But she is blessed with bags of common sense.'[26]

Peter Shore MP, her contemporary at Transport House in the 1950s, is equally supportive: 'She is doing it very well. A Speaker needs quickness of mind, which she has. You also need a presence, to establish your authority, and she has that too. She handles difficult questions well. If the House once senses that a Speaker can be caught out, you can imagine how merciless they would be. I see no threat at all to Betty from that sort of parliamentary barrack-room lawyer, of which there are quite a number. She has been pushed, but she has held her ground.'[27]

On the Tory side, the congratulations are more muted, because Betty's decision to allow a vote over the Maastricht Social Chapter infuriated many government back-bench loyalists, though they were probably more worried about losing their seats if it was lost than any perceived threat to parliamentary tradition. However, sources close to Sir Edward Heath, Father of the House and former Conservative Prime Minister, concede, 'Her rulings have been right,' and choosing her for the job was 'one of the few sensible moments' in recent Commons history. Even so, it was said, 'She does go over the top occasionally.'[28]

Another Tory constitutionalist MP of the Biffen stamp argues, 'I would not fault her on partiality. She is not a boss's Speaker. That is what the Whips don't like. She is unlike Speaker Thomas. She thinks the House is a place for backbenchers. This place operates by virtue of "the usual channels" and to that extent it is a very good Speaker who can resist being sucked into the usual channels because life is so much simpler when they are operating. Like Speaker Weatherill, she has done quite well to keep herself at a distance, so that she is a Speaker at a distance as well as a Speaker for the usual channels.'[29]

Betty has no doubt as to how she would like to be remembered. 'I don't want stardom. I just want to be a good Speaker,' she confessed on 'Desert Island Discs'. Alas, minor stardom at least has already come her way. She has also said, 'I would like to go down in history as a good, fair and just Speaker but no one is ever going to say that while I am in the chair. They will only say it when my toes are turned up.' So, the final verdict on just how good was her Speakership will have to wait for some years.

Judging by Betty's remarks to her friends, it is clear that she will go for a second term as Speaker in 1996 or 1997, whenever John Major calls the general election. Asked if she will go into the next parliament, her deputy Geoffrey Lofthouse confides, 'I am sure that she will, and I certainly hope that she will. She is much admired and much loved.'[30] There is certainly no problem about her being returned at the next election. The Labour Party has changed its rules so that she cannot be challenged by one of its members, and the Conservatives are virtually certain not to oppose her. If she does not have a free run at West Bromwich West, Betty will only have to contend with a fringe party – perhaps Militant Labour – and she will be returned with the biggest majority of her life.

Political commentators are less inhibited in their views about Betty's Speakership, though they too often feel they have to watch their step. Matthew Parris, himself a former Conservative MP and now parliamentary sketch writer for *The Times*, says she has performed 'superbly', while adding, 'But she has yet to face any major test.' Maastricht came the nearest, 'but in the end the Maastricht rebels behaved'. Betty, he argues, is greatly helped by being a 'Labour' Speaker because dissent is more likely to come from the Labour side. 'It is easier for her than Jack Weatherill [her Conservative predecessor] to tame Labour dissidents.' Equally, 'she is not without a trace of vanity, which I think is important for a Speaker. The Speaker is a bit of a showman, and must be.'[31] Betty will be remembered, Parris believes, as 'a great popularizer of her office'.

Michael White, political editor of the *Guardian*, regards Betty as a success 'almost from day one. She has natural authority, a theatrical temperament and seems to enjoy the limelight. Betty also has poise. She *looks* like she is in charge, though there is a danger that she sometimes stands on her dignity a bit too much. She can sound a little regal. When she says, "Time's Up!" she sometimes reminds me of the landlady of an extremely smart country pub in the North Riding of Yorkshire throwing out unruly customers!'[32] Like other commentators, he thinks Betty will be remembered quite simply as the first woman Speaker.

In the judgment of Trevor Kavanagh, the well-informed political editor of the *Sun*, Betty will not go down in history as a great Speaker. 'But she is a warm personality, genuinely liked by MPs on both sides of the House. Any flaws in her Speakership are widely ignored and tolerated.' He also observes how theatrical Betty can be, and is amused when her speech slips from 'carefully cultivated Yorkshire into Molly Sugden of "Are You Being Served?".' This happens, he says, when she is under pressure.

Kavanagh considers, 'Her worst moment came when she had to adjudicate on Michael Mates. She effectively lost that one. Mates came out the winner. That was seen as a serious moment for her – but that has all faded into the past. There have been times when she has been seen by Labour as favouring the Tories, and by the Tories as favouring Labour, which may actually mean she is being pretty good at being impartial. I think she is good, but I don't think she is great. She is better than the people who were standing against her. She has made a better job than Peter Brooke would have done. She is very popular with foreign viewers. She gets stacks of mail from the USA and else-where in the world.'[33]

Simon Hoggart, radio wit and political editor of the *Observer* who moved over to become parliamentary sketch writer for the *Guardian*, argues, 'She is doing very well. They love her. There is an element in the Tory Party that just loves being bossed around. Betty's a strict disciplinarian. They like that.' It is harder to please Labour MPs. 'Labour Speakers, like George Thomas and Horace King, are invariably accused of being too soft on the Tories, as a reaction against what they were. In fact, she did very well on the big decision on Maastricht. She was actually quite brave.'

Speakers always have to pretend they are working from a precedent in Erskine May, the parliamentary procedure bible, Hoggart points out, 'but of course they have a great deal of choice. And she came down against the government on that one.' In the Mates case, however, she came up against an MP determined to defy her, and Betty was 'a bit weak. Mates simply spouted on and on, because he had to get it read into the record. You cannot really throw a man out for trying to explain his own behaviour – whereas Dennis Skinner and Ian Paisley want to get thrown out.'

Hoggart, too, sees something of the pub landlady in her style, singling out Annie Walker of the Rovers' Return in the Granada soap 'Coronation Street' – actually played in the 1960s by Betty's friend, the actress Doris Speed, who regularly campaigned for her. 'When she shouts, "Order! Order!" you always expect her to say, "If this goes on, I will put the towel over the taps."' Hoggart concurs that she will be best remembered as the first woman Speaker, 'but a bit more than that. All Speakers in the end are deemed to be a great success. She is also very good at the humorous interjection, which often defuses a problem. It makes her more of a character to the viewers.'[34]

These interim assessments have a number of points in common. Betty is seen as a popular, dedicated holder of her office, not without faults but usually right on the big decisions. Nobody holds her difficulties with Michael Mates against her, and everyone agrees that she brings a certain theatrical glamour to the chair. Naturally enough, they all see her as she is now, without Betty's own long perspective of a lifetime in politics. Betty herself has said she wishes to be judged on how she handles the Speakership. But this would be only a partial evaluation of her contribution to public life, and in particular the advancement of women and the interests of working people. Taken all in all, it has been a remarkable achievement – and it is not yet over. When she does choose to retire, Betty will be honoured with a peerage, possibly even a hereditary title of the kind bestowed on Willie Whitelaw and her forerunner George Thomas. Having no issue, of course, the title would die with her.

When Betty calls 'Time's up!' on her career in the Commons, she will be sanguine about it. 'I don't think people should go on and on and on,' she has said . . .[35] 'The time comes when we've all got to go and I don't mind that at all. When I retire, I shall travel as much as I can. I shall go to the theatre. I shall see friends. I shall make new friends. I shall have people come and see me, and I shall go and see them much more. And I shall dig my garden. All the things that I've neglected to do I shall do. It sounds very humdrum, but I shall do that.'

What is more, she will be able to do it secure in the knowledge that she has done something that no other woman before has done, and that must bring a very special peace of mind. And should anyone fear that there is a secret *'je regrette'*, she has already given the answer. Asked if, looking back, she would change anything, Betty replied firmly, 'Nothing. I hope that doesn't sound smug. But it's the truth.'[36]

Notes and References

Chapter One: Making History

1. Source for this quotation and for Parliamentary quotations on the following pages: *Hansard*, vol. 207, col. 2–26.
2. Glenys Kinnock and Fiona Millar, *By Faith and Daring*, Virago 1993, p. 18.
3. *Mail on Sunday*, 10 July 1988.
4. 'BBC Westminster Daily', Uncut interview video, 27 April 1994.
5. *The World of Interiors*, May 1994, pf. 68.
6. John Biffen, *Inside the House of Commons*, Grafton 1989, p. 16.
7. Philip Laundy, *The Office of Speaker*, Cassell 1964, p. 155.
8. Interview with author.
9. Letter to author, 18 July 1994.
10. Statement to author, 18 July 1994.
11. Interview with researcher, Brigid Walsh, 24 March 1994.
12. *The Times*, 1 July 1982.
13. Rebecca Abrams, *Woman in a Man's World*, Methuen 1993, p. 191.
14. 'A Descriptive Account of Dewsbury', approx. date 1900, p. 2.

Chapter Two: A Yorkshire Upbringing

1. Interview with researcher, BW, 6 January 1994.
2. *Yorkshire Life*, April, 1993.
3. Interview with sisters, BW, 1 April 1994.
4. Rebecca Abrams, op. cit., p. 177.
5. Ibid, p. 176.
6. Ibid, p. 177.
7. Ibid, pp. 175–6.
8. Victoria Mckee, interview, *Times Saturday Review*, 7 November 1992.
9. Ibid.
10. Kinnock and Millar, op. cit., p. 14.
11. Interview with researcher, BW.
12. Interview with researcher, BW, 10 December 1993.

13. *Yorkshire Life*, op. cit.
14. 'Eastborough WMC History', 1960.
15. *The Times*, op. cit.
16. Rebecca Abrams, op. cit., p. 178.
17. *Yorkshire Life*, op. cit.
18. Abrams, op. cit., p. 177.
19. Interview with researcher, BW.
20. Ibid.
21. Ibid.
22. 'Eastborough History'.
23. Abrams, op. cit., p. 179.
24. Ibid, p. 176.
25. *The Times*, 7 November 1992.
26. Interview with researcher, BW.
27. Interview with researcher BW, 10 December 1993.
28. Ibid.
29. *Yorkshire Life*, op. cit., p. 9.
30. *The Times*, 7 November 1992.
31. Fiona Millar, interview, *The House*, 20 July 1992.
32. Interview with author.
33. Interview with researcher, BW.
34. Interview with researcher, BW, February 1994.
35. Fiona Millar, op. cit.
36. Interview with researcher, BW.
37. Abrams, op. cit., p. 177.

Chapter Three: Adventurous Years

1. Kinnock and Millar, op. cit., p. 15.
2. Abrams, op. cit., p. 179.
3. Ibid.
4. Interview with author, 6 January 1994.
5. Interview with author, 15 December 1993.
6. *Daily Mail*, 29 April 1992.
7. Ibid.
8. Interview with author, 15 December 1993.
9. *Daily Mail*, op. cit.
10. Interview with author, 15 December 1993.
11. *Daily Mail*, op. cit.
12. Interview with author, 15 December 1993.
13. *Daily Mail*, op. cit.
14. Interview with author, 15 December 1993.
15. Abrams, op. cit., p. 174.
16. Ibid., p. 176.

17. Interview with researcher, BW.
18. Interview with author, 3 January 1994.
19. Interview with researcher, BW.
20. Interview with researcher, BW, 22 February 1994.
21. Interview with researcher, BW, 10 December, 1993.
22. Doremy Vernon, *Tiller's Girls*, Robson Books 1988, pf. 9.
23. Kinnock and Millar, op. cit., pp. 15–16.
24. *Scotsman*, 11 February 1988.
25. *Wolverhampton Express and Star*, 27 July 1987.
26. *The Times*, 1 July 1982.
27. Abrams, op. cit., p. 179.
28. Official letter from Tiller school to new entrants, 2 March 1948.
29. Interview with author, 2 March 1994.
30. Interview with author.
31. Vernon, op. cit., p. 131.
32. Letter, 11 May 1992; copy in possession of author.
33. *Evening Standard*, 28 April 1992.
34. *Letter to author*, 12 May 1994.
35. Interview with researcher, BW.
36. 'Desert Island Discs', tape.
37. Abrams, op. cit., p. 180.

Chapter Four: Politics Beckon

1. Death certificate, 25 March 1948.
2. Abrams, op. cit., p. 178.
3. *Yorkshire Life*, April, 1993.
4. Abrams, op. cit., p. 180.
5. Interview with author.
6. Interview, 3 March 1994.
7. Barbara Castle, *Fighting All the Way*, Macmillan 1993, p. 180.
8. Ibid., p. 188.
9. *Batley Reporter*, 22 March 1952.
10. *Dewsbury News and Chronicle*, 10 May 1952, p. 1.
11. Interview with author, 6 January 1994.
12. Denis Healey, *The Time of My Life*, Penguin 1990, p. 132.
13. Interview with author.
14. Kinnock and Millar, op. cit., p. 16.
15. Interview with author, 22 March 1994.
16. Castle, op. cit., p. 163.
17. Abrams, op. cit., pp. 180–1.
18. Ben Pimlott, *Harold Wilson*, HarperCollinsPublishers 1992, p. 174.
19. Castle, op. cit., p. 160.
20. Abrams, op. cit., p. 181.

21. G. and H. de Freitas, *The Slighter Side*, privately published 1985, p. 11.
22. Ibid., p. 53.
23. Andrew Roth, biographical details from unpublished study of Parliamentary Profiles.
24. Ibid.
25. Kinnock and Millar, op. cit., p. 16.
26. *The Times*, 1 July 1982.
27. Interview with author, 2 January 1994.
28. *The Times*, 1 July 1992.
29. Kinnock and Millar, op. cit., p. 16.
30. Labour Party Annual Report 1957, p. 118.
31. Text of official speech, Leicester University, 16 July 1993.
32. *Tribune*, 22 November 1957, p. 16.
33. *The Times*, 25 November 1957.
34. *Manchester Guardian*, 27 November 1957.
35. Interview with author, 13 December 1993.
36. Ibid.
37. *Peterborough Citizen and Advertiser*, 15 September 1959.
38. *Daily Herald*, 14 September 1959.
39. *Peterborough Citizen and Advertiser*, 29 September 1959.
40. Ibid.
41. *Peterborough Citizen and Advertiser*, 2 October 1959.
42. *Peterborough Citizen and Advertiser*, 13 October 1959.
43. G. and H. de Freitas, op. cit., p. 98.
44. Abrams, op. cit., p. 182.
45. *Rossendale Free Press*, 30 May 1970.
46. *Yorkshire Evening Post*, 25 May 1973.
47. *Yorkshire Evening Post*, 8 November 1960.
48. *Evening Standard*, 1 April 1961.
49. Interview with author, July 1994.
50. Abrams, op. cit., pf. 182.
51. Interview with author, July 1994.
52. Abrams, op. cit., p. 182.

Chapter Five: The Girl Most Unlikely to Succeed

1. Interview with author, 14 February 1994.
2. Interview with author, 28 April 1994.
3. Abrams, op. cit., p. 183.
4. David Owen, *Time to Declare*, Penguin 1992, p. 205.
5. *Daily Mirror*, 4 May 1964.
6. Interview with author, Dec 1993.
7. *Evening Star*, 23 April 1968.
8. Election Address, Nelson and Colne, June 1968.

9. Interview with author.
10. *Evening Star*, 23 April 1968.
11. *Evening Star*, 11 May 1968.
12. Pimlott, op. cit., p. 507.
13. *Evening Star*, 11 June 1968.
14. *The Times*, 17 June 1968.
15. Interview with author, Dec 1993.
16. Interview with author, 3 January 1994.

Chapter Six: Parliament at Last

1. Healey, op. cit., p. 345.
2. Telephone interview with author, 15 March 1993.
3. *Birmingham Post*, 16 May 1973.
4. Interview with author, 21 February 1994.
5. *Observer*, 20 May 1973.
6. *New Statesman*, 18 May 1973.
7. *Yorkshire Post*, 17 May 1973.
8. *Sunday Times*, 13 May 1973.
9. *Birmingham Post*, 17 May 1973.
10. *New Statesman*, 18 May 1973.
11. Interview by author with party chairman, John Edwards, 22 February 1994.
12. Labour Party news release, 21 May 1973.
13. *Wolverhampton Express and Star*, 25 May 1973.
14. *Daily Telegraph*, 12 June 1973.
15. *Hansard*, 18 July 1973, p. 538.
16. Ibid., p. 540.
17. Pimlott, op. cit., pf. 607.
18. *Wolverhampton Express and Star*, 29 October 1974.
19. Biffen, op. cit., p. 80.
20. *Sunday Express*, 27 October 1974.
21. *Wolverhampton Express and Star*, 21 November 1975.
22. *The Times*, 30 March 1976.
23. Labour Party, annual report of 1976 conference, p. 166.
24. Ibid., p. 173.
25. *Birmingham Post*, 28 September 1976.
26. *Wolverhampton Express and Star*, 18 November 1976.
27. Ibid., 1 February 1977.
28. *The Times*, 19 March 1977.
29. *Wolverhampton Express and Star*, 27 May 1977.
30. Tony Benn, *Conflicts of Interest, Diaries 1977–80*, Hutchinson 1991, p. 43.
31. Ibid., p. 91.

32. *Labour Victory*, Number 3, October 1977.
33. *Wolverhampton Express and Star*, 22 December 1977.
34. *Birmingham Post*, 10 May 1978.
35. Healey, op. cit., p. 462.
36. Benn, op. cit., p. 494.

Chapter Seven: Eyes on the Prize

1. Healey, op. cit., p. 466.
2. Benn, op. cit., pp. 584–5.
3. *The Times*, 18 July 1980.
4. Owen, op. cit., p. 204.
5. Tony Benn, *The End of an Era, Diaries 1980–90*, Hutchinson 1992, p. 70.
6. *Daily Telegraph*, 10 February 1981.
7. Interview with author, 14 February 1994.
8. *Sunday Express*, 21 October 1979.
9. Interview with author, 22 February 1994.
10. Interview with author, 21 February 1994.
11. *Birmingham Post*, 6 April 1981.
12. *Wolverhampton Express and Star*, 4 April 1981.
13. *Glasgow Herald*, 23 July 1981.
14. *The Times*, 8 September 1981.
15. Benn, op. cit., p. 222.
16. *Guardian*, 24 June 1981.
17. *Daily Telegraph*, 28 October 1982.
18. *Labour Herald*, 12 November 1982.
19. Healey, op. cit., p. 499.
20. *Daily Telegraph*, 13 June 1983.
21. *Wolverhampton Express and Star*, 17 June 1983.
22. Interview with author, 21 April 1994.
23. *Wolverhampton Express and Star*, 2 July 1983.
24. Benn, op. cit., p. 303.
25. Annual Report of the Labour Party, 1984, p. 256.
26. Ibid., p. 261.
27. *Sunday Times*, 22 July 1984.
28. *The Times*, 15 March 1985.
29. *Hansard*, 18 June 1985.
30. *Guardian*, 14 November 1985.
31. *Guardian*, 3 October 1985.
32. *Guardian*, 9 December 1985.
33. Telephone interview with author, 20 July 1994.
34. Telephone interview with author, 22 September 1994.
35. *The Times*, 17 June 1986.

36. Annual Report of the Labour Party, 1986, p. 150.
37. *Daily Telegraph*, 30 September 1986.
38. *The Times*, 31 March 1987.
39. Healey, op. cit., p. 535.

Chapter Eight: Choose Me for What I Am

(General Note: for this chapter I have drawn substantially on interviews conducted with MPs and other Westminster sources 'on lobby terms': that is, for use but not for attribution. To protect those sources, I was sometimes obliged to guarantee anonymity. I hope the reader will understand.)
 1. Interview with author, 19 March 1994.
 2. Interview with author, 28 April 1994.
 3. Interview with author, 18 May 1994.
 4. *Yorkshire Post*, 3 February 1988.
 5. *Scotsman*, 11 February 1988.
 6. *Mail on Sunday*, 10 July 1988.
 7. Interview with author, 29 March 1988.
 8. *Guardian*, April 1992.
 9. *Financial Times*, 29 April 1992.
10. Roth, op. cit.
11. Alan Clark, *Diaries*, , p. 352.
12. Interview with author, 20 April 1994.
13. Interviews with author over several days, March 1994.
14. Interview with author, 22 February 1994, for this reference and the following pages.
15. Interview with author, 6 September 1994.
16. Biffen, op. cit., p. 26.
17. *Hansard*, vol. 207, col. 2, and six following pages.

Chapter Nine: Order! Order!

 1. *Daily Mail*, 7 May 1992.
 2. *Today*, 5 November 1992.
 3. *Wolverhampton Express and Star*, 31 December 1992.
 4. *Observer*, 25 April 1993.
 5. George Thomas, *Mr Speaker: The Memoirs of Viscount Tonypandy*, Century 1985, p. 143.
 6. *Evening Standard*, 5 May 1993.
 7. *Guardian*, 5 May 1993.
 8. *Observer*, 5 May 1993.
 9. *Daily Telegraph*, 30 June 1993.

10. *Financial Times*, 30 June 1993.
11. *Independent*, 8 July 1993.
12. *Financial Times*, 22 July 1993.
13. *The Times*, 22 July 1993.
14. Interview with author, 21 February 1994.
15. *Observer*, 8 August 1993.
16. *Scotland on Sunday*, 1 August 1993.
17. *Observer*, 21 November 1993.
18. 'PHS Diary', *The Times Saturday Magazine*, 12 February 1994.
19. *Daily Telegraph*, 30 April 1992.
20. Kinnock and Millar, op. cit., p. 19.
21. *The Times*, 1 March 1994.
22. *Hansard*, col. 415, 14 April 1994.
23. *Independent on Sunday*, 20 March 1994.
24. *Hansard*, col. 415, 14 April 1994.
25. Ibid., col. 432.
26. *Observer*, 17 April 1994.
27. *Hansard*, col. 732, 19 April 1994.
28. *Independent*, 12 May 1994.
29. *Guardian*, 13 May 1994.

Chapter Ten: Time's Up!

1. University of Cambridge, Order of Proceedings, Presentation of Honorary Degrees, 9 June 1994.
2. Press release from Cambridge University, 9 June 1994.
3. *Washington Post*, 29 September 1993.
4. Kinnock and Millar, op. cit., p. 17.
5. *Washington Post*, Ian Katz interview, 29 September 1993.
6. Interview with author, 15 December 1993.
7. Interview with author.
8. Author's interview with Sheila Goodair, 24 March 1994.
9. Interview with author, 6 July 1994.
10. Interview with author, 10 Deceember 1993.
11. Interview with author, 19 July 1994.
12. Interview with author, 13 December 1993.
13. Abrams, op. cit., pp. 182–3.
14. Interview with author, 14 February 1994.
15. *Wolverhampton Express and Star*, 25 May 1993.
16. *The Times*, 1 July 1982.
17. *Yorkshire Life*, interview, April 1993.
18. Abrams, op. cit., p. 183.
19. Kinnock and Millar, op. cit., p. 17.
20. *Elle*, September 1992.

21. *Sunday Times Magazine*, 1990.
22. Report from author's informant, a senior journalist in Colombo, Sri Lanka, known to the author for a decade: dated 10 March 1994.
23. Abrams, op. cit., p. 190.
24. Letter to author from Betty Boothroyd, 17 November 1993.
25. Interview with author.
26. Interview with author, 5 July 1994.
27. Interview with author, 24 February 1994.
28. Information supplied, July 1994.
29. Ibid., March 1994.
30. Interview with author, as above.
31. Interview with author, 12 October 1994.
32. Interview with author, 13 October 1994.
33. Interview with author, 13 October 1994.
34. Interview with author, 12 October 1994.
35. Abrams, op. cit., p. 190.
36. *Yorkshire Life*, 1990.

Index